'Sex' at 'Work'

Also by Jeff Hearn:

Birth and Afterbirth: A Materialist Account, Achilles Heel, 1983

The Gender of Oppression: Men, Masculinity, and the Critique of Marxism, Wheatsheaf, 1987

Men in the Public Eye: The Construction and Deconstruction of Public Men and Public Patriarchies, Routledge, 1992

'Sex' at 'Work'

The Power and Paradox of Organisation Sexuality

Revised Edition

Jeff Hearn
and
Wendy Parkin

St. Martin's Press
New York

"SEX" AT "WORK": The Power and Paradox of Organization Sexuality, revised edition

Copyright © 1995 by Jeff Hearn and Wendy Parkin

St. Martin's Press, Scholarly and Reference Division, 175 Fifth Avenue, New York, N.Y. 10010

This edition first published in the United States of America in 1995

Printed in the United Kingdom

ISBN: 0-312-12956-4 (cloth)
ISBN: 0-312-12957-2 (paper)

Library of Congress Cataloging-in-Publication Data

Hearn, Jeff.
  "Sex" at "work".

  Bibliography: p.
  Includes index.
  1. Organization.   2. Sex.   3. Sex role.
I. Parkin, Wendy.   II. Title.
HM131.H372   1987   302.3'5   86-27997
ISBN: 0-312-12956-4 (cloth)
ISBN: 0-312-12957-2 (paper)

'For the invasive presence and the
intent are both audible and inaudible,
visible and invisible'.

(Daly, 1978, 323)

Contents

Figures

Foreword to the First Edition

One dominant image of writing, and especially academic writing, is of the male writer tucked away in quiet seclusion. In contrast the process in our case has been social rather than secluded, and therefore in reality very far from this supposed 'ideal'. The backcloth is domestic, and the writing has been done both in spite of and because of its domestic base.[1] Most books and most authors remain silent on these matters of their own production(s). This could be for many reasons — the assumption that it is 'too trivial'; the actual protection of The Writer from the 'intrusions' of domestic life; the likelihood of much writing being done elsewhere and typically by men; the relative status of women's writing, so producing 'writers' and 'women writers'. Large parts of women's experience still remain unspoken and unwritten (or at least rarely published) in academic contexts — partly because of the shackles of domesticity. All this can affect the content, style and flavour of dominant writing, academic and other.

Writing this has been both stressful and fun. Joint planning sessions have usually been on Monday, Thursday or Friday evenings, and usually interspersed with child care, requests for salad sandwiches, encouraging children to bed, giving in, asking for the radio to be turned off, becoming hysterical at a good new idea, searching for the 'right word', and postponing going to the loo for more than half an hour. Interruptions have been a normal constituent; long periods of being 'shut away' undisturbed have been an impossibility.

In addition to writing in domesticity, we have done so without a common organisational context, being paid by different organisations, in different capacities, with no organisational hold over each other. We have therefore worked on this text for our own individual reasons not as part of some pre-defined organisational project. Before working together in this rather discontinuous non-organisational way, we were neither friends nor colleagues.

Most of the writing of the final draft of the text has been by Jeff Hearn. This has arisen from a variety of reasons. In particular while he has remained in a full-time university lecturer post, Wendy Parkin has moved from a combination of part-time social worker and part-time temporary college lecturer to full-time social worker and back to part-time social worker and part-time permanent polytechnic lecturer. These shifts symbolise in part the different realities of the male and female narratives. Equally important to these changes have been shifts for both in domestic commitments as children enter school or leave home, and as parents age and die.

So how have our own separate personal, working and domestic lives got mixed up with the study of sexuality and organisational life? Our explicit interest in gender and organisational sociology began in 1977 with the planning, through student participation, of an undergraduate sequence on 'Groups and Organisations'.[2] A predominantly female student group expressed great interest in relating such issues as 'sex discrimination' and the 'sexual division of labour' to the study of organisations. This led to the examination of literature as a back-up to a series of seminars labelled 'Women and Organisations'.[3] It was quickly discovered that although there was a mass of information available on women and work, and sex discrimination in paid work, this was not reflected in most organisational sociology (see chapter 2).

From 1980 we worked together on the relationship of gender and organisational dynamics. Initially this was in trying to construct a reader on 'Women, Men and Organisations', a project later abandoned. When it became apparent that certain basic issues around sexuality in organisations were not described in the literature, we realised we would have to write about them ourselves. This realisation was reinforced when quite separately we were asked to write a chapter specifically on sexuality for another text on organisation studies. Thus the realisation of the importance of sexuality in organisations came through a number of concrete practical activities in trying to do research. It also came through the parallel and overwhelming evidence for the importance of sexuality in organisations in everyday experience. Increasingly the 'research activity' and the 'everyday activity' have become one and the same. In several senses it would be mistaken to say that we chose this area of research: it was the one most difficult to avoid. The issues studied are *there*, like it or not; they do not vanish through not being studied. Thus, the myth that sexuality is purely a personal matter, for private life, the family, leisure and the night, has been exploded once and for all. Recent feminist and other critical scholarship has demonstrated that sexuality is a public issue and an issue of power. One major area for both the control and expression of sexuality is provided by organisations, especially as workplaces.

This text attempts to engage with these issues, in such a way that the process of narration becomes part of the subject matter under scrutiny. In other words, it is not enough to simply produce disinterested, academic analyses and 'results', as in the all-possessing 'male sexual narrative' (Dyer, 1985). At each point the potential richness and complexity of sexuality and organisational life needs to be appreciated. We write within a process of the dialectical development of our subjectivity and the objects in question: our changing consciousness, and social and political change in the oppressive uses of sexuality in organisations.

The necessary structure of this book belies an important qualitative process. The text moves from the initial appearance of sexuality in organisations, through to the analysis of the major factors affecting the relation of sexuality and organisational life, to the recognition and exploration of the phenomenon of 'organisation sexuality'. Throughout, issues of *power* and *paradox* recur. Organisation sexuality is powerful and paradoxical, and is beset and determined by further power and paradoxes.

The first part of the study, 'Background and Contexts', provides a detailed introduction to the subject of sexuality and organisational life. Chapter 1, 'Sexuality Appears', notes the frequently attributed opposition and contradiction of sexuality and organisation, their historical location and development and, despite processes of desexualisation, the discovery of the sexualised organisation. Chapter 2 surveys the contribution of organisation theory and organisational sociology to the study of sexuality in organisations, and some of the major sources of literature that have been of use in our 'search for literature'. The following chapter traces some of the major ways in which the subject of the research, sexuality and organisational life, have become intertwined with 'the process of research'. This process is thus more than just a methodological framework; the questioning of abstract research method and dominant orthodoxy is an inherent part of realist research into sexuality and organisations.

Part 2, consisting of chapters 4, 5 and 6, focuses on questions of 'Power and Dialectics'. Matters of power determine sexuality in organisations, while sexuality has a powerful impact upon organisations. Power resides both in social structures 'beyond organisational boundaries', and in internal organisational structures. Chapters 5 and 6 outline the major ways in which organisations construct sexuality, and sexuality constructs organisations, and are thus in a dialectical relationship to each other.

In the final part, chapter 7, 'Organisation Sexuality: A Paradox', describes the simultaneous and paradoxical occurrence of the qualities of organisation and sexuality. Organisations exist as sexuality and sexuality sometimes as organisation. Organisation sexuality persists as physical, movement and proximity; emotions and feelings; ideology and consciousness; and language and imagery. The final chapter restates some central issues and considers some implications for change, and concludes with brief statements from each of us on the differential impact and implications of organisation sexuality, both personally and for our respective genders.

January 1986, Bradford

Foreword to the Revised Edition

Since the publication of *'Sex' at 'Work'* in 1987, there have been many developments in the theorising of sexuality and its relationship to power, gender and organisational processes. This revised edition includes the full original text, with only essential minor amendments, followed by a postscript which summarises new developments in theory and practice.

In the foreword to the first edition, we wrote about the process and context of our writing. Changes have occurred in both of these areas and have exerted their influence on our work and thinking. We continue to have no organisational hold over each other; our individual reasons for writing remain primarily personal and political, though now academic publishing is at the very least complicated by the politics of research funding and research ratings exercises. Both of us are now required to produce research and writing for our organisations. This was always implicit in that undertaking research was necessary for academic career progress but is now much more explicitly tied into competition for scarce resources.

Jeff Hearn is now a Reader in Sociology and Critical Studies on Men and remains at the University of Bradford. His recent research has been on historical change in, particularly, managements and men, and men's violence to known women. Wendy Parkin has moved from a mixture of temporary and permanent work to a permanent full-time post at the University of Huddersfield as Senior Lecturer in Sociology and Social Work. She is involved in research into sexuality in residential care settings. For both, in addition to pressures to produce publications, increasing student numbers and levels of responsibility have increased workloads.

In an additional postscript we refer to a number of contextual changes since the first edition that have resulted in different aspects of sexuality being brought to public awareness, as well as further developments around, for example, sexual harassment. These issues include the spread of HIV/AIDS; evidence of numerous sexual scandals in children's homes; wider publicity regarding the sexual abuse of children including the setting up of Childline and increasing research on sex offenders; more sexually explicit behaviour on television, films and advertisements; continuing sexually violent abuse of women and children; globalisation of pornography and prostitution through the 'sex tourism' industry; control of sex education in schools. These and many other contextual changes provide the background for exploring research, theoretical developments, controversies and practices in theorising sexuality, gender and organisation(s).

January 1995

Acknowledgements

Many people have helped us in producing this text by exchanging ideas, providing information and commenting on the script. These include John Barker, Dr John Birch, Gibson Burrell, David Collinson, Jan Davis, Nancy DiTomaso, Alan Goater, Julia Graham, Janette Griggs, Tim Griggs, Barbara Gutek, Jacqui Halson, Dave Hardwick, Jay Hearn, Rose Hearn, Peter Hitch, Wendy Hollway, Martin Humphries, David Lloyd-Hughes, Andy Metcalf, Sue Moody, June Rossington, Deborah Sheppard, Nigel South, Andrew Spence, Peta Tancred, Hugh Valentine, Sue Webb and Viv Whittaker.

We would particularly like to acknowledge the encouragement and support from Romesh Vaitilingam, formerly editor of Wheatsheaf Books, in the production of the first edition of this book and Christina Wipf in the production of the revised edition. We appreciate the labour of other workers at Wheatsheaf; the helpful and perceptive suggestions of the copy-editor, Janet Tyrrell; and the useful comments of anonymous reviewers. Christine Parton was kind enough to be a third proof-reader. A special acknowledgement is also given to Sue Moody, Valerie Bentley and Susan Hanson for their outstanding speed, accuracy and patience in the typing of various scripts.

Many others have contributed anonymously either at seminars and lectures or in the supply of information about sexuality in organisational life.

Finally this book would not have been possible without strong commitments from our families. We thank Jay Hearn and Malcolm Parkin for all sorts of support and especially for being there; Amy, Tom and Molly Hearn for their enlivening impact, and Carolyn and Alison Parkin for their continuing encouragement.

We are grateful for permission to include an extract, prior to publication, from B. A. Gutek and V. Dunwoody 'Understanding sex in the workplace' in *Women and Work: An Annual Review, Vol II*, ed. A. H. Stromberg, L. Larwood and B. A. Gutek (Sage Publications, Beverly Hills, 1987).

Part One
Background and Contexts

1 Sexuality Appears

Sexuality appears mysterious. It uplifts and afflicts us. It appears part of our other nature, that is animal or spiritual, devilish or platonic, desperate or ecstatic; it certainly seems other than the mundane, everyday world we live in. It is the 'wild card in the pack' (Brake, 1982, 13), the elusive combination of 'the fervour of knowledge, the determination to change the laws, and the longing for the garden of earthly delights' (Foucault, 1981, 7). In effect we all know sexuality through its unknownness, perhaps its unknowability – and this remains as true in the commonplace and routine meeting of eyes in mild flirtation as in the much advertised goal of orgasm. Contrary to what it seems, the unknown nature of sexuality is with us daily, by the minute and the second.

Enter most organisations and you enter a world of sexuality. In addition to foyers, lifts, corridors, shopfloor machinery, filing cabinets, computers, paper work, desks and telephones, there is usually much (else) that can be called 'sexuality'. This can include a mass of sexual displays, feelings, fantasies, and innuendoes, as part of everyday organisational life, as well as sexual relationships, open or secret, occasional sexual acts, and sexual violations, including rape.

THE INVISIBILITY OF SEXUALITY

And yet read the 'mountainous' literature on industrial sociology, organisational sociology, organisation theory, management theory, industrial relations and so on, and you would imagine these organisations, so finely analysed, are inhabited by people who are devoid of sexuality. There has been in effect a booming silence. This is partly a reflection of the more general neglect of gender within the study of organisations. Although a great deal of information on sex discrimination in paid work has become available in recent years this has only slowly been recognised and appreciated in the study of organisations and is certainly not reflected in most mainstream or malestream (O'Brien, 1981) texts in, say, organisation theory. Many of the 'classics' on organisation theory avoid the issue of gender in a way that is bizarre (Hearn and Parkin, 1983; Sheriff and Campbell, 1981). In many cases the lack of even the most basic information and observation on gender shows a distinct carelessness.

Sexuality is in many ways the most obvious aspect of gender relations, and yet despite or perhaps because of this has been even more neglected within the study of organisations than other aspects, such as the sexual, or more precisely gender, division of labour. What is apparent is that even basic questions around sexuality in organisations are usually not referred to in the literature. We appear to be encountering here an obscure and hazy nether-world that professes to describe and analyse organisations yet for some reason fails to see what we all know is important within them. We can see this in a number of ways. There is first the amount of time, effort and involvement that goes into conversation, gossip and rumour on sexual matters. We therefore take it for granted that for many people, sexual reality is a significant part of organisational reality, and conversely that organisational reality is a significant part of sexual reality. An additional point is that sexual practices at 'work' are becoming increasingly recognised as a public and indeed political issue in their own right. This applies particularly but by no means solely in the growth of trade union and other campaigns, usually led by women, against sexual harassment (e.g. Leeds TUCRIC, 1983). In one sense this book is itself an attempt to contribute towards that shifting relationship of what is recognised as public. Another way in which sexual reality is important is the dramatic impact that sexual relationships, real and alleged, can have upon particular organisations, leading occasionally to the exposure and possible 'fall' of those in high office.[1]

The neglect of sexuality within organisation theory, management theory and the like is in simple terms an example of the sexism of such theories. It is a particular instance of making invisible that which is already visible, a dominant process which has been recognised by Oakley (1974, ch. 1) amongst others as applying to 'woman' and 'women'. It is an interesting example of ideology and how theoretical disciplines which attempt to uncover the underlying structures and systems of organisations can in doing so ignore the 'obvious'. This can be a convenient means to removing the obvious from contention, from political argument. More broadly still there remains the question of the relationship, often reciprocal, between the ideology of theory, say management theory, and the ideology of that which is theorised about, say management. The sexism of one may conveniently feed the sexism of the other. Thus, for example, management theory can provide both technical prescriptions and implicit legitimation for management just as much in relation to sexuality as issues of work, division of labour, management method, power and authority.

These questions of visibility and invisibility are central to our task and will recur throughout, in a number of ways and at a number of levels. They are just as important in the academic study of organisations and management, as they are in the everyday perception (and non-perception) of sexuality, and its construction through ordinary language. Organisation theory's ignorance of sexuality is in these terms a very similar phenomenon to that everyday language which says sexual harassment is 'only a bit of a laugh really'. Both phenomena are products of deeply-rooted power relations between women and men, that deny major and huge elements and aspects of reality, along gender lines. This process may be called 'patriarchy'.[2]

THE PUBLIC AND THE PRIVATE

To put all this in more concrete terms, we may usefully draw on the broad distinction between the public domain and private domain. Organisational life clearly comprises part of the public domain. Sexuality is often considered primarily biological, and socially part of the private domain. Both these assumptions are disputed. Within organisational contexts sexuality clearly becomes part of the public, though sometimes unrecognised as such or only recognised with great reluctance. The public—private division has in recent years been seen by many feminist writers (e.g. Elshtain, 1981; Stacey and Price, 1981) as crucial in understanding gender relations and the distribution of power between women and men, and indeed children. O'Brien (1981) in particular draws a parallel between the relationship between the public and private domains for understanding gender, and the relationship between the economic classes for understanding the capitalist economy. Men tend to dominate explicitly in the public domain and more implicitly but not less powerfully in the private. Organisations both constitute part of the public domain, and are themselves structured in accordance with the 'rules' and ways of that domain, for example, in divisions of labour and hierarchy. Men accordingly dominate twice over, in the public domain over the private, and within particular parts of the public domain—that is, organisations. The attempt here is to build on such approaches in the understanding of sexuality, within one aspect of the public domain, namely organisations, and particularly work organisations. Thus it is the public forms of sexuality that are here of most interest in contrast to the more usual emphasis on the private nature of sexuality.

The public forms that sexuality takes are significant for a number of reasons. Firstly, they provide images of both women and men that may be influential in the development of different notions of masculinity and femininity and different possibilities for personal (and sexual) identity. Secondly, they provide visible and more accessible indicators of sexuality that may be linked with private sexuality. Thirdly, the public forms of sexuality, particularly as they are affected by public inequalities, may need to be understood in order to fully understand the private forms. They provide both the context and causes of certain private forms. Fourthly, and more obviously and importantly, they exist! They are a major element in the everyday relations between women, men and children. To quote Cixous (1980, 96): 'Phallocentrism *is*'.

There are also several further reasons for looking at sexuality in the specific context of work organisations. First, the public world is largely produced by and through work organisations. Secondly, work organisations themselves both construct sexuality and are constructed by and through sexuality—they are in themselves, areas of sexual practices. Thirdly, there are many work organisations whose task is explicitly defined in terms of sexuality, including dating agencies, strip joints, pornographers, and fashion houses. These are clear embodiments of the sexual power of the work organisation in action.

Organisations, and particularly work organisations, are arenas that, though public, offer opportunities for the continual definition and redefinition of the public and the private. They offer opportunities for 'private' conversation, for quiet enclaves and 'cubby holes', for discussions 'behind closed doors', for intimacy; they also exist in public worlds like an uneasy truce over the *possibility* of the private. They both create the private and dispel the private. An interesting comparison can be made with the organisation of hospital childbirth as another 'routine' yet special place and moment where the private is created within the public. In such situations men are even allowed to break the number one rule of masculinity: to cry, or at least to cry in public. Sexuality is rather similar, in that it forever grants the possibility of breaking a host of rules of organisational life: to *not* remain in organisational role, to be private in public, to be personal, and so on. It is therefore to these fundamental contradictions between sexuality and 'work', sexuality and organisations that we now turn.

SEXUALITY VERSUS 'WORK' AND ORGANISATION

The idea that sexuality and 'work' are somehow at odds with each other is widespread. This is both an issue of theory and an issue of personal experience:

If I reflect on this, this supposed division of sex and work, I still feel a certain uneasiness, even embarrassment, in connecting my own paid work with my own sexuality. I realise intellectually that there are strong connections. But there are also strong emotional, perhaps puritanical, hangovers which say, on the one hand, to introduce or acknowledge the sexual issue at work, 'my' work, is to complicate and even denigrate the real purpose of work; while, on the other, to link work with my sexuality is to interfere, to impersonalise *my* personal sexuality. The hangovers say that work should be left to be instrumental, and that sexuality should be expressive; to mix them is to offend both.

(Hearn, 1985a, 110)

But of course, and this explains the bracketing of 'work', it is *paid, organised* work that is seen to be the offending article, not work in general, unpaid work, domestic work. These oppositions are drawn in various ways and on various historical planes. Rationalisation, capitalism, bureaucracy, instrumentality, the wage relationship, we could go on, are all often seen as opposed to sexuality, love, eroticism—a general historical process of 'desexualisation'. It is often held that this process has led us to a present-day situation 'in which human features such as love and comfort are not seen as part of the organisational world' (Burrell, 1984, 99). Burrell has traced historically the apparent exclusion of sexuality from the workplace, concluding that 'sexuality and labour power are not compatible' (*ibid.*, 113). While disagreeing with this particular element of his findings, we recognise the importance of a broad historical view of the relationship of sexuality and organisational life. Burrell's basic thesis is that, firstly, organisations have been sites of desexualisation, involving the suppression of sexuality, during the post-medieval period; and secondly, this process is frequently resisted by a variety of forms of resistance that reassert sexuality against this suppression. This analysis is cast very much within a Foucauldian framework, so that forms of knowledge and control produce silences and margins, which may then be effectively transgressed. There are thus several important elements to this kind of historical analysis: an attempt to understand the present by searching back to historical times when 'things', in this case sexuality in organisations, were different:[3] a focus on broad historical processes of desexualisation, very much in keeping with a Weberian thesis of rationalisation;[4] and attention to the continuing *antithesis* of that rationalisation, particularly within total institutions, that *seek* to control sexuality totally as other parts of human life.[5]

In common with much of Foucault's own work, this scheme is the outline of a (meta-) discourse, which produces its own contradictory reaction, within itself, to almost but not quite form a complete closure. The total institution and its reactive underlife represent a microcosm of such a macro-historical process. More will be said on this way of conceptualising sexuality, within discourse in chapter 4.

Of particular interest here are the various ways in which Burrell accounts for the process of organisational desexualisation. These are principally 'the civilising process' (Elias, 1978); the development of religious morality; the development of calculative rationality; the development of control over time and over the body. These are clearly not mutually exclusive, for example, control of the body may be one part of the development of religious morality, and the control of time may be part of the development of calculative rationality. Indeed what they have in common is that in each reference can be made both in practice and analysis to an abstraction that transcends individuals and individual preferences (including sexualities), and *which may be mediated in particular situations through organisations and organisational practices*. This applies in both paid work organisations with respect to workers, through, for example, the invoking of calculative rationality, and in total institutions with respect to residents, through, for example, the invoking of morality. In such ways organisations, and especially paid work and residential organisations, can appear to be inherently at odds with sexuality.

One of the most important insights of such broad historical views is their appreciation that the way organisations tend to be seen in relation to sexuality at any given historical time is itself to be understood in relation to the place of organisations in that society. Organisations, like work, are not inherently asexual or desexualising. Burrell makes special mention of the role of the early Catholic Church in suppressing sexuality as part of a grand plan for its organisation and the organisation of its 'sub-units', its monasteries, convents and so on. In creating a centralised, bureaucratic hierarchy, the Catholic Church focused on the 'evils' of sex, and in doing so it effectively *created* strong sexual taboos. This institutional development was subsequently felt more broadly throughout society. According to Cleugh (1963) and Elias in particular, the exclusion of sexuality and nudity from the public realm, and indeed the idea of obscenity, are relatively modern phenomena dating from the fifteenth century. Thus:

In the course of the civilizing process the sexual drive is subject to ever stricter control and transformation. The development of social *con*straint is matched by individual *re*straint in these matters. Pressure is placed on adults to privatize all their impulses, there is a conspiracy of silence when children are present . . . the monogamous marriage takes on the form of a social institution.

(Burrell, *op. cit.*, 103)

These constraints and restraints receive a specific reinforcement and a specific organisational aspect with the modern, industrial separation of home and paid work. Most people do not have sex where they do paid work. Many women do have sex in the same building, the home, where they do (unpaid) work.

It would be mistaken to see this privatising of sexuality as a single or remorseless process. For example, the Second World War had the impact of throwing many accepted moral values into confusion (Costello, 1985). A more specific example is changing practices around breast feeding in organisational settings. The frequent practice of breast feeding in the mills and factories of the Industrial Revolution represented a response to economic exigency *and* an introduction of the 'sexual' into the public arena. More recently the Second World War brought on a modified, more ordered version of such practices with the mushrooming of workplace nurseries. Now workplace nurseries are much less common and where they do exist usually only take children after weaning from two and a half or three. The separation of sexuality and work is thereby reaffirmed. Against that, some women have been partially successful in their attempts either to desexualise breast feeding in its practice in public places or, in doing so, to promote the sexual in public. While this may be more usual in cafés, restaurants, and other public places, in paid work organisations it remains very unusual.

Thus the (wrongly) *supposed* opposition and separation of sexuality and work parallels and may be premised upon a particular and misleading view of work, and what work is. The facile reduction of work to 'paid work' makes for its easy opposition to both sexuality and unpaid work. Both sexuality and unpaid work share an unspoken invisibility. Although frequently devalued, they refuse to be defined away by organisational criteria. The fact that 'work' is so often used in both everyday and academic language to mean 'paid work' is itself part of the problem. Work, and especially domestic work and the care of children, clearly does not become less onerous by virtue of being unpaid. Lack of payment may or may not change the *immediate* relations of control of that work but may merely serve to increase its unattractiveness. If work is taken to mean that which one does not wish to do, unpaid work may be more 'like work' than paid, rather than being presumed to be enjoyable through being unpaid.

Furthermore, these remarks on the ideological construction of 'work' are equally relevant in the undervaluing of various forms of organised work or work in organisations. These include 'domestic' tasks that become organised, like childcare in residential establishments and nurseries, and a range of 'voluntary' unpaid activities, i.e. work, that is performed in and around the boundaries of formal organisations. Sometimes such 'voluntary' work is performed by formally recognised volunteers; often it is not.

A rather similar problem surrounds the identification of what an organisation is. There are numerous links between the recognition of *paid* work and the recognition of organisations. The boundaries of paid work, rather than 'voluntary' work or unpaid work, are assumed to be equivalent to the boundaries of organisations. Such an approach neglects the work of unpaid spouses, of the wives of executives and others, who are expected to entertain spouses' work colleagues and so on. The dominant models of organisations and organising are derived from, firstly, work organisations and secondly paid work organisations. The focus upon paid work organisations that is characteristic of organisational sociology in general thus rests on and to some extent obscures broader debates around the definition and nature of work, and thus more indirectly of sexuality itself.

Particular complications surround the analysis of voluntary organisations or volunteer organisations, where the definition of the organisation is wholly or partially separated from the definition of paid work. In these organisations one might expect to find a lesser contrast of work and sexuality; yet the impact of organisational controls often remains. The contradictions of sexuality and work, and sexuality and organisation are themselves here more complicated. Members may feel their sexuality is *none* of the 'organisation's' business, because of their own voluntarism. In practice there may be many reasons why their sexuality is of interest to the organisation, for example, if they are volunteer carers of children. Similarly volunteers may subject their sexuality to the scrutiny of organisational controllers or other members because they wish to retain membership of the organisation for other reasons, for example, obtaining subsequent employment.

These historical relationships of sexuality, work and organisation are frequently glossed over in dominant intellectual traditions. The supposed antagonism of 'love' and 'work' has been promoted by a whole range of social theorists and political positions (Rubenstein, 1978) from the romantic right, through to liberal individualism, psychoanalysis, humanistic psychology, libertarianism, to left radicalism and most versions of socialism. It is as strong within marxism as within Freudianism. In the former, wage labour is seen to diminish and alienate the worker, so that 'the worker feels himself only when he is not working; when he is working he does not feel himself. He is at home when he is not working, and not at home when he is working' (Marx, 1975, 326). The worker thereby feels his true self, however falsely, when not at work, but off work, at home, in bed.

The contrast is drawn more starkly still in the 'work' (or perhaps sexuality) of Freud. He sees the two worlds and the two aspects of the person as opposed and subject to limited personal reserves of energy. In *Civilization and its Discontents* he writes of 'the antithesis between civilization and sexuality' (Freud, 1962, 55). More precisely, work itself involves drawing on libidinal energy and diverting it into the work objects rather than the sexual objects. Freud (*ibid.*, 50) thus explained that:

Since a man does not have unlimited quantities of psychical energy at his disposal, he has to accomplish his tasks by making an expedient distribution of his libido. What he employs for cultural aims he to a great extent withdraws from women and sexual life.

Forgetting the heterosexism of this statement, it usefully presents a plausible account of the sublimation of sex in work. No wonder we have such colloquialisms as 'on the job', 'hard at it', 'having a go' or just plain 'busy'.

Seen in this light the long-running attempt to relate or reconcile the insights of Marx and Freud does not seem so daunting, for both share certain dualist tendencies in their treatment of work and sex. Although both may have drawn the line between sexuality and work too firmly, they did lay the basis for understanding the close interrelationship that the two realms enjoy. Indeed it is interesting that two of the principal reconcilers, Reich and Marcuse, have been at their most fluent and influential in their writing on sexuality. At first sight Marcuse is the more relevant here, with his replacement of the antagonism between work and Eros (the pleasure principle) with the antagonism between alienated work and Eros (Marcuse, 1955). Accordingly Marcuse became the champion of the sixties and in this way members of the 'permissive society' could fight capitalism and sexual repression at the same time. As a Parisian May 1968 slogan had it: 'Work—It Will Make You Ugly' (cited in Jenkins, 1974, 40).

Although then less fashionable than Marcuse, Reich's ideas are in some way more revolutionary and of more lasting significance. He linked the development of political ideology and especially conservatism and fascism, with the control of sexuality within the authoritarian, patriarchal, family. Thus the antagonism of sex and work, and specifically the desexualisation of work, are themselves ideological. The limitation of sex to the family is seen as repressive—and by implication the recognition of the interrelation and even possible reconciliation of sex and work is potentially liberating. Thus Reich's ideas, although rigid and patriarchal in some respects, are in accord with the current concern for the interrelation of the public and the private, the potential unity of 'sexuality and achievement', 'work and love' (Reich, 1942, xvii-xx). Marcuse certainly saw the personal as political but saw the form of the division rather than the division itself as crucial. It is the fact of the division and the development of practical ways of transcending it that have been such an important part of modern feminism.

Of all modern social and political movements, and in contrast to most, feminism is the prime example of the attempt to relate the personal and the political. In this context to connect the personal experience of sexuality and the public conditions of organisations and work is no longer obscure, or difficult, or sensationalist, but altogether rather obvious. They are related to each other because we all know and experience them as related, if we are honest. The ways we talk, walk, flirt, touch and so on, as women or as men, may all be instances of being sexual at work, and at the same time be means to displaying different sexual identities, that are at least partly work-based and organisationally-determined.

THE DISCOVERY OF THE SEXUALISED ORGANISATION

Now that connections have been made it becomes rather difficult not to see them throughout all aspects of organisational life. Organisations, both those of paid work and those serving other purposes, now become obvious places for the development of sexual relationships, be they unspoken glances, mild flirtations, passionate affairs or life-long arrangements. For example, two popular surveys have reported fairly high levels of explicit sexual activity at work. In what is probably a rather unusual sample of men, half of those who replied to a questionnaire conducted by the British women's magazine *Cosmopolitan* admitted to making sexual advances at work (McIntosh, 1982). Another much publicised survey of 645 readers of the magazine *Wedding Day* found that a quarter had met their marriage partners at work, school or college (Parry, 1983). According to R. Miles 'the workplace is still [*sic*] the prime area for making social/sexual contacts, especially for a newcomer to a city' (1985, 112). An Audience Selection Survey of 349 husbands and wives found that 'the most common place for affairs to start is at work' (Laming, 1985).

In a more qualitative way, Michael Korda in his review of male chauvinism at work suggests: 'The amount of sexual energy circulating in any office is awe-inspiring, and given the slightest sanction and opportunity it bursts out' (Korda, 1972, 108). In another recent study of the British newspaper industry, Cynthia Cockburn (1983, 134) notes:

The social currency of the composing room is women and women-objectifying talk from sexual expletives and innuendo through to narrations of exploits and fantasies. The wall is graced with four-colour litho 'tits and bums'. Even the computer is used to produce life-sized print-outs of naked women.

Such 'sexual events' do not occur randomly. They are the result of the relationship of definite social structures within organisations and sexuality.

In many ways the 'discovery' of sexuality in organisations, represents a development of the 'discovery' of the small group and informal process within the Hawthorne Experiments and the Human Relations approaches. This particular tradition which has led on to group dynamics, organisation development, motivation studies, job design, humanistic psychology and other approaches to organisation and management is forever focusing on the informal, the emotional and the interpersonal, without quite moving on to consideration of the sexual.[6] These issues are clearly of particular importance where the task has a strong emotional element.

These brief comments on the relationship of the emotional and the sexual take an even greater significance in those organisations which have a more explicit sexual ideology. This can apply both in organisations that explicitly exploit sexuality as a major part of their task, for example, brothels, and other 'sexploitation' organisations, and in organisations which focus on gender consciousness or gender liberation, for example, gay and lesbian information services.

'FIRST YOU SEE IT, NOW YOU DON'T'

The appearance of sexuality in this introductory chapter has been fleeting and somewhat shrouded. It has appeared as a mistaken opposition to work, paid work and organisation. It has temporarily resided in the private and the personal, only to then become apparent within the 'confines' of the public domain and productive institutions. It has appeared more by dint of it not quite being there, being constructed through organisational and 'work'-based factors. Like the use and exploitation of sexuality in both advertising and pin-ups its apparentness grows in its concealment, and yet in allusion to it. Such elusiveness means that sexuality is revealed by and in allusion. It is shown by 'signs', it is (a) sign(s). It signals relations with other gender stereotypes and job sex-roles. In this sense the chapter and indeed the whole of this book is an attempt to demonstrate the argument, to dismantle the organisational definitions, to show as well as to just say the argument. To do this necessitates unmasking organisational defences,[7] to reveal that which exists behind and below them. Organisations exist very much as such social defences and it is this aspect of their structure and dynamics that needs attention if sexuality is to become more fully apparent.

It is for this reason that this book does not seek a first cause either of sexuality or by sexuality. We therefore do not dwell on the possible 'hierarchy' of social structures that might be related to each other in the effort to work towards a *particular reduction* of sexuality and organisational life.[8] Thus we do not assert a simple and particular point of generation of sexuality within organisations. The relationship of sexuality and organisational life appears to relate to and at times derive from a variety of other important relationships, for example, between unpaid and paid work, the private and the public, the reproductive and the productive, even patriarchy and capitalism. At different times sexuality shows and is shown in organisational life as part of one or more of these dualisms. To capture the full subtlety and complexity of sexuality in organisations involves *holding on* to all of these and other dialectics in the analysis of 'sex' at 'work'.

2 The Search for Literature

Many texts follow a convenient tradition of 'reviewing the literature'. Here we do not so much outline a conventional literature search, as search for literature. Although there is a considerable amount of literature relevant to the analysis of sexuality and organisational life, for most of it a concerted act of interpretation is needed to display that relevance. The literature review includes both 'classic' studies and general theoretical positions in organisation theory; in most, sexuality is implicitly constructed, rarely explicit. Rather than determining research 'findings', we are more concerned with the shifting 'problem' posed by sexuality in the study of organisations and managements. This chapter is also written partly as an historical flashback to help understand how overt consciousness of the significance of sexuality in organisational life has grown. Literature on organisation and management is best read as ideology, emphasising the question as to how sexuality could possibly have been avoided in the first place.

CLASSICAL THEORY

Industrial sociology, organisational sociology, organisation theory, management theory, industrial relations, as well as the range of related sub-disciplines such as work study, personnel management, operational research, all describe, analyse and theorise about organisations and organisational life. All of these areas of study, some predominantly theoretical, some predominantly practical, share a similar historical and intellectual tradition. This goes under a number of names—'Scientific Management', 'Classical Theory' or simply 'Taylorism'. Because of its continuing importance some comments are necessary about this broad approach, and its implications for an understanding of sexuality within organisations.

The Classical approach to management is rooted in the attempt to produce universalistic rules and prescriptions for managers faced with the perplexing task of managing the large, multi-unit organisations that developed towards the end of the last century and the beginning of this century. It has become something of a conventional wisdom within 'radical organisation theory' to explain the growth of Classical Theory as a manifestation of the development of corporate or monopoly capitalism from the previous factory form of capitalism. Accordingly, the establishment of limited liability, the refinement of the joint stock company and the increasing separation of ownership and control, together are seen as producing the profession of management and in turn the need for management thought and management theory.[1] A practical problem and a problem for the practice of managers led to the devising of relatively straightforward theoretical statements, that overrode practical contradictions, in the characteristic manner of ideology.[2] Such marxist or neo-marxist accounts place fundamental emphasis upon the development of the mode of production for their explanation of management theory and Classical Theory in particular. They fail to notice that the development of the modern profession of management and its associated and legitimating theory and thinking represent a development of patriarchal authority.

Taylor's prescriptions are a detailed set of suggestions for how men should be, both as organisers and as the organised (Taylor, 1947). This 'management of men' by 'scientific methods' is both a technical and a more loosely ideological schema for defining and *restricting* men's behaviour. It focuses upon men as little more than the sum of their visible and effective behaviours. Although aware of the need for the 'functional foreman', who would look towards the morale of the men, Taylor was much more interested in the strictly instrumental aspects of the work organisation. Thus he observes: 'Perhaps the most prominent single element in modern scientific management is the task idea.' He continues: 'The work of every workman is fully planned out by the management at least one day in advance, and each man receives in most cases complete written instructions, describing in detail the task which he is to accomplish, as well as the means to be used in doing the work' (p. 63). The man is little more than the performer of the task, the user of specified means for the specified end. Furthermore, in order to do the task (and perhaps the man) in the 'one best way', it is necessary to eliminate all false movements, slow movements and useless movements. The model of men and the model of masculinity are precise, behavioural, controlled and instrumental. The man is the work. For the manager he has the further responsibility for the control of other men, precisely as the teacher gives 'definite, clear-cut tasks' to students, since 'all of us are grown-up children'.[3]

What has all this to do with sexuality, one might ask. Organisations, work and management are, for Taylorism in its various continuing forms, the concerns of men. All three spheres are reduced to an instrumentality, and so desexualised. The workman is, potentially at least, nothing more than the doer of the task, without feelings and emotions. The ideal workman would appear to almost lose physical presence, or be a mere disembodied bearer of role, in effect part of a machine system. And yet paradoxically in this desexualisation, a very explicit model of masculinity and thus sexuality is given. This model conforms closely to the Freudian patterning of super ego, ego, and id, as corresponding to the parental authority of management, the reality—testing of the workman, and the to-be-feared irresponsibility of both. Organisations, according to Classical Theorists, can become through appropriate management control a harmonious 'joint effort' between super ego and ego.[4] The sexuality of the id, as sexuality in organisations, is both excluded, 'relegated' to outside work, and yet dominated by the more conscious pairing. Masculinity and the implied sexuality of men is *split* between the consciousness in 'work' and the unconscious outside. Above all the model developed is one of supposedly stable, taken-for-granted power and authority, as in the patriarchal family.[5]

In this scheme of masculinity women vanish, or very nearly so. The prescriptions made are for men and for male society.

'Scientific' management is assumed to be concerned with the management of men by men. It is this tradition which informs men that they may remain asexual worker-beings, while in contrast women presumably have special qualities, by virtue of their sexuality, as sex objects, features of organisational adornment, and so on. More significantly and in some contrast, is may be observed that these peculiar emphases, or short-comings, of Classical Theory are all the more interesting in the light of major changes in the gender division of labour that took place during, and prior to the establishment of 'scientific' management. That particular period of industrial capitalism was characterised not only by increased corporation but also a great increase in the employment of women in clerical tasks. While in the mill and the factory the work gang and sub-contracting systems were being replaced by bureaumatic management, in the office new machine technology and women workers superseded the old manual methods.

Braverman (1974) charts some of these changes in his brief but useful account of the mechanisation of clerical work and the associated introduction of women workers. In 1851 there were less than 100 women clerks in the British Isles, while at the turn of the century about a quarter of clerks in the United States were women, and at present levels in excess of three-quarters of all clerks are female. He also identifies 1885 as the beginning of office mechanisation with the invention and application of a machine for counting punched cards. The beginnings of mechanisation, such as the marketing of the typewriter in 1873 by Remingtons, thus coincided with the major shift in the gender division of labour in the office. We may well wonder whether the then attempted elimination of thought from work which just happened to occur in mechanisation, in scientific management methods, and in the control of women workers at about the same time was coincidental. Through these organisational and managerial changes what was initiated was a new level of precision in the control of *the body*.[6] Post-Taylor 'management scientists' were keen, for example, to emphasise the similarities in both office work and factory work as forms of *manual* work, which can be measured, evaluated and prescribed. Thus office Organisation and Methods (O & M), which is the clear successor to Taylorism, is frequently directed towards women workers as its objects. Movements of hands, eyes, feet, arms are given detailed attention, for the sake of measurement. *A Guide to Office Clerical Time Standards* (Systems and Procedures Association, cited in Braverman, 1974, 320−5), in American companies, published in 1960, lists recommended times for all manner of minute motions−walking (over different distances), getting up from chair, sitting down in chair, applying rubber band, removing same, and so on. All work is measured as motion. In this context it is perhaps not so surprising that Mumford and Banks (1967, cited in Braverman, 1974, 337) in their study of bank computerisation found that personnel managers were 'recruiting girls [*sic*] of too high an intellectual calibre for the new simple machine jobs'.

The influence of Classical Theory on the practice and theory of management and organisation has been immense. This broad yet limited approach continues to provide a mass of taken-for-granted expectations about how organisational life is meant to be. There are, for example, deeply embedded assumptions that organisational leadership is something to be performed by men, that leadership implies maleness, and that maleness carries inherent qualities of leadership that women lack (Hearn and Parkin, 1986−7; Parkin and Hearn, 1987). Classical Theory and its associated practice ignores sexuality, conflates masculinity and asexuality, and creates the possibility of the conflation of femininity and sexuality. It sets up a firm framework for the control of the bodies of women and men in minutely detailed ways. There is no mind in the worker. There is also little of the body, except the visible, perceivable surfaces, apparent to the behaviourists. It creates persons−sexual, asexual or contradictory.[7]

HUMAN RELATIONS THEORY

The Human Relations tradition within organisation theory and its associated disciplines is often seen as a reaction against the formalist strictures of Classical Theory. While this tradition may partly be understood in those terms, its origins lie strictly within the discipline of organisational psychology that developed in the immediate wake of 'Taylorism', almost as a putting of

Classical Theory to the practical test. Mayo's early work grew from the organisational psychology studies of the First World War and subsequent years into the causes of fatigue and monotony in industrial settings.[8] Initial approaches to the industrial fatigue problem were strongly physiological, so much so that it was even suggested that doses of acid sodium phosphate might do the trick of dealing with 'fatigue toxins' (Mayo, 1960, 5). Mayo's own work in 1923-4 on the very high labour turnover of a mule-spinning department in a Philadelphia textile mill raised in a preliminary way the significance of *'emotional* labor turnover' (our emphasis), induced by the 'mental preoccupations—pessimism and rage' of the workers through the conditions of their work. He notes how:

At the beginning of the inquiry there were difficulties of observation owing to the fact that this was merely the latest of many investigations. The men were restless under observation, and the management were uneasily aware of this. We were greatly helped . . . in the placing of a small dispensary in the plant with a qualified nurse in charge . . . . She found that the majority of those who visited her were glad to 'give a very detailed personal account' of themselves. . . . When not occupied in her small office or clinic, she would walk in her uniform through the factory—visiting all departments but giving the greater part of her time to the workers in the spinning department. Any confidences made to her and there were many, were regarded as inviolable and not communicated to anyone unless professional need arose.[9] . . . In this way she came to know the attitude and personal background of every worker on 'the mules' with some detail and intimacy. . . . If any one of them [the workers] was permitted to talk at length, either in the nurse's office or to her in the department, the preoccupations he expressed whether about himself, his life, his home, or the work, appeared to be almost invariably morbid.

(pp. 44-5)

It was after this information was obtained that management agreed to institute experimentally a number of rest periods. The nurse's introduction is interesting on several counts; its passing over as merely informative is particularly notable in view of the interest of Mayo and his associates in the process of research, including the Hawthorne Effect itself.[10] The nurse's passive intervention was a means of access to the emotional life of the male workers by a lone woman who was especially permitted to walk throughout the factory.[11] A lack of an emotional life between the men workers may be implicit; lack of communication between the men workers and the men managers is left unstated. When Mayo comments that the nurse became 'something of a social nexus for the group' (p. 45) he was thinking of the workers, but he might more accurately have referred to the larger 'group' of researchers, workers and managers. For the nurse was what the three male 'sub-groups' had in common; men were communicating by way of a woman.

This leads on to what is usually considered the major contribution of the Human Relations School: the 'discovery' of the informal organisation and the power of the social group. The Hawthorne Experiments were initiated in April 1927 in a period when organisational psychology was undergoing a transition from a physiological and behaviourist to a social psychological base. As an example of this Mayo refers to Wyatt and Fraser's report to the Industrial Health Research Board in Britain in 1929 which stated that boredom was less liable 'when the operatives are allowed to work in compact social groups rather than isolated units' (Wyatt and Fraser, 1929, 43, cited in Mayo, 1960, 44). The first stage of the Hawthorne Experiment was conducted on six women workers in the Relay Assembly Test Room, and involved the introduction, with consultation, of a series of fifteen different changes in payment system, rest periods, arrangements for lunch and refreshments. Significantly, steady increase in production could not be accounted for by the environmental changes themselves, and instead recourse had to be made to psychological, emotional and social factors and explanations. In constructing such explanations it needs to be noted that from the start of the experiment attention was directed towards the 'mental attitude' of workers. Accordingly an attempt had been 'made to discover the home and social environs of each girl [*sic*] worker' (Mayo, 1962, 68) as part of the research records.[12] Though the development of a compact social group in the process of the experiment was certainly one relevant factor explaining work productivity, at the time the research team was unclear about this. Their strategy was to begin a large-scale interview programme of social psychological attitudes to work, covering in two years 21,000 of the 40,000 employees. This extensive intervention demonstrated the degree of disquiet amongst the workers, and the power of the emotional relationship to work in overriding the environmental conditions of work.

It also raised the possible impact of the interview process itself in eliciting emotional responses and becoming a part of the work situation.

The Hawthorne Experiments developed from a rather abstract observation of mental attitudes, such as that the women of the Relay Assembly Test Room 'have ceased to regard the man in charge as a "boss"' (Mayo, 1960, 75), to a more intimate interest in the lives and emotions of particular, often women, workers. The men researchers, and thus subsequently the men managers, had as part of their concern and supposed responsibility the personal and emotional lives of the workers. Management of the Human Relations type is beginning to own not just asexualised labour, or the controlled body, as in Classical Theory, but the 'person' as well, mind, body, emotions, a form of psychic totalitarianism.[13] There follow more in-depth observations from Mayo and his colleagues. Examples of such 'case studies' include the following:

she dislikes this . . . supervisor merely on the ground of a fancied resemblance to a hated relative; . . . she is 'nervous' . . . eighteen, unmarried . . . lives at home, . . . restrained by severe parental discipline, especially from her mother . . . spends her time when not at her most active either resenting the constraints of her elders or suffering a 'headache';

(pp. 87, 99)

'nervous' . . . about forty, a widow with two children doing well at school, . . . thinks much of 'child-welfare', has few friends, . . . is inordinately anxious about her children; . . . she 'overthinks' her situation in true obsessive fashion.

(p. 99)

Organisation theory and managerial practice were taking something of a leap forward. The work organisation is reorganised as a place for the *re-introduction* and residence of the private, the personal, the familial, and the emotional. Work was a psychodynamic process;[14] with a general tendency for 'emotional release' (Mayo, 1962, 67) from work constraints and indeed from self: 'If an individual cannot work with sufficient understanding of his work situation, then unlike a machine, he can only work against opposition from himself' (Mayo, 1960, 115). The Hawthorne research group thus showed considerable interest in the Freudian notion of 'compulsive obsession' (p. 103

passim) within which individuals become caught in a vicious circle. Embedded within the work of the Human Relations theorists is a multi-levelled framework for understanding the emotional life of organisational members, as the product both of individuals' relation to group dynamics and organisational structures, and of their own intrapsychic development.

The relevance of Human Relations thinking for this study is that a number of facets of the person that are relevant to or part of sexuality could be understood as organisationally located, if not organisationally determined. These include appearance, image, attractiveness as well as social and emotional relations.

The catch is that these insights were usually implicit in Mayo's theorising and that of his associates: they were not fully *recognised*. This general problematic of the place of the emotional—sexual—familial within organisations has been taken up within a number of subsequent theoretical approaches, perhaps most notably within humanistic psychology and motivational studies on the one hand, and ego psychology and psychoanalytic approaches to organisation and management on the other. However, this cannot be said to have been the most important legacy of the Human Relations Theory, for its major impact has been in terms of facilitating change in management methods and styles. Human Relations theory in effect opened up a new set of personal factors as of interest to management, at the same time liberalising and obscuring its operation. Management could legitimately take a 'more complete' view of the worker, including their emotional life and 'personal situation'. In doing so there was the possibility of more sympathetic and responsive management, existing alongside the reality of more of the worker being sold as labour. Worse still more of the worker was becoming known to management with the possibility of being patronised and manipulated. Human Relations Theory can give ready-made justifications to management, sometimes via female supervisors or personnel officers for seeking information of various personal matters. Indeed 'Human Relations' may be a metaphor for the 'authoritative' male investigation of the 'awkward' female, a little like the Victorian treatment of female 'hysteria', or the medicalisation of gynaecological problems.

FEAR IN THE 'WAR FACTORY'

Classical Theory and Human Relations Theory may have found their theoretical synthesis in systems theory but their practical synthesis lay in the managerial practices of the managers of the war factories in the Second World War. Anxious to maintain discipline and increase the productivity of their new charges, these men took to the task of managing in a manner that took account of 'human relations'. The metaphorical ownership of the 'whole person' in Human Relations Theory had soon become a reality, with wartime state direction of labour. The not-so-hidden agenda of a 'classic' study[15] by Mass Observation of factory life in the early war years was how men managers could coax and cope with 'the irresponsible and carefree outlook [of] the machine-shop girls' (Harrison, 1942, 68). Like Mayo, Harrison, the editor of the study, was extremely fearful of the onset of anomie and apathy within society. However, the latter was more explicit in fearing the anomie and non-cooperation of *women*: as he says 'Underlying the life of young working women today there is a background of aimlessness . . . and boredom . . . . The *laissez-faire* of leisure, and its dangerous separation from work, is immediately and primarily responsible' (Harrison, 1943, 6).

Throughout the *War Factory* study there is a constant preoccupation with the incompetence, unsuitability and vanity of the women workers held to be more interested in their appearance than their work. There is a series of 'unfortunate' diversions around clocking in, the cloakroom scramble, 'clock watching', doing of hair and 'lavatory-mongering'. Pen portraits of six of the women are drawn within the problematic of the antagonism of 'leisure' and 'work'. Of these, three are seen as particular problems for management. Sadie is described as 'a slow, very good-natured girl, with a round red face and dark hair' (p. 40). She resents her lack of leisure; finds the work from eight a.m. till eight p.m., with lunch and tea breaks exhausting; gets home at half past nine. She prefers her previous work in a greengrocer's shop, where she finished at five or half past and she 'could meet her boy when he got back, and . . . go to the pictures or anything like that' (p. 41).

Peggy appears as:

a lively very good looking girl of twenty, with lovely naturally-wavy hair, which she wears loose on her shoulders . . . . Every possible evening she gets off at half-past five . . . and goes off with a crowd of friends, who with much shrieking and laughing and waving, manage to secure lifts to where she lives. . . . evenings she usually goes to some dance or other, . . . staying up till two in the morning; as she has to be up at six to catch the bus to work; it is not surprising that she often fails to catch it, and then has a day off.

(p. 33)

As regards the work itself, this:

bores her intensely, and her slapdash manner with the machine results in frequent breaking of drills—always an occasion for laughter. . . . In the same carefree spirit, she always wears nice dresses and stockings to work, regardless of . . . dirt and oil of the machine shop they are going to be ruined very quickly.

(p. 34)

This is a true sign of moral indignation, that she is not only harming productivity but herself and her 'nice dresses'.

As for fifteen-year-old Claire, though it is added that: 'she might easily be taken for twenty she is so tall and well developed' (p. 36). The diagnosis for Claire is quite unequivocal:

She does not seem to be a bad worker, but is invariably so tired and sleepy that it is hard to tell what her real potentialities are. The main reason . . . is that she goes around with a young man of twenty-five or more, who takes her home, to dances, socials, pictures etc., and she rarely gets to bed before one or two in the morning.

(p. 36)

What is more the man is a charge-hand on the bench where she works so that even though, being under eighteen, she cannot work beyond 5.30 p.m., she stays till he finishes at eight 'to walk home with him—also to prevent him flirting with any of the other girls, which he usually does whenever she is not there' (p. 36). The complication this relationship raises, for the woman, is 'that anyone who gets off with an authority of any kind, even a charge-hand, is usually looked on slightly askance by the others [the women workers]'.

In marked contrast we find Hilda, 'a heavy, plain girl of above twenty-eight . . . a large pasty face, glasses and dark hair cut in a bob and drawn off her face with a slide, like a school girl' (p. 32), and Molly, '[a] queer, old-fashioned looking, little thing

with glasses, a rather high childish voice, wears her clothes and
her hair [that make] her look well over thirty, though actually she
is twenty-four' (p. 37).

Hilda reportedly does not feel the lack of leisure, has no
special friend, and yet what do we find? She is said to be 'as
good-natured as she is stupid . . . one of the most contented of
the machine-shop girls, and probably one of the best at her
work' (p. 32). Similarly, Molly has no close friends in the
factory or in the town, hardly ever goes out in the evening and
only attends Sunday afternoon tea at her chapel. In particular
she takes care with her appearance, if in an 'old-fashioned' way.

It's terrible the way the dirt gets through onto your clothes. I was ashamed of
my petticoat this week, it was all quite black . . . I was brought up to take
more care of my under things than my top ones. . . .My mother always used
to say, suppose you were run over.

(pp. 39–40)

By this stage, the conclusion is clear: 'Molly is one of the
happiest, most contented girls in the factory' (p. 40).

There is, however, a middle way and it is found in the only one
of the six who happens to be married. Edith, '[a] very sweet,
gentle girl of twenty-two, small and very pretty . . . [who] thinks
of . . . and worries about [her husband] continually; carries
photographs which she shows to us all at odd times . . . [she]
disliked the work, finding it dirtier and more monstrous than she
had expected . . . ' and yet 'being by temperament very
conscientious, did not do it badly or try to dodge it' (pp. 34–6).

The whole study is written for management, an exercise in the
reinforcement of the taken-for-granted sexism of managerial
practice. It suggests that 'girls of the machine-shop type are far
more influenced by a personality than . . . by any number of
abstract appeals to patriotism, or by impersonal regulations and
penalties'. The managers respond: 'This should be made more
use of' and 'every three months it is my intention to make a
statement in person' (p. 69). The stated conclusion of *War
Factory* is that women workers remain a problem, because of
their different attitude to earning money and to penalties or
suspensions, as 'little more than a holiday and a big joke'
(pp. 19–20). An alternative interpretation is that sexuality in the
guise of 'doing hair', 'getting off', going to dances and staying

out late, let alone possible undermining of male authority, created a problem for management. The desire to subjugate the moral and sexual life of newly mobile women workers to the demands of paid employment appeared to catch them off balance: *War Factory* represents an almost archetypal statement of this particular 'organisational problem' for men.

GROUP DYNAMICS

Human Relations theories and wartime experience both appeared to make sexuality more visible, and yet, in important ways, contributed to its obscuring within post-Human Relations theorising. In particular group dynamics, psychoanalytic approaches, and systemic analogies for organisations, share a common tendency to *incorporate* expressive and emotional elements of social reality, within their own neutralised and all-embracing language. While operating at different levels of generality each provides an analytical framework for apparently opposing elements, for example, the formally and informally structured. Organisations, and indeed groups, are thus seen as organised processes of change, rather than primarily formal structures or informal relations. There are numerous ways in which group dynamics, psychoanalysis and systems analysis have drawn on each other, culminating in Parsons' theorising of systems, at individual, family, group, organisational and societal levels.

The growth and establishment of group dynamics as a recognisable discipline was predominantly concerned with the measurement of the more qualitative aspects of groups, often in very detailed ways, in both laboratory and non-laboratory situations. For example, the sociometric studies by Moreno and others developed sociograms, 'friendship indices' (Dimock, 1941) and the concepts of 'sociogroups' and 'psychogroups'[16] to quantify the informal relationships within groups. The Second World War action research in the United States Air Force and Navy, the War Office Selection Boards (WOSBs) in Britain, and elsewhere, focused on leadership, task performance and stress in task-centred groups. Subsequently, researchers such as Leavitt (1951), and Josephine Klein (1956) produced detailed evaluations of group structure and patterns of communication, such as 'stars', 'chains' and 'circles', in terms of effectiveness, social participation and enjoyment.

The crucial problematic of such group dynamics work centres on the tension between the task, leadership and structure of groups on the one hand and the emotional, experiential and interpersonal aspects of groups on the other, generally addressing the latter in relation to the former. It does not usually speak of sexuality as such but uses a variety of euphemisms: 'interpersonal attraction', 'sense of belonging', the 'socio-emotional', even 'cohesiveness'. In these terms, the structural evaluation of groups, whether single-sex or mixed-sex, can be seen as a translation of emotionality and sexuality into desexualised 'structures'. The *implicit* project of the group dynamics tradition becomes clear from more recent work such as that by Mayes (1979) that *explicitly* looks at the impact of women group leaders on sexuality.

PSYCHODYNAMICS

The psychoanalytic tradition in group dynamics appears at first to have developed in a rather different direction, being concerned as much or more with the intrapersonal as the interpersonal, and more explicitly focusing on sexuality, albeit at times within a determinist framework. Its development was also greatly facilitated by the events of the Second World War, and in particular in Britain the involvement of the Tavistock Group in the machinery of government (Dicks, 1970; Sofer, 1972; 194–215). Their work was not only in the wartime selection of leaders but also in the rehabilitation of military men and ex-prisoners of war in therapeutic communities and Civil Resettlement Units. Much of this work, by Wilfred Bion, John Rickman, Tom Main, A.T.M. Wilson and others attempted to use group approaches in dealing with psychiatric and neurotic disturbance, both during the war and its aftermath.

The post-war period saw a series of attempts, by the Tavistock Group and others, to codify and clarify the experiences of dealing with the trauma of war, and to draw out 'lessons' for 'peacetime'. In some cases these were directly concerned with the conceptualisation of sexuality within social situations, and especially groups; more usually sexuality was ostensibly a minor component of these analyses. Bion's work brought together the development of group dynamics, the therapeutic community and psychodynamics. He pointed to the unconscious preoccupation of group members with certain basic assumptions, of which one is the tendency to pairing in group communications manifesting underlying sexual purposes (Bion, 1948, 1949, 1950).

The recognition of, if not the ubiquity then at least the frequency of, sexuality in groups is overridden by his concern for the presence of projections in groups causing them to become immobilised and ineffective. According to de Board (1978, 116), Bion's explanation of behaviour in groups corresponds to Melanie Klein's ego psychology of the individual, whereby projection as an ego defence against anxiety blurs the boundary of the person, re-stimulating the paranoid-schizoid and depressive anxieties of childhood.

Bion's approach to groups has a relevance for the analysis of sexuality, in that events outside 'the group', 'the organisation', the meeting or the room, including sexuality, can also have profoundly projective effects. Sexuality is not to be feared because it makes 'bad workers' (cf. Harrison, 1943), but it can produce confusion, illusion and misperception, through projections and other processes.

A stricter ego psychology synthesis was developed by Jaques, who had joined the Tavistock Institute in 1946, and was to work in particular on the functioning of social defence systems. Jaques expanded the Kleinian idea of ego defence to the social context, whereby aspects of organisations and institutions are taken on and used by individuals to reinforce individual defences (1955, 478). Menzies (1960), who had been in the Civil Resettlement Unit Team in the wartime Tavistock, extended this approach in her study of how hospital nurses cope with anxiety of the job. Her study elaborates on the impact of the work itself, which in the case of nursing was often intimate, emotional and yet involving dependence from and possible hostility to patients, upon the behaviour of nurses. The intense and contradictory emotions generated by nursing work have a remarkable resemblance to those infantile anxieties proposed by Klein, so leading to a variety of defensive actions by nurses, such as retreat into ritual task performance, so desexualising the task.

This kind of theorising is appropriately enough capable of contradictory interpretations. On one hand it represents a means to psychologising social and political problems. Jaques' work can be read alongside the work of Bowlby, another Tavistock researcher, and especially his classic study (1953) of maternal deprivation as the cause of all sorts of personal and social problems, including 'sexual misdemeanours'. In this sense such explanatory psychodynamics fitted well in Britain at least with post-war reconstruction and welfare statism.[17] On the other hand, social defence systems theory indirectly raises novel questions for an understanding of sexuality, as a major source of anxiety, within organisations and groups. Such theory provided an opportunity for considering the way aspects of organisations are used, often collusively, by members to deal with and defend against the anxieties of sexuality.

Neo-Freudian and psychoanalytic approaches to groups and organisations have clearly promoted the importance of intensely personal, emotional and indeed sexual aspects of organisational life. This has, however, generally not led to a recipe for expressivism. Bion, Jaques, Menzies and others had raised some sensitive and difficult areas of organisation but the tradition was largely swallowed by the rising popularity of all-consuming models of the system. From the system perspective, anxiety, projection, intimacy and sexuality are but functions or means to the satisfaction of needs. The confluence of psychodynamics and systemic analysis is seen not only in the Tavistock Group's work, but was most significantly of all to be explicitly furthered in the structural functionalism of Parsons, Bales and their associates.

SYSTEMS

The Parsonian synthesis (e.g. Parsons and Bales, 1955; Parsons, Bales and Shils, 1951) may be seen as a *means of incorporating* some of the insights of psychoanalytic theory, particularly at the intrapersonal level, into a more comprehensive framework. Alternatively, Parsonianism may be a *continuation* of a process of neutralising sexuality accomplished within psychodynamic approaches to organisations. Either way, Parsons' theorising attempts an overarching reconciliation of structural and instrumental facets of group and organisational dynamics, and a variety of expressivist tendencies, including those relating to sexuality.

The interesting point about this synthesis for present purposes are the linkages made by Parsons, Bales and others between such divisions as task/maintenance, instrumental/expressive, and gender. The nuclear family with a clear gender division of labour between the 'externally-orientated' male and the 'integrative' female is drawn as a paradigm case for application to groups and organisations (e.g. Strodtbeck and Mᵃrn, 1956; Hare, 1962, 208–9). In such formulations sexuality is unambiguously part of the maintenance, expressive and thus 'female' 'functions'. The female is accorded the role of the carrier of sexuality, and is not part of the goal-orientation of the male. Furthermore, systems themselves have 'male' and 'female' facets. When men are behaving 'socio-emotionally' or sexually, their behaviour comprises part of those 'female' functions. In terms of system management both sexuality and the 'female' are relegated to a secondary role, in terms of performance, adaptation and goal-orientation. This kind of theorising can be used to justify and perpetuate the 'maintenance' roles of women in less powerful and lower paid organisational positions.

THE NEUTERING OF ORGANISATION THEORY

Systems thinking has in many respects become the new orthodoxy of management thought and theory. The 'system' may incorporate human relations processes, bureaucratic dysfunctions, hierarchical structures and much more. It has become part of the post-war 'commonsense' of management, whereby 'neutral' concepts and language may be used to incorporate virtually anything, including sexuality. Technology theory, contingency theory, open systems theory, inter-organisation theories and the rest are usually genuinely sexless. Adaptations of the organismic system, such as people-changing organisations as contrasted with the people-processing

(Hasenfeld, 1972) might be said to centre on internal 'maintenance' rather than external 'task', but in systems theories as a genre such issues are implicit.

Within the dominant post-war strands of organisation and management theory, the so-called 'functionalist paradigm' (Burrell and Morgan, 1979, 118–226), the most usual approach is either to neglect gender completely, or to use relatively simple descriptive, sometimes stereotypical, models, or somewhat more critically to see gender as no more than a variable of which account should be taken (Hearn and Parkin, 1983). Many of these functionalist texts conform to Feldberg and Glenn's (1979) 'job model' within the sociology of work. According to this, work (by which they mean largely paid, organisational work) that people do is the primary, independent variable in explaining behaviour both on and off the job. Feldberg and Glenn argue that the job model is most usually applied to men, while the 'gender model', emphasising personal and family relationships, is often used to explain women's behaviour both at and away from 'work'.

Another feature of some 'functionalist' theorising is its not so very implicit concern with men. Texts about organisations turn out to be discussions of men, men's behaviour and masculinity. In this sense 'classics' such as *The Organization Man* (Whyte, 1956) and 'Bureaucratic man' (Kohn, 1971) deserve critical re-examination. In addition to these, many mainstream texts can be reviewed in terms of their treatment of male roles and masculinity (Acker and Van Houten, 1974; Morgan, 1981). Discussions of, say, organisational goals, hierarchy or management function are virtually always euphemisms for discussions of men.

These firm traditions of organisation theory and management theory as legitimate, sexless disciplines are, however, only part of the changing picture. The same period in which systems thinking was consolidated and organisation theory institutionalised also saw the acceleration of critical approaches to organisations.

GENDER AND ORGANISATIONS

The 1960s and 1970s involved both corporatism and managerialism on one hand, and a radical questioning on the other.

Critique took various forms: anti-positivist, ethnomethodology; neo-marxism and New Left politics; and the recognition of the gendering of organisations as a serious question for organisation analysis. Relevant 'early' studies included in Britain those by Lupton (1963) and Cunnison (1966) on factory labour and in the United States that by Simpson and Simpson (1969) on the relationship of the 'semi-professions' and gender.

Beynon and Blackburn's (1972) analysis of a British food factory examined internal divisions between women and men workers, as well as between day shift and night shift, and full-time and part-time workers. However, although such early studies established 'gender' as a reasonable area of inquiry they did so largely with an emphasis on the industrial division of labour rather than on organisational processes and dynamics, and generally without a feminist perspective or one informed by feminism.

FEMINIST CRITIQUES

From at least the late 1960s onwards the impact of the (modern) women's liberation movement and feminist theory and practice have been increasingly evident in the study of organisations. It is difficult to characterise this political development; by their very nature, feminist critiques are varied, emphasising the importance of practice by women for women.[18] Though much feminist literature in the late 1960s and early 1970s tended to stress either general societal processes and means of oppression or specific issues and experiences of women, it is hard to underestimate the reformulation of organisations that has taken place. This critique has thus brought into view both structural and personal matters that make it clear once and for all that organisations are gendered institutions and collectivities. This means that most if not all organisations possess a distinctive genderic structure, typically with men occupying the most powerful organisational and occupational positions (Davies, 1975; Mackie and Pattullo, 1977; Lewenhak, 1980; Game and Pringle, 1983). Few organisations are genderically random.

Until relatively recently the impact has generally been indirect with few feminist analyses of organisational dynamics or types of organisation. In the last decade this has been remedied by such writers as Wolff (1977), Kanter (1975, 1977), Pollert (1981), Cavendish (1982) and Cockburn (1983). Feminist critiques have not only been directed against the *distribution* of women and men throughout organisations, but also against the very structure and hierarchy of organisations.[19] Most of these studies have however, been concerned primarily with the gender division of labour, work, power and authority, so that sexuality where it is addressed follows from these factors rather than being a dynamic of itself. Feminist scholarship has opened up many new questions about organisations, and it is in relation to these that the present study is conducted.[20]

The two most prolific feminist or feminist-influenced sets of literature on gender and organisations have come from marxist and socialist feminism; and writing on 'women in management', especially from North America. Thus the dominant concepts for analysing the gendered organisation have included the 'dual labour market', the 'reserve army of labour', 'direct' and 'indirect discrimination', 'affirmative action' and so on. Sexuality has still not generally been the central focus of interest.

SEXUAL HARASSMENT SURVEYS

Explicit analyses of sexuality in organisational settings are found in surveys and studies of sexual harassment. Interest in and outrage at the nature and scale of sexual harassment in work organisations has increased throughout the 1970s and 1980s, initially in the journalistic media and in North America, but also in Europe and elsewhere. This represents part of the broader concerns of women against male violence and objectification in its various forms.

The making visible of sexual harassment constitutes a major empirical contribution to the study of organisations and exemplifies the way the understanding of organisations is being changed by feminist research. There have been numerous surveys of the occurrence of sexual harassment particularly in Britain and America.[21]

These have led on to more detailed analyses of the factors that appear to affect either level or perception of harassment.

Such studies may focus on the 'characteristics' of individuals, for example, attractiveness and personality; the nature of the relationship between the participants, for example, discrepancies in motives or authority increasing perception of harassment; or more organisational considerations, such as sexual structuring or sex ratios, and associated sex-role spillover (Gutek and Morasch, 1982; Gutek and Nakamura, 1982; Gutek and Dunwoody, 1987).

These surveys also give some indication of the complex form and process of sexuality in organisations, compulsory heterosexuality, heterosexism, routine oppression. They show sexuality in organisational life is a matter of power. These surveys have also acted (for us) as an incitement to find out more, to expose the way sexuality often is at work, in both senses. The harassment studies are promoted by and reinforce a political and personal awareness. Unlike some of the previous studies, research is not conducted through objectification but from a position of commitment and nurture.

STUDIES OF SEXUALITY

The sexual harassment surveys have a specifically political and a more loosely academic significance. They have made visible, analysable, and challengeable those things that were previously, more often than not, taken for granted. The focus on sexual harassment has had another more diffuse effect: the legitimation of more general studies of sexuality in organisational contexts, including actual or potential sexual relationships, their differential perception and repercussions, both subtle and dramatic.

One of the earliest of these recent and wider-ranging studies was that by Bradford, Sargent and Sprague (1975) on the impact of sexuality, by which they mean heterosexuality, upon managerial women and men, particularly with the increasing number of women in management positions. Their analysis is thus at one level broadly historical, arguing that these changes in the division of paid labour, together with changing social and cultural norms, increasing opportunities for (heterosexual) contact, and reduction in traditional controls, are likely to lead to an increase in sexual relationships in organisations, especially at the managerial level. They also stress the implications of such possibilities for 'disrupting' relationships between men in previously all-male groups. Sexuality thus has a political impact on power structures and relations in organisations (see chapter 4) (Korda, 1976).

In particular there has been a growing number both of empirical studies and of policy-orientated commentaries on 'romantic relationships' (Quinn, 1977), 'managers and lovers' (Collins, 1983), 'romance in the workplace' (Gray, 1984), and 'love at work' (Harrison and Lee, 1986). While these studies suggest likely increases in such relationships, they analyse the phenomenon with a mixture of 'liberal tolerance', an emphasis on non-harassment in love or sexual relationships, and an unwarranted assumption of heterosexual norms. On the one hand, the possible conflict of particularistic sexual relationships and universalistic organisational 'rationalities' is noted (Quinn, 1977); on the other, doubts are expressed as to whether 'romance' can be left to 'individual discretion . . . commonsense or outmoded rules', (Harrison and Lee, 1986). The implication is clear that it may be advisable *for management* to develop 'corporate rules for the game [*sic*] of love' (Gray, 1984).

Problems of these tendencies to homogenise, and so reduce, sexual and similar relationships are illustrated in qualitative studies, such as Horn and Horn's (1982) investigaton of 'power and passion in the office', which elaborates the *differences* between flirting, the fling, dating, the affair, commitment, as well as harassment. This is, however, not to suggest that sexual harassment and sexual relationships are necessarily so distinct: a theme that has been explored in depth as 'social-sexual behaviour', by Gutek with a number of colleagues since the late 1970s. Many of the insights of this work have recently been drawn together in Gutek's (1985) major study of *Sex and the Workplace*.

POPULAR AND CULTURAL SOURCES

Finally, any account of 'the search for literature' would be incomplete without mention of the variety of popular and cultural sources that provide useful empirical and occasionally analytical information on sexuality in organisations. Magazines such as *Cosmopolitan* in Britain and *Ms.* in the USA, journalistic sources, newspapers, advertisements, trade materials, film and television can be resources not only about particular organisations featured but also about the organisations themselves that produce the material. For example, in 1982 the *News of the World* magazine, *Sunday*, published a feature on pin-up calendars and their history, with the stunningly sexist title of 'How long could you spend with this girl?' (1982). Its 'usefulness' in research terms was in terms firstly of certain historical information and, secondly, of the portrayal of sexist image, rather than in the terms probably intended by the publishers. Thus popular and cultural sources are not only diverse but have meaning and significance at a number of levels, sometimes in a contradictory fashion.

Popular articles such as 'Sex on the job' (R. Miles, 1985), '. . .if you've got to cry, then cry in the loo' (Watts, 1978), and 'Sex and the power lunch. Touching moments at table' (Dienhart and Pinsel, 1984), attend more to sexuality than do most academic texts on organisations. This sort of material has for some reason been largely ignored, as not significant and perhaps even frivolous, by most 'academic' (male) organisation theorists. Topics such as the stereotyping of secretaries, women's and men's sexual self-image, clandestine relationships, and sexual fantasy are given more regular attention in these cultural resources than they are as significant organisational processes within the academic literature on organisations. Supposedly desexualised academia appears slow at noting certain aspects of organisational reality, that do not easily fit into recognised malestream theories and traditions.

3 The Process of Research

The neglect of the study of sexuality within organisations presents several challenges to organisation theorists. These are partly challenges of substance: how to counteract the near exclusion of the topic from organisation theory, as a subject for serious academic study. They are also, however, challenges of method, that is research into sexuality may itself represent a challenge to orthodox research methods. This is particularly so as researching sexuality continually demonstrates fundamental 'methodological difficulties', which themselves could be part of the explanation of the topic's neglect. In other words, the methods of research become increasingly intertwined with the substance of research.

For example, the search for literature just described was initially perceived by us as a necessary first stage in the research process. In the event it then became much more than that: it is a part of the problem and a problem in itself. Searching the literature has become an integral part of the research process: a process which involves interpretation at different levels, a way of opening up new dimensions of organisational life. Thus in our experience in researching sexuality and organisational life we have found it necessary to question the adequacy of any abstracted research methods, as practical difficulties that appear in 'doing methodologies' merge with personal, political, organisational and other difficulties and issues.

This chapter therefore begins by examining some of the problems of dominant research methods; moves on to consider issues arising in the practice of researching; and concludes by redefining so-called 'methodological difficulties' as organisational processes, worthy of study in their own right.

RESEARCH METHODS AND THEIR PROBLEMS

Social science research is often assumed to proceed through a series of ordered stages, from setting out methodological assumptions and devising hypotheses through to operationalisation and the production of results (cf. Silverman, 1985). This approach is *ideally* 'straight line' and 'hygienic', with objectivity at each stage, and the expectation of *answers* to follow. This remains within general debates around quantitative versus qualitative research methods, despite an increasing readiness to go beyond positivism in social science. In social science there is thus characteristically a combination of quantitative method and qualitative inquiry.

The 'pros' and 'cons' of quantitative and qualitative research, important as they are, in many ways do not go far enough. Both styles of study may indeed preserve high levels of 'epistemological privilege' and 'ontological privilege' for both their observation-languages and their whole enterprise (Keat and Urry, 1982, 17−22).[1] What is necessary in moving towards a realist approach to research is the inclusion of the relationship, and especially the emotional relationship, of researchers to the research undertaken as part of the research. Stanley and Wise (1983, 153) put this perspective with the following clarity:

> Presenting the research process as orderly, coherent and logically organised has consequences. . . . most social science researchers start off believing that what is presented in these descriptions is a reasonable representation of the reality of research. Most of us get a nasty shock when we come to do research ourselves . . . the point at which we begin to realise that this 'hygienic research' in which no problems occur, no emotions are involved, is 'research as it is experienced', is frequently a crucial one . . . . One problem all researchers have to cope with is their actual experience of the research process.

These general research problems have an immediate applicability to the study of sexuality within organisations, with the added complication that the subject itself−sexuality−is of a qualitative nature. Sexuality is private, intensely felt, and often kept secret in organisations, as elsewhere. As Brake (1982, 13) suggests:

> The nature of sexuality . . . is a subject which ranges into the difficult area of the personal and political . . . . Sexual passion is . . . the one area where

the trappings of respectability and success have been thrown away for pleasure
. . . . Yet sexual activity is shrouded in mystery, everyone has subjective
experience of it but little objective knowledge. It is surrounded by myths
and taboos.

The topic is clearly a delicate one, involving as it does research
into sensitive areas. If one compares sexuality in organisations with,
say, corruption in organisations, a number of interesting points can
be made: (i) it is more personal to individuals; (ii) it usually involves
more than one person; (iii) it cannot be locked away in a drawer;
(iv) it has different and more subtle repercussions, for example,
the display of emotions after an affair may be more visible than
any change after the sacking of an embezzler; and (v) it is often
outside the rules of many organisations, whereas corruption simply
breaks the rules.

Researching sexuality either in private, clinical[2] or organisational
settings is clearly not easy. This is of course not to say that there
is no quantitative research on sexuality in organisations,[3] rather
that such research typically strives to quantify qualitative, subjective
experiences. For example, the various recent surveys of sexual
harassment in the paid workplace attempt to measure the reported
frequency of its occurrence.

In the *Cosmopolitan* survey 11 per cent of women workers
reported that they had been subject to persistent, unwanted advances
at work (McIntosh, 1982); the Liverpool branch of NALGO (1982)
indicated that a quarter of the women had experienced harassment
in their current workplace, and a half at some time in their working
lives; Alfred Marks Bureau (1982) found that 51 per cent of the
women respondents had experienced some form of unwanted sexual
advance during their working lives; Cooper and Davidson (1982)
discovered that 52 per cent of women managers had suffered in
this way; and Camden NALGO produced a response of 70 per cent
(cited in Tysoe, 1982) and the Inland Revenue Staff Association,
75 per cent (cited in R. Miles, 1985). Typically such surveys use
formal questionnaire methods, sometimes coupled with interviews.
Questionnaires have usually been directed at members of
workforces, trade unionists or respondents of more randomised
samples.

Questionnaire research on sexual, as other, harassment does,
however, carry with it several difficulties. The information obtained
is constrained by the form of questionnaire; and is unlikely to be

fully commensurate with the lived experiences of those harassed. Questionnaires are also likely to attract or distract interest from different types of people. The Lesbian Employment Rights survey (Taylor, 1986, 3) suggested: '. . . the concept of using questionnaires as a means of providing information is a very white, middle class, academic approach to research. This is reflected in the race and class of women who responded to the survey and, in itself, has a significant effect on some of the conclusions which can be drawn from the results'.

One of the clear implications of this is the need for more detailed qualitative study of harassment and related forms of sexuality (for example, Mahony, 1985). Farley (1978) refers to the use of tape recording during job interviews to discover the existence of sexual harassment. In slightly different vein there was the description of how a secretary kept a diary which logged more than 100 incidents of sexual harassment by her boss against her, an example of quantification of very qualitative, subjective experiences (Corless, 1983; 'Secretary kept diary. . .', 1983).

Research into sexual harassment also illustrates a further problem, namely the difficulty of definition (see chapters 4 and 6). 'Sexual harassment' covers many activities and actions; eyeing up and down; suggestive looks at parts of the body; regular sexual remarks and jokes; unwanted cheek kissing on meeting and parting; asking out on dates despite refusals; unwanted touching or patting; pinching or grabbing; direct sexual proposition; forcible sexual aggression; the pinning up and maintenance of pin-ups.[4]

Most research on sexual harassment has focused on the 'heterosexual' harassment of women by men. Such harassment takes on a further level of offensiveness when directed at lesbians, whether they are sexually 'out' or not. In many organisations, lesbians and gay men are also subject to directly oppressive actions. Probably the first research survey directed specifically the experience of lesbians both in employment and unemployment is the extremely useful Lesbian Employment Rights (Taylor, 1986), *All in a Day's Work*. From the 171 women respondents, the following types and numbers of harassment were recorded:

Co-workers assuming that women are heterosexual	143 incidents
Anti-lesbian remarks	124 incidents
Lack of promotion	28 incidents

Dismissal threats	21 incidents
Dismissal	12 incidents
Other types of anti-lesbian discrimination	58 incidents
None of the above	8 incidents

'12 women did not answer the question, . . .151 lesbians had experienced at least one, and frequently more than one, of the above types of anti-lesbianism' (p. 27).

Sexual harassment is, however, more than just a list of actions: it is a process of harassing actions performed, usually by men, and actions received, usually by women. Furthermore, even this 'process' view of harassment may neglect issues of intentionality, of visibility, of ambiguity.[5] Moreover there is the question of how harassers, usually men, get themselves into the social and physical position to do such things to others, usually women, in the first place. Sexual harassment is, like pornography, often more to do with violence and power than sexuality, 'so mindless and impersonal that any but the most hardened are likely to be turned off by it' (Betzold, 1977).

Another genre of sexual harassment studies has measured people's evaluation of imagined situations: 'Many of these studies use similar research designs, all classic analyses of variance designs, in which students, employees, or managers are asked to rate one or more scenarios' (Gutek and Dunwoody, 1987).

Both quantitative and qualitative methods are useful to certain extents in producing information about sexuality in organisations. However, limited reliance on such methods to generate research results is unlikely to produce an adequate account of the *complexity* of sexuality within organisational life, including the relationship of the researched to the researcher. The interaction between the qualitative nature of the topic and any methods adopted, in our experience, is such that the process of researching sexuality in organisations has a *doubly qualitative* character.

METHODOLOGY IN PRACTICE

This critique of dominant research methods is partial; it is not an argument against the validity of such methods or the results produced. It is a commentary on their *limitations* when researching a qualitative subject, sexuality, that permeates organisational life, in a continuing, powerful and dynamic process.

Much research consists of trying to answer questions that are pre-determined within a given paradigm; our experience has differed. Our research began with a growing awareness of unaddressed questions including the seeming lack of research on sexuality in organisations rather than hypotheses to test. The *significance* of the lack of research has become one focus of the research itself. Additionally as noted, early in the research process we recognised some of the problems around methodology and consequent 'methodological difficulties' in studying the subject. It has become increasingly apparent that fixed answers were unlikely to be found in this particular field. Instead we have tried to develop a view of organisational reality that allows analysis of both what is known and obscure, 'seen but unnoticed' (Hearn, 1985b), and what is only revealed by successive peeling back of layers of structure and meaning. We have also been obliged to attend to the recurrence of issues of power and our own relationship to them. Both sexuality and research on sexuality are processes not results. These complications now clearly seem a major deterrent to organisational theorists from study of the subject, particularly in view of the dominance of positivism within organisation theory.

Acknowledging and accepting 'methodological difficulties' has been an important part of our own changing relationship to the research; it has given us a methodological freedom that is at the same time exhilarating and confusing. The excitement of alternative ways of researching has developed from and interrelated with the elusiveness of sexuality and the resistance of the research process to rigid structuring. Limiting the definition of what constitutes research clearly also limits what one may possibly research.

The activity of researching sexuality in organisations can be now seen as the product of, at least, a three-way relationship. Each element in this process is itself subject to power relations, and in particular dominant forms of ordering.[6] This applies as much to the obscuring of sexuality through certain kinds of organisational 'order', as it does in the research methodology.

Figure 1: The three-way research relationship

There is thus a need to move beyond the simple contrast of quantitative and qualitative methods. Several possible avenues have presented themselves as ways forward, and each one has in different ways been important in our research.

(i)   strategies of *conflict methodology*—'a willingness to utilize any and all situationally available techniques to gather data' (Lundman and McFarlane, 1976, 507), particularly where free flow of information is impeded by élites.[7]

(ii) *feminist* research methodology and other attempts to interrelate *theory and practice* (e.g. Stanley and Wise, 1983).

(iii) reconceptualisation of research as the *critique of language* in use (e.g. Manning, 1983).

Taken together these constitute a condemnation of simple abstracted research methods: instead they demonstrate the need for methodology itself to be opened up to a process of critique and reconstruction. This facilitates a *variety* of research methods, contributing to a composite picture. We have over the last seven years engaged in participant observation of organisations as occasional though regular visitors; observed our own employing organisations; conducted structured and unstructured interviews; elicited written descriptions and statements from organisational members on apparently significant 'incidents'; used the presentation of our research ideas as opportunities for gathering further information on reactions to the topic; searched organisation theory and 'non-organisational' academic literature; and scoured 'quality', the 'popular' and magazine presses, as well as advertising, television and films. This involves not only the use of 'mixed media' but also re-interpretation at several levels of the information gained, in the light of the power of élites to control information, gender power and the power of language. Furthermore these complications are repeated *within the research activity itself*. The doing of the research has in a number of ways provided material for the research.

We have already referred to our own personal involvement with the topic. The topic is not just a sensitive topic to be studied; it is a sensitive area *for us* to work on. This applies in our own working relationship, which has had to be challenged and reviewed in the light of the sensitive material that arises. It also points to the usefulness of two viewpoints, two genders and the dynamic nature of dialogue in research that is not easily captured in the starkness of the written word. It also applies in relation to our own working/employing organisations. Increasingly, as our interest in and awareness of the 'topic' has grown, we have been drawn to look more closely at what is happening under our noses, in our employing organisations. They are rich sources of material. This is despite the fact that turning one's attention to 'one's own' organisation can accentuate the personal, ethical and political problems of participant-observer research. Thus we do not advocate a 'free-for-all' approach to research where 'muckraking' is done for the sake of it. Instead we see our own organisational situations as unavoidable resources or places for our own experience, against which to test what we write. For these reasons it is difficult to separate our organisational analysis from our own organisational experience.

Another important aspect of the research activity has been the way in which our presentation of the topic has elicited strong reactions and differences of opinion from academic audiences. These have often been emotionally rather than academically based. One seminar participant noted how in his (all male) research field he had discounted attention to sexuality partly because it was not the sort of thing usually studied in organisational sociology and partly because it involved activities (showing of blue movies on public property) that were probably illegal. The first time such a response was evoked we merely noted it but when we continued to receive such responses we saw it as valid research material. At times some men's reactions seemed comparable to the titillation evoked by 'soft porn'.[8] Some women's reactions were anger at the men's reactions; both occurring within the same formal organisational situation.

These micropolitics of research merge with another much larger issue, that of *gender divisions* in research. This issue has been unavoidable with a special relevance for research on sexuality. The gender of researchers and gender divisions in research projects clearly have implications for the ability to gather information. For example, men studying men may be able to direct attention to causes and accounts of men's sexual harassment of women rather than just considering sexual harassment as forms of behaviour received by women.

Mixed research obviously has the advantage of gathering more information from more sources, from women and men. It does have definite dangers and limitations including: the danger of trying to see women's accounts and men's accounts as comparable to each other; the danger of not being truthful between researchers; the danger of information on women being passed to men; different justifications for the research in the first place.

FROM METHODOLOGICAL DIFFICULTIES TO ORGANISATIONAL PROCESSES

So far we have given a rather generalised account of some of the 'difficulties' of researching this area, and some strategies to cope with them. However, even this has been somewhat abstracted and therefore wanting, for the reality is that our own perception of 'difficulties' was part of the substance, not just the method, of research.

This diagram was *originally* produced as an attempt to overview and make some sense of the 'methodological difficulties' we were meeting. The ordering that this involved stressed two main 'factors': elusiveness and secrecy. Though this diagram was subsequently abandoned it did enable us to re-interpret the problems outlined. What were initially perceived as 'methodological difficulties' became worthy of study in their own right as organisational processes. To put this another way, part of the way in which sexuality in organisations was obscured for us was by our perception of its study through the eyes of methodological difficulties rather than organisational processes.

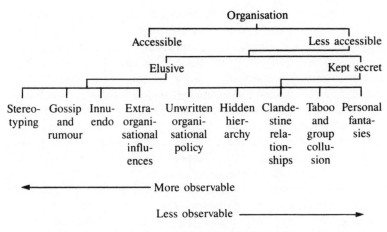

Figure 2: Types of methodological difficulties

These processes are all the more powerful because of the variety of ways in which sexuality is further obscured in most if not all organisations by a series of 'fronts'. This applies even when sexuality is used explicitly in organisations, for example, the hiring of female 'models' at motor shows. Organisations can be understood as having many 'fronts', of different types, that deny and cover up the full presence of sexuality in organisations. Indeed one possible 'front' is that which denies all this, a further element of the ideology that sexuality and organisations are incompatible.

Within this critical approach organisations themselves become problematic. This is but another attack on the reification of organisations, in the tradition of anti-organisation theory (Burrell and Morgan, 1979) and other deconstructions. Thus when someone, often a man, says they are in 'possession' of the 'facts of the case', whether organisational or sexual, this can be understood as merely one layer of organisational life, even a sexual metaphor.

Likewise in research, 'possession of the facts' is an appearance, permitted and accepted, that derives from underlying structures yet particularises and obscures them. Promoting research as a mere means to an end is both limited and limiting; with the merging of ends and means, research becomes more interesting, more exciting and more fun.

Researching sexuality in work organisations makes a number of difficult and interrelated demands upon the researchers. There are immediate questions of material distributions within organisations, but there are broader issues of locating both organisations in particular, and the quality of 'organisation' in general, predominantly in relation to the structuring of the public domain to the private. Within organisations themselves, the process of sexuality cannot be just 'read off' from organisational factors. There is a continual need to attend to the interpersonal and intrapersonal subtleties of sexuality, in terms of not just the multiple meanings of social situations, but also the complex layering of interpretation available to individuals. This last facet of the research process applies as much to researchers as it does to those workers and other organisational members being researched. Furthermore, these 'psychodynamics' of sexuality, although a matter of consciousness, are not spates of autonomous ideas, but rather exist and change as and in relation to material relations. This complex realism, this sexual materialism, is explored more fully in the subsequent chapters.

Part Two
Power and Dialectics

4 Sexuality and Power

'Possession of the facts' is a dominant and restrictive mode of power. Undermining such possession, as well as those 'facts', reveals series of powers and dialectics. This process is particularly important in appreciating the subtlety and complexity of sexuality in organisations.

In this chapter we pursue this theme in considering two fundamental questions already raised in the previous section. Firstly, what is to be understood by sexuality, and secondly, how is an understanding of sexuality informed by the consideration of power. These two questions are interrelated, so that 'definitions' of sexuality presume a statement on power, and statements on power extend definitions of sexuality.

WHAT IS SEXUALITY?

It has already been made clear that the organisational literature tends to see sexuality, if at all, through euphemisms. That literature which does focus on sexuality usually does so in a rather fragmentary way, as a variable (Zetterberg, 1966), as romantic relationships (Harrison and Lee, 1986), as sexual liaisons (Burrell, 1984), as a form of threat (Bradford, Sargent and Sprague, 1975), as stereotype (Kanter, 1975), and as harassment. What is now necessary is to develop a broader definition and approach to sexuality in relation to organisational life than are to be found in such approaches.

An obvious starting point is consideration of the status and relevance of biological explanations of sexuality. Rubin

(1984, 275) has critically recognised the power of 'sexual essentialism—the idea that sex is a natural force that exists prior to social life and shapes institutions'. The dominance of this thinking in folk wisdom has been reinforced through much recent theory and practice of medicine, psychiatry, psychology and the academic study of sex, and other 'possessions of facts'.[1] Accordingly she continues:

> These fields classify sex as a property of individuals. It may reside in their hormones or their psyches. It may be construed as physiological or psychological. But within these ethnoscientific categories, sexuality has no history and no significant social determinants.
>
> (*ibid.*, 276)

Although a solely biological interpretation of sexuality is hardly tenable, it is difficult to avoid taking account of biology in at least two ways: the fact that sexuality is in part a matter of physical contact, actual or possible; and the likelihood that most people appear to have sexual instincts and sexual states, and experience sexual drives. To say this does not negate the immense variability in people's instincts, states and drives, and more importantly the numerous ways in which these can be subject to expression, repression and oppression; nor do they in themselves add credence to biological explanations, based solely or even primarily on hormonal levels, territoriality, heterosexuality and monogamy. There should be no confusion between the inevitability of the biological within sexuality and normative accounts of what it is to be supposedly 'natural' sexually or to have a supposedly 'natural' sexuality. Just as biology plays a part in arrangements for eating both within and outside organisations, so it does in sexuality. However, it cannot be said to determine sexuality simply because of the immense social and cultural variation that exists between societies, within given societies historically, and between different parts of a society at a given time. To understand such variation demands attention to social, economic, cultural and political structures and experiences.

The most usual set of social structures to which sexuality is related in a determinate way is the family. In the work of Parsons (for example, Parsons and Bales, 1955) as well as of others working within a similar framework, sexuality is seen as a fairly natural (in both senses) by-product of the family system(s) conflating the biological division of labour and system needs. Similar foundations lie behind freudianism and its emphasis on the impact of early heterosexual family life upon the development of the child's sexuality. Adult sexuality is understood to stem in large part from infantile experience, internal conflicts, typically not fully resolved, and repressions of instincts in early life. Parsonianism and freudianism have a great many points of contact, and taken together may provide a social structural model of sexuality based upon the family, its 'normal' functioning and its 'pathological' variations. That the family has a major impact on sexuality is undeniable. What is more questionable are, firstly, that the particular formulations of the family within Parsonian—Freudian theory are adequate; secondly, that the family is the final determining *base* of sexuality; and thirdly, that the focus on the family avoids the tendency to equate sexuality with 'women' and thus to neglect the problematic sexuality of men.[2]

The major critical traditions of phenomenology and marxism represent ways away from and out of these difficulties. On the first count sexuality becomes an interactional process, sustained in the fragility of social relationships and performances. For example, Henslin and Biggs (1978) and Emerson (1970) analyse the desexualisation of gynaecology through the dramaturgical and ethnomethodological perspectives respectively. In this kind of approach: 'Masculinity and feminity [*sic*] must cease to be regarded as properties owned exclusively by subjects called male and female, and must instead be seen as character-functions and relations distributed throughout all subjects' (Kosok, 1971, 69).

Different emphases are to be found in marxist and indeed most marxist-feminist approaches to sexuality. Here much more credence is given to the impact of paid, 'productive' work and the associated divisions of labour in the development of femininity, masculinity and sexuality (for example, Bland *et al.*, 1978; Barrett, 1980). As noted in chapter 1, this approach, though dialectical, does not necessarily transcend the assumed antagonism of sexuality and 'work'. In such accounts 'personal' matters of sex and family are often seen as constrained and determined by the 'needs' of 'public' activity, particularly in the demands of capitalist production and division of labour. This approach is developed by a variety of writers focusing either on predominantly heterosexual (Zaretsky, 1976; Red Collective, 1978) or on homosexual (Fernbach, 1982; Mieli, 1980) relations. In some accounts (over-) attention or, worse still, reification of 'personal' life which would include sexuality is held to be highly diversionary.[3] Increasingly sexuality is appreciated as a problem within marxist analysis, that is not and perhaps cannot be fully explained away through the traditional conceptual apparatus of marxism.

It is against this background that what might be called the 'new sexual debates' are being developed. These debates arise from the uncertainties over the determinacy (or possibility of determinacy) of social structures, the family, capitalism, or whatever, for sexuality. They are concerned not just with the factors that 'affect' sexuality and cause 'it' to vary, as is so with the vast sexology studies of Kinsey, Hite and others,[4] but also with the production, construction and determinateness of *sexuality itself.*

Much of the interest in sexuality over the last ten years or more arises from the interrelation of feminism, gay liberationism, Foucauldian analysis and, once again, psychoanalysis. Sexuality is being increasingly described and analysed as a complex set of phenomena, that includes but is distinct from sex, sexual relations, sexual practices and so on (Coward, 1983).[5] Foucault's contribution occurs at several levels and in several directions: the ubiquity of power; the conceptualisation as discourse, rather than, say, biology; the central importance of speech, language, gaze, ordinary practice in maintaining discourse; and the presence even of silences, margins, and transgressions within discourse so that even those at the margin, the deviant, the excluded, retain a power to act otherwise.[6]

Some feminists and gay scholars have made considerable use of Foucault's insights in the analysis of sexuality and related areas, despite the fact that Foucault himself is remarkably implicit and even obscure on questions of gender.[7] Feminism has changed both the understanding of sexuality and the importance given to sexuality in many ways: the making of women's experiences visible,[8] the realisation of both women's and men's power, the theorising of (the control of) sexuality as the central dynamic of patriarchy (MacKinnon, 1982, 2). Major themes in the study of sexuality within gay studies are also partly about the making of the invisible visible: the rediscovery in history and culture of forbidden and labelled types of love and sex (Weeks, 1977). Paradoxically, gay and feminist insights have brought both a distancing from the family as a focus, and a return to it, sometimes though not always from a psychoanalytic perspective. Thus Coward, Lipshitz and Cowie (1978, 7) assert that 'it is in the familial relation that we find what is specific to women's oppression'. Much feminist, psychoanalytic work has been informed by the insight that sexuality frequently has effects on non-sexual behaviour, characteristically mediated through symbolisation and sublimation.[9] At minimum, projection may be one routine element and one way of analysing many instances of 'falling in love' (Goodison, 1983); at worst, it is women who become the symbols of men's powers and objects of men's projections, to the point of assault. In other works, intra-psychic processes of projection may 'conveniently' parallel and use social divisions and hierarchies in organisations and elsewhere. An interesting self-defeating example of the psychological use of hierarchy in this way is to fall in love with someone who is quite unattainable.

Several things can now be said: sexuality is not simple; it is not just to do with sex and sexual acts; it has itself 'come out'.[10] The dominant view of sexuality emphasises, first, its privateness and covertness, and, secondly, sexual contact, especially heterosexual acts. When we first began to research this area our focus was initially on sexual liaisons and relationships as an assumed index of sexuality, a documenter of pattern. We now find this very questionable. The conduct of research has reconstituted what we have come to recognise as sexuality. We have found it necessary to broaden our definition in at least two ways: firstly, to see sexuality as an ordinary and frequent public process rather than an extraordinary and predominantly private process; and secondly, to see sexuality as an aspect and part of an all-pervasive body politics rather than a separate and discrete set of practices.

Thus the term sexuality is used here specifically to refer to the social expression of or social relations to physical, bodily desires, real or imagined, by or for others or for oneself. Others can be of the same or opposite sex, or even occasionally of indeterminate gender. In addition, Stone remarks that 'Despite appearances, human sex takes place mostly in the head' (1977, 483); indeed imagined or fantasised sexual relations may be as important a part of sexuality as actual sexual practices. Sexual practices may range from mild flirtation to sexual acts, perhaps with orgasm, even with enclosure and/or penetration. Such acts may be accomplished willingly, unwillingly or forcibly by those involved. It is important to emphasise that sexuality includes narcissistic, bisexual, homosexual and heterosexual preferences and practices (as well as the variety of sexual 'perversions') and it also includes fantasy. It should be added that a major focus of attention will be heterosexuality, necessitated by its dominance of most organisations (Rich, 1980). This emphasis should not be interpreted as a commentary on 'normality' or 'naturalness' in sexual relations or preferences. Sexuality is best seen as both a specific, and a wide-ranging, necessarily open-ended topic.

In addition to the question of desires within sexuality, there is a range of other relevant bodily states and experiences that relate to these desires, including puberty, pre-menstruation, pregnancy and menopause. Thus, to summarise, the definition of sexuality used here is the social expression of, and relations to bodily desires, real or imagined, by or for others or for oneself, together with the related bodily states and experiences.[11]

Sexuality is thus a specific set of phenomena and practices, as defined above; but it is also diverse. To reduce this broad range of powers, actions, thoughts and feelings just to sexual acts is likely to give an inaccurate, even sexist, view of sexual realities. Sexuality is no monolith; it includes and *refers to* the body and touch, emotion and desire, thought and fantasy, image and appearance.

POWER AND POWERLESSNESS

Sexuality is always political; it entails action and activity with power. This is visible most obviously in the overlap with violence—in harassment, assault, rape, pornography and so on, but also throughout the 'ordinary' conduct of inter-person, interbody relations—body politics. The task of the remainder of this chapter is to provide a theoretical statement of the place of power in the analysis of sexuality and organisational life. This follows from Rubin's (1984, 275) characterisation of 'a radical theory of sex' as one that 'must identify, describe, explain, and denounce erotic injustice and sexual oppression'.

Like sexuality 'itself', politics and power(s) operate both at different levels, and through complex dynamics. To borrow from Lukes' (1974) typology, one can conceptualise power relations as immediate behavioural control, as indirect behavioural control and influence, and as non-immediate social structuring. Thus even body politics should not be thought of as merely operating at the behavioural level; they are equally subject to the controls and constructions of social structure. Power relations, including those of sexuality, are characterised by dialectical and changing forms. As, for example, Giddens (1979, 149) suggests:

The dialectic of control operates even in highly repressive forms of collectivity or organisation . . . the dialectic of control is built into the very nature of agency, or more correctly put, the relations of autonomy and dependence which agents reproduce in the context of the enactment of definite practices. *An agent who does not participate in the dialectic of control, in a minimal fashion, ceases to be an agent* . . . all power relations, or relations of autonomy and dependence, are reciprocal: however wide the asymmetrical distribution of resources involved, all power relations manifest autonomy and dependence 'in both directions'.

(emphasis in original)

Power (Power 1) may create powerlessness; but (apparent) powerlessness will often bring forth resistance (Power 2); moreover that 'powerlessness' may obscure its own potential or counter-power (Power 3) (as in labour-power); and that potential power is likely to bring forth the resistance of the powerful (Power 4). These simplified dialectics can apply at the levels of behaviour and persons, or at the level of social structure. They can also apply in terms both of the subjection of sexuality to other powers and controls and of the power of sexuality itself. Thus 'non-sexual' power, for example capital (as Power 1) can control sexuality, which in turn may bring forth resistance (as Power 2), such as making love rather than commodities in 'works time', and/or the realisation of the potential power of sexuality (Power 3), such as the use of seduction to undermine authority, and/or resistance of the powerful (Power 4), such as tightening up procedures for appointing managers to test for certain 'sexual tendencies'.

There are a number of linked generic powers that appear to subject sexuality and act as controls over it. These include:

(i) the power of men (over sexuality, and over women);
(ii) the power of the public realm (over sexuality and over the private);
(iii) the power of production (over sexuality and over reproduction);

and indeed
(iv) the power of reproduction (over sexuality).

These powers appear to exist not only over sexuality as a complex whole but also over particular forms of sexuality. For example, 'productive' sexuality, as is used and exploited in advertising, and 'reproductive' sexuality, as in heterosexual reproduction, are themselves more powerful than 'non-productive', 'non-reproductive' sexuality, such as homosexuality and bisexuality.[12] The domination of heterosexuality, heterosexuals, heterosexual ideology and practice, and particularly their patriarchal heterosexist variants, over homosexuality is characteristic of most organisations; this is evidenced by managerial policies, everyday practices, discriminations against and dismissals of homosexual people. For lesbians 'oppression (in and around work organisations) is in conjunction with the other forms of discrimination which are faced every day' (Taylor, 1986, 20).

Thus powers exist (i) *over sexuality* from other sources such as capital; (ii) *of sexuality*, in terms of its own impact on other powers; and (iii) *within sexuality*, where these two forms intersect.

However, powerful to the point of violence though these powers are, they are not all-powerful. They are not absolute efficient systems; they vary greatly culturally and historically; and as noted they meet both resistance and other forms of potential and actual power. Thus counter-powers exist for women, for the private realm (in the shape of mothers, fathers, families, households),[13] reproduction, and, most importantly, for sexuality. The power of sexuality exists for all, for women (Hollway, 1983) and for men, for gays and for straights. This power operates through both the unconscious and consciousness; and both socially and personally.

Sexuality although often subjugated to the demands and powers of organisations has a power and a *potential power* of its own. It is after all labour. As Dorn and South (n.d., 37) express it: 'Sex is a particular way of turning the body's labour back on itself (i.e. on the person of self and/or other), thus engaging the "mental" and "physical" aspects of labour together'. This potential power might be thought of as sexual labour-power, [14] paralleling productive and reproductive labour-power (O'Brien, 1981): it is the potential of labour to create desire of some value between people (or for a person), of use or for exchange.

Our conception of power is thus complex. Power certainly has material bases in the structures of reproduction and production, the public and the private, but these do not operate in terms of *strict* determinations of sexuality. Sexuality's own power, a form of body politics, exists in both alliance and contradiction with other powers. Additionally and crucially, power is not to be abstracted from real situations to 'determining' structures. It exists in the immediate activity between persons, in experience, and in the psyche. As with earlier comments on the research process, this is not to idealise power, for interpersonal, experienced, and intrapersonal power itself only exists in relation to, or even as forms of, material relations.

Organisations and organisational life are characteristically combinations, and sometimes awkward and unhappy combinations, of these powers and counter-powers. Thus organisations can exert power over the un-organised and less-organised. Organisations institutionalise and formalise some of these dynamic relations. Particular organisations, notably the state and the professions, institutionalise sexuality in law, welfare services and medical work. Organisations and organisational life are a frequent means of exerting the variety of asexual powers over sexuality and, in turn, of resisting the power of sexuality.

Organisations and organisational life do not only exist socially but also spatially. Most space, in cities or elsewhere, is dominated by 'heterosexual' organisations, by heterosexuals and by organisations, in a mutually reinforcing process. In some of the larger cities there may be significant gay 'communities' and gay organisations, that in effect hold sway over a particular area of geographical space. This form of spatial power is certainly part of the general process of urbanisation and urban migration of the Industrial Revolution, whereby cities were in effect able to offer political economies (and indeed sanctuaries) of scale to particular social concentrations. To quote Rubin (1984, 286) again:

In the United States, lesbian and gay male territories were well established in New York, Chicago, San Francisco, and Los Angeles in the 1950s. Sexually motivated migration . . . had become a sizeable sociological phenomenon. By the late 1970s, sexual migration was occurring on a scale so significant that it began to have a recognisable impact on urban politics in the United States, with San Francisco being the most notable . . . example.

Thus the growth of the 'pink economy' mainly in urban areas is typically also a spatial and an organisational phenomenon. This 'example' is beginning to be emulated by other sexual groups: 'Bisexuals, sado masochists, individuals who prefer cross-generational encounters, transsexuals and transvestites are all in various states of community formation and identity acquisition. The perversions [*sic*] are not proliferating as much as they are attempting to acquire social space, small businesses, political resources' (*ibid.*, 287), in short their own organisational lives.

Organisations are not only purveyors of power; power is also distributed throughout and within them, through their own internal structures, hierarchies, goals and ideologies. Organisations express, maintain, reinforce and supplement these power relations. The particular power of management and other organisational leaders, the resistance and labour power of workers, the bureaucratic and other organisational divisions, are but further realms of power that may both subject sexuality, and be a means of displaying sexuality.

5 The Organisational Construction of Sexuality

While sexuality is clearly not a passive clay waiting to be moulded by the array of organisational powers, there are many ways in which organisations and their characteristic features do construct the form and expression of sexuality of and between members. This chapter considers some of these ways in which organisations construct sexuality, as a prelude to the analysis in subsequent chapters of the sexual processes of organisations.

Organisations are recognisable social collectivities of people, in structured relationships to each other, or at least some of each other. Accordingly, organisations consist of a number of elements that bear on both power and sexuality, not as a magic formula, but as determining factors. In particular, organisations do much to control the physical and emotional distance and proximity between people, that in turn affects the sexuality of and between organisational members. Thus one simple, initial model of sexuality in organisations is as follows:-

$$\left.\begin{array}{l}\text{Organisational} \\ \text{Characteristics}\end{array}\right\} \quad \left.\begin{array}{l}\text{Physical control} \\ \text{Emotional control}\end{array}\right\} \quad \begin{array}{l}\text{Sexuality of} \\ \text{organisational} \\ \text{members}\end{array}$$

Figure 3: Organisational control and sexuality

Organisations routinely structure the distribution of members throughout their territory, as well as the extent of their travel beyond their boundaries. One of the defining powers available to managers, usually men, is the control of organisational space and the movement of people, often differentiated by gender, within those spaces.

Organisations act as a means both of aggregating people and of giving them a collective relation to the outside world—what might be thought of as an *external* organisational form. They also act in a contradictory way as a means of disposal and distancing of people from each other through *internal* organisational divisions. The external and the internal are in a dynamic relation, so that, for example, in bureaucracies and total institutions people may be both brought together and kept apart, by rules, regulations, and indeed sometimes solitary confinements or ostracism. These external forms and internal divisions create and maintain further dialectical relations and resistances within the organisation. Indeed 'Resistance can be incorporated and utilized and displaced so that it is never in a position of exteriority' (Burrell, 1984, 100). These questions of organisational underlife, of the alienative effects of labour process, of interstitial social and sexual relations, and so on, are integral parts of organisational forms, structure and process, and not mere reactions thereto.

External organisational form has a number of interrelated elements all of which have a bearing on sexuality. Firstly, organisations have a certain territoriality, that is a certain size and degree of control over space and members. Secondly, the external form refers to overt organisational goals and beneficiaries of the organisation. In particular, this refers to the extent to which sexual purposes are part of these processes. Thirdly, external organisational form refers to the openness or closure (i.e. closedness) of the organisation, its separation from and interdependence with the outside world. Closure and openness necessarily imply differential controls over the use of time, bodies and sexuality within given organisational contexts. Where the goals are contrary to the interests of members, the boundaries are impermeable or controls are coercive, severe resistances may often arise from within. All these elements of external organisation form represent powerful and sometimes implicit types of control that pre-determine more overt and particular systems of control, for example managerial directives and procedures.

Internal divisions of organisations arise from both *division of labour* and *division of authority*. Organisations have identifiable ways of working and organising labour, in particular through the relations of technology to organisational members, the labour process. These labour processes produce and exist within broader, often formalised, divisions of authority. These further aggregate people and divide them from each other, facilitate and inhibit interaction and communication, and generally account for the development of inequalities within organisations. Organisational divisions and structures also produce *interstices*, that is spaces between structures, that are thus often only indirectly controlled.

External organisational form	{	Territoriality Goals and beneficiaries Closure and openness
Internal organisational divisions	{	Division of labour Division of authority Interstices

Figure 4: Elements of organisational construction of sexuality

The organisational features as above are frequently interrelated with each other. For example, a particular labour process or type of organisational structure may be associated with a given size of organisation. Particular organisations are subject to a combination, and moreover an interplay, of organisational conditions and structures. Furthermore both organisational form and organisational divisions interrelate with gender divisions and divisions around sexuality. In other words the ubiquity of division and inequality in organisations has a recurrent relationship with the ubiquity of gender divisions and gender inequality, particularly between women and men, and between homosexuality and heterosexuality.

EXTERNAL ORGANISATIONAL FORM

Territoriality
Organisations occupy space over geographical areas; they have a determinate mass; they control the aggregation of members. This territoriality of organisations is thus a fundamental determinant of the conditions that construct the sexuality of members. Organisations are a means of amassing people, of

bringing them together, physically, emotionally, normatively. They are also a means of separating people from the outside world through, say, the creation of corporate identities.

Large organisations may produce a gathering together of like minds, with resultant implications for individual and collective change and consciousness.[1] They may become both more bureaucratic, and at the same time more cosmopolitan than small organisations. They may bring together more people but on a less intense emotional basis. They operate like small cities, with an increased 'choice' of potential partners, possible or fantasised, whether as lovers or sex objects; increased likelihood of minority or oppressed communities of interest, for example of gay men or lesbians; divisions between 'sexual locals' who seek their pleasure with other members and 'sexual cosmopolitans', who keep the two worlds apart; and so on. These permutations may, however, conflict with bureaucratic ways of working that restrict mobility and access between members. Organisations, and especially large, complex ones, are characterised by contradictory social and spatial processes. They concentrate people in typing pools, shop floors, 'open-plan' offices and so on, thus facilitating social meeting but impeding intimacy, and create relatively autonomous cultural enclaves,[2] 'sub-units', and spaces behind closed doors. Some of these impacts are summarised in figure 5 below.

SMALL ORGANISATION ◄─────────► LARGE ORGANISATION

SMALL ORGANISATION	LARGE ORGANISATION
Less sexual heterogeneity	More sexual heterogeneity
Fewer potential partners in organisation	More potential partners in organisation
Closer relationships (However, the potential closeness of relationships may include resistance to closeness)	Less close relationships (However, distance of relationships may include resistance producing closeness)

Figure 5: Summary of impact of territoriality on sexuality

Small organisations, and indeed to some extent the more autonomous departments of larger organisations, raise a rather different set of issues. If large organisations are like cities, small organisations are like villages: there is a limitation on availability of possible partners in the organisation, while minority or oppressed sexualities are likely to remain hidden or seen in individual ownership rather than collective properties. Small size may also entail regular and close social contact, relatively less bureaucratic procedures and interaction, and opportunities for personal even charismatic control and leadership. Without the 'convenience' of bureaucratic rules to fall back on, small organisations can develop in various and idiosyncratic ways: autocratic and repressive, gossiping and flirtatious, openly sexual. The awareness of the intensity of potential sexuality may be greater, and yet more controlled, because of the perception of its possible disruptive effects in a relatively small-scale social context. This fear of disruption, whether from management and/or workers, may be reinforced where the task is perceived as asexual, for example, in a small religious sect. For these reasons, and not simply the lack of 'choice', the members of small organisations may take a particular interest in outsiders, clients and representatives of other organisations, like shopkeepers taking an interest in their customers. Clearly, territoriality of organisations has both a spatial and social dimension, a theme which will be further developed.

Goals and beneficiaries: the control of sexual purposes
Organisations vary according to their goals, manifest task, purposes, and prime beneficiaries. Despite the problems that exist with the goal perspective on organisations, particularly if applied within a rigid and positivist framework (Georgiou, 1973), it does focus analysis on what is often the most public aspect of organisations—what they, or significant, powerful members, managers, owners or other representatives, claim they attempt to accomplish.

Some organisations do have explicit sexual goals, such as to provide sexual services to 'clients'; in most, however, sexuality both collectively and individually, is, in terms of officially stated goals at least, subordinated to other organisational tasks. In contextualising the status of sexuality within organisational goals, two questions need to be addressed: the extent to which sexuality is expressed or repressed within organisational goals; and where it is expressed, whose interests are dominant, who in or outside the organisation is the prime beneficiary. This second question is similar to that posed by Blau and Scott (1963) in their 'cui bono' frame of analysis. Accordingly, rather than speaking of business, service, mutual benefit and commonweal organisations, consideration may be given to how, if at all, the sexual component of organisational goals is of direct 'benefit' to managers and owners, 'clients' and customers, members, or none of those. Thus we may recognise:

(i) *sexploitation organisations*, where sexuality is exploited for the benefit of managers and owners, either commercially or sexually, for example, the pornography industry;

(ii) *(sexual) service organisations*, where the organisation has the goal of serving 'clients' for their sexual benefit, for example, sex therapy;

(iii) *mutual (sexual) organisations*, where members come together for their mutual sexual benefit, for example, gay liberation organisations;

(iv) *subordinated (or perhaps repressed) (sexual) organisations*, the most common type, where the sexuality of members and others is subordinated to the 'non-sexual' organisational task. This type therefore contrasts with the first three where sexuality forms part of the overt goals of the organisation.

These should be seen as broad types, for particular organisations may well include aspects of more than one type, for example, where a 'non-sexual' commercial organisation (iv) uses sexuality for the advertising and promotion of its products (i). There, sexuality is the means to 'non-sexual' ends (see figure 6). The four types share some of the characteristic problems of Blau and Scott's business, service, mutual benefit and commonweal types. Thus in sexploitation organisations managers and owners may meet the characteristic problem of maintaining motivation of workers. In service organisations, the contradictions of using professional knowledge and giving professional service may be heightened by the emotional and deeply felt nature of the client's experience; professionals working in this area may also have to deal with counter-transference and the restimulation of their own sexuality.

Furthermore, the concepts of 'sexual service' and 'sexual benefit' may, in some organisational situations, need to be interpreted without normative assumptions. This particularly applies to those, often medical, psychiatric, or custodial organisations that have 'sexual' policies, formal or informal, on clients seen as 'sexual deviants'. 'Sexual service' there may extend to the use of drugs to diminish sex drives, programmes of counselling of transsexuals, and unofficial counselling for sterilisation of mothers who have murdered children.

Mutual organisations may face the problems of oligarchy amongst supposedly equal members, perhaps expressed through tensions between *sexual* benefits and other social mutual benefits. And in subordinated organisations members may find the formal organisational tasks less interesting and absorbing than sexuality, with sexuality in effect disrupting or threatening accountability. Indeed in this last type sexuality may form part of the resistance to the organisational task or goal.

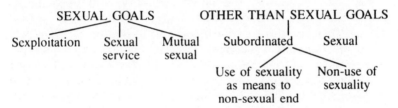

Figure 6: Types of organisational goals

Of particular interest are those organisations which subordinate sexuality to the major organisational task, but where that task is explicitly concerned with the physical expression and/or repression of the body. Thus, for example, military establishments, and particularly those specialising in military training, are constantly concerned with the exertion of the bodies of organisational members. Bodies are trained, rearranged, packed close, and in the final analysis expendable. The potential for arousal of the body, and especially homosexuality, is often intense. Sometimes male heterosexual arousal is specifically exploited as a means to 'more effective' performance in aggressive tasks, as in sexually-based 'war chants', whether by rugby teams or army units. As Strange (1983, 23) notes:

Power in the army involves the humiliation and hatred of women. During basic training, recruits are commonly called 'faggot' or 'girl', the insult screamed at close quarters by a drill instructor. Chants such as 'Your sister is a whore, your girlfriend is a whore, and your mother because she had you', exploit the sexual basis of violence.

However, more usually and certainly in an overarching way, too much sexual arousal and certainly male homosexuality are at odds with the major military task. Comparison can be made with the situation of nurses, subject to intense emotional involvement with the bodies, life and death of patients, and thus accepting of the 'institutional defences' of relatively bureaucratic procedures (Menzies, 1960). Dixon (1976) argues along rather similar lines that the military faces a particular and contradictory problem, in that aggression and violence are engendered against potential enemies, but have to be severely controlled—in internal interaction between members of the same army—hence the development of military 'bullshit' and other forms of often petty disciplines. Similarly, the latent sexuality, and particularly homosexuality, of such organisations, that arouse sexual possibilities in the face of a broad subordination of sexuality, often necessitates especially rigorous rules and sanctions concerned with various, particularly homosexual, sexual conducts. Repressive rules on sexuality are thus characteristic of those organisations that subordinate sexuality yet are explicitly physical and implicitly sexual. More will be said on this in the next section.

Furthermore, those organisations in which sexuality is completely subservient to the task, for example, security or espionage organisations, are the very ones where sexuality is often closely monitored, guarded against, or sometimes used against members. Thus there develops a dialectic between the exclusion of sexuality and the obsession with sexuality, as exemplified in sex scandals involving spies, diplomats, politicians, and members of the armed forces or military scientific establishments. The organisations that preclude sexuality are 'bedevilled' by it.[3]

In stark contrast 'sexploitation' organisations trade on sexuality. They are many and various: Adams and Laurikietis (1980, 93) list as sexploitation jobs: 'fashion and photographic modelling . . . through to prostitution. In between these two extremes are the hired escorts, the hostesses, the bunny girls and·pets and strip-tease dancers.' Burstyn (1983, 86) includes within the 'sex industry': 'prostitution, massage parlours,[4] gay and heterosexual gathering places (i.e. [*sic*] steam baths), live sex shows, peep shows, telephone fantasy services, pornography of the film, video, magazine and literary varieties, and sexual aids from lingerie to whips and chains'. She also comments that the 'commodification of sexuality is not restricted to these . . . but forms part of many other (not directly sexual) enterprises'. In addition there are sex shops, clip joints, sex palaces, 'kissagrams', certain clubs, and advertising agencies, marriage agencies, contact magazines, protection rackets,[5] and worst of all, apart from the sponsors of 'snuff movies', sexual slavery (Barry, 1984). Most of these ventures involve the exploitation of the sexuality of girls and women; some exploit the sexuality of boys and gay men, a few exploit men's heterosexuality. Some powerful sexploitation organisations have the potential of producing any sexual possibility imaginable, in whatever combination imaginable, to those who can pay. Many women and men doing a wide range of 'non-sexual' jobs are of course exploited in these organisations through their wage labour regardless of their sexuality. Indeed the selling of sexuality is itself often and probably usually boring, degrading, alienating, dangerous work.[6]

Sexploitation organisations are big business; at one estimate larger than all other entertainment industries combined (Burstyn, 1983, 63). Mustang Ranch, the world famous 500-acre Nevada brothel, was acquired in 1985 for $18 million (Scobie, 1985). The sex industry, like any other, is subject to technological change, as well as to the capitalist processes of diversification and concentration (Tomkinson, 1982). The launching of 'girlie calendars' at the turn of the century ('How long . . .?', 1982) reflected the development of increasing linkages between companies within monopoly capitalism. In the post-war period technological innovation has facilitated the spread of mass production pornographic films and videos. The spread of gay organisations in localities of some large cities may represent a significant expression of power for gay people, but they also constitute new possibilities, often by gradual infiltration, for capitalist development in the guise of the 'pink economy', particularly the male gay economy rather than the lesbian economy (Kane, 1984).

Finally, in this section, it is necessary to note an important sub-category of sexploitation organisations, namely what might be called glamour organisations, often associated with the 'entertainment' industry, that exploit sexuality in a less direct way. This can apply as much to the entertainment industry of pop musicians, and their much advertised 'affairs' for their own promotion, or indeed to the entertainment industry of royalty, and their supposed likes and loves. In this sense, large sections of the popular media are fringe members of the sexploitation industry; in some cases they are 'leaders of the field'.

Closure: the control of sexual time and sexual bodies

Variation in organisations' size and purpose, and their associated contradictions are often closely interlinked with organisations' relations of closure, separation and interdependence with the outside world. For example, relatively closed organisations may share some of the characteristics and contradictions of small organisations: a greater potential emotional intensity—the 'hothouse' phenomenon—but also a need to continue working and sometimes living alongside each other, to maintain routine, to survive. They may also show other characteristics and contradictions of larger organisations, especially those with a strict regime. It is for these reasons that total institutions (Goffman, 1968), where people eat, sleep, work and play—and have whatever sexual relations they do have—under a unified organisational regime are of special interest. Total institutions are above all places where the more usual division between the public domain and the private domain is redrawn, blurred or even abolished. Where the whole of the day's time (or even the lifetime) of the residents is spent within the organisation, as in the classic total institution, sexuality is bound to be an important feature of organisational life. In such situations the control of sexuality, of the 'inmate' qua (often naked) body, epitomises the (totalising) body politics of the total institution. An institution which fails to address or achieve this is failing to be a total institution. Thus the 'successful' completion of the task and the planned regime of the total institution necessitates powerful rulings on sexuality. This applies even where that involves a deliberate liberalisation of sexual practices or even an 'acceptance' of sexual acts publicly visible to insiders.

Total institutions are primarily institutions where the total control of the bodies of residents is attempted, including their sexuality, sexual relations, sleeping arrangements and night practices. Thus although total institutions have existed since ancient times, they arise in definite historical and social structural contexts. Burrell (1984, 108–10), following Foucault (1977, 1981), has discussed the association of the discourses of sex, the development of bio-politics and the proliferation of control institutions, particularly in the eighteenth and nineteenth centuries. Numerous links are to be noted between the development of military institutions, prisons and factories, as controllers of labour, bodies and sexuality, particularly with the spread of categorisation, segregation, and incarceration as approaches to 'social problems'. The ultimate and most horrific of all these has been the creation of the 'death factories' of the Holocaust: in Auschwitz-Birkenau over four million people were killed. Sexual atrocities were routine in the concentration camps; the body was naught, to the point of elimination. The attempt was made to make bodies beneath perception.

Total institutions are rarely random in their recruitment; they tend to gather the old, the young, the sick, the criminal, the poor, the rich, and very rich, ethnic and sexual minorities, and so on.[7] The control of sexuality within these institutions has to be understood in this broad social context, that is, provision is being made *for other* people, whether in atrocious or luxurious conditions.

Entrance to total institutions is characteristically by way of standard procedures – 'degradation ceremonies' in Goffman's words. New residents are typically both inducted by staff and initiated by other residents. On entry the resident is sometimes stripped bare, sometimes emotionally, sometimes physically; sometimes washed, shaved, reclothed, labelled, numbered. This process may occur once or many times as when remand prisoners are strip-searched before and after visits to courts. Pauline McKinney, a Republican prisoner in Armagh jail, Northern Ireland, was strip-searched 225 times on her way to and from court during the Christopher Black trial. This is carried out although the women do not leave the sight of security or prison guards during visits out. Even the description of 'organised sexual harassment' ('Armagh picket', 1985) falls short of recognising the full brutality. In mortification and degradation processes, the organisation is made and re-made through the making and re-making of bodies—as in 'strip cells' in British prisons, 'prisoners are left naked in a completely bare cell' (Fitzgerald and Sim, 1979, 101).[8]

In most non-total organisations formal induction is less severe;[9] it may consist merely of suggesting that a certain style of dress, self-presentation, or polite talk is appropriate 'here'. Initiation rites and rituals amongst co-members can be severe, sometimes including pronounced sexual and/or physical assaults. We have numerous examples of these sexual initiations from the armed forces, from junior cadets, the fire brigade, hospitals, coal mining, and engineering, chemical and textile factories. These may involve the use of glue to stick and smear on genitals, use of rope to tie, perhaps symbolising the intimacy of the bonds. Usually they are led by men, are common in men-only organisations and often part of male culture in mixed organisations. Vaught and Smith (1980) describe the sexual themes of American coal-mining underlife, and the inclusion of women in the sexual initiations when they became part of the workforce. Formerly men-only homosexual overtones may become complicated by the mixed-sex and indeed sexually harassing nature of the ceremonies, as with the entry of a woman into the London Fire Service.[10] This may suggest that a 'polymorphous' sexuality overrides homosexuality or heterosexuality or, more likely, the imposition of dominant male culture upon women.

Boundaries are also important in structuring sexual or potentially sexual or fantasised contact with non-members across and beyond them. The possibilities for this clearly depend on their permeability, with prisons again an obvious example of severe restriction. Indeed most imprisonment can be seen as primarily a restriction of contact and communication, and particularly sexual contact, from lovers, partners, spouses and other sexual intimates. In Britain informal visits for prisoners are at a minimum of one every twenty-eight days (two visits for young offenders), and usually in practice two per month. Visits are generally in the presence of prison officers, who remain in sight, but not generally in hearing. Rules forbid any physical contact between visitor and prisoner, separated by the table, glass or grille, with fears of drug traffic currently particularly acute. In practice some prisoners are allowed a brief embrace at the beginning and end of a visit. Category A prisoners are permitted no physical contact with visitors whatever.

Conjugal visits do not occur, although there have been various attempts to introduce them in Denmark, Sweden, the Netherlands, Mexico and parts of the United States.[11] Visits between spouses, both of whom are prisoners, can be arranged under close supervision every three months, there being relatively few establishments for the accommodation of both sexes. Marriages can be arranged in a registry office under escort, and since 1983 in prison chapels ('Lords approve marriages in prison', 1983); on very rare occasions marriages may take place while on parole and thus unescorted. Lower security category prisoners serving sentences of more than two years may apply for short periods of home leave of two or four nights, towards the end of their sentences. In many total institutions, contacts are limited to 'leave', 'binges' (cf. Goffman, 1968, 52) and the adoption of sexual 'mascots' as by ships and regiments ('Navy scuttles Gilly . . .', 1982).

Many total institutions maintain explicit rules against the expression of sexuality within them, as for example in the subjugation of the body and neutering of appearance within boarding schools and similar institutions for bringing up girls,[12] and the prohibition of sexual relations between residents, and between residents and staff, as within prisons. This inhibits the making of cross-sex appointments, especially of men in women's prisons (Dean, 1983). Frequently such organisational policies towards sexuality are complicated by the single-sex nature of the institutions, and the central importance of homosexuality and attitudes towards it (Buffum, 1982). In the armed forces, and many other total institutions, homosexual activity is contrary to the rules of the organisation. However, in many institutions anti-homosexual 'norms' are overlain by degrees of persecution, for example, the investigations into lesbianism, leading to the discharge of women sailors, on United States Navy ships ('Women sailors quit. . .', 1982). The persecution of homosexual monks (Burrell, 1984), and lesbian nuns is a well established historical practice—silence on these activities and orientations is only now being broken (Curb and Manahan, 1985). Tatchell (1985, 78–9) has recently described this phenomenon in military contexts as follows:-

The armed forces have an obsessive fear and loathing of same-sex relationships and these are treated as violations of the military discipline Acts—even when the homosexual relationship is with a civilian and is limited to off-base liaisons in off-duty hours. Though male homosexuality has been legal in civilian society between consenting men over the age of 21 since the 1967 Sexual Offences Act, that legislation specifically excluded members of the armed forces. Gay personnel are frequently charged, imprisoned and dismissed under the catch-all Section 69 of the Queen's Regulations which forbids 'conduct prejudicial to good order and military discipline'. Lesbianism has never been an offence under civil law and, as with male homosexuality, there is no military regulation explicitly banning it. Nevertheless, what is perfectly legal in civilian society is treated as a crime under military law. According to an internal memo, Female Homosexuality in the Army, lesbianism is punishable by dismissal on the grounds that it is 'unacceptable' and 'detrimental to unit discipline and morale'.

Though a few individual liberal-minded officers may turn a blind eye to discreet gay personnel, usually the slightest hint of either male or female homosexuality is sufficient to launch widespread investigations, interrogations and purges by the Special Investigation Branch of the Military Police. These can include the raiding of personal lockers (no search warrants required), interception of mail and telephone calls, covert surveillance of off-duty suspects, interviews by psychiatrists, strip searches and intimate body inspections. Any soldier discovered to be gay is put under very strong pressure to identify others, including civilians whose names are often handed over to the police for filing or prosecution. This pressure sometimes involves virtual blackmail, whereby military investigators offer an administrative discharge in exchange for the names of sexual partners (instead of a court-martial and prison sentence).

Between 1976 and 1980, 200 gay service personnel were dismissed from the army and RAF following a court-martial. More than half of them served a military prison sentence before discharge. A further 500 homosexuals were dismissed administratively without court-martial, ...

In Britain the formal status of homosexuality is rather more complex in prisons than in the armed forces. Homosexual activity is, as in the armed forces, generally considered contrary to the rules of prison discipline, without formal exception. On the other hand, there are no specific rules or regulations regarding homosexuality as such. Indeed in a judgment in the Divisional Court on 20 September 1982 (R v. Board of Visitors Highpoint Prison, ex parte McConkey) the court held that, in the absence of any contrary indication disciplinary offences under the Prison Rules should be construed no more harshly against prisoners than equivalent criminal offences. To be precise, since the 1967 Sexual Offences Act legalises consensual homosexuality activity between men over twenty-one in private, homosexuality becomes punishable if in public, if non-consensual, if one or both (or more) of the participants are under twenty-one, or if general prison discipline is broken. An organisational ploy indirectly controlling homosexuality is the allocation of prisoners one, three or four, rather than two to a cell. To complicate the situation further, 'soft pornographic magazines', both 'homosexual' and 'heterosexual', are allowed as long as their distribution is not considered by the governor to be inflammatory. Many single-sex institutions thus both prohibit and facilitate homosexual relations.

It would of course be mistaken to characterise all total institutions as punitive. There are, for instance, attempts to cater more fully for the emotional and sexual needs of patients in hospital. A relevant example is the North Lincolnshire initiative introducing double beds for spouses in the Special Care Baby Maternity Units. Furthermore, some total institutions are in fact entered voluntarily and even peopled by powerful, affluent residents. Though such residents are often more able to express their wishes within the institution, it remains for the staff and management to develop policies on the *conditions* if not the *conduct* of sexuality. Even hotel and guest house managements explicitly or implicitly have to be aware of the sexual possibilities for residents, to impose visiting or time restrictions, 'turn a blind eye', make arrangements for blue movies, 'call girls' or whatever.

The day-to-day form of sexual relations in closed institutions exists at the intersection of the official regime and the underlife. As a nun has explained it, 'There's a tremendous [sexual] energy there, it's not suppressed, it's just channelled in a different direction' (quoted in Coles, 1978, 82). Residents' culture frequently stands in opposition to the formal rules, and may entail all manner of 'secondary adjustments', including sexual ones. Burrell (1984, 110–12) conceptualises such sexual practices as forms of *resistance* to formal desexualisation, and cites examples from the Navy, concentration camps, women's prisons and coal mines. Total institutions such as prisons present differential opportunities for and attitudes towards single-sex friendships, homosexual relations and a more general social contact, thus producing a complex social and sexual culture. A useful summary of differential emotional and sexual patterns in male and female prisons is that by Edwards (1975). Drawing on the work of Giallombardo (1966), Ward and Kassebaum (1965) and others, she notes how men's friendships tend to be modelled on economic, contractual or violent (or potentially violent) relationships, while women's relationships within prisons tend to follow familial patterns, homosexual dyads and friendship cliques. Tittle (1969) takes some of these findings further in noting the more stable nature of women prisoners' lesbianism as against the more casual nature of men prisoners' homosexuality. Perhaps the important point about all these relationships is the fact that they exist at all, often necessitating elaborate ruses in the face of official proscriptions.

It is hardly surprising that the power of total regimes and the complexity of institutional underlives can sometimes lead to sexual abuses and sexual scandals. Total institutions face the paradoxical problem of being made separate from the outside world for certain specific reasons, yet that separatism produces the conditions, the 'closed doors', that may subvert the achievement of those ends. Homosexual rape and exploitation in prisons is well documented (Scacco, 1975; Weiss and Friar, 1974; Wooden and Parker, 1982). There have also been cases of the sexual abuse of young people both by other residents, as in the 'kangaroo court' incident in Styal prison (Davies, 1985) and homosexual assaults by staff at the Kincora boys' home, Belfast, Northern Ireland. The inaccessibility of total institutions is a metaphor for sexuality: an institutional voyeurism so beloved by the 'Sunday papers'.

Sexual purposes and institutional closure are two major ways in which sexuality in organisations may, through organisational construction, have more impact and sometimes be visible to the point of sexual acts in public. In organisations with either of these properties, sexuality is likely to be an explicit aspect of organisational life. This might also suggest that the most sexualised organisational life is to be found in total institutions which also pursue an overt sexual purpose.

The sexual prohibition and opportunities of closed institutions compare interestingly with those of the opposite case, the permeable or open organisation (see figure 7).

CLOSED ORGANISATION ◄────► OPEN ORGANISATION
IMPERMEABLE BOUNDARIES ◄─► PERMEABLE BOUNDARIES

More sexual time within organisation	Less sexual time within organisation
More potential partners in organisation	Fewer potential partners in organisation
Fewer potential partners outside	More potential parnters outside
Closer relationships	Fewer close relationships
More potential control of sexuality	Less potential control of sexuality
(However, closed organisations may be associated with rigid, mechanistic, even authoritarian ways of working including (i) control of close relationships and (ii) resistance to such a regime producing closeness.)	(However, open organisations may be associated with flexible organising of ways of working, including closer relationships)

Figure 7: Comparison of closed and open organisations

Closure and openness are compounded in particular organisations by the complexity of organisational conditions. For example, an army unit may be relatively closed to the outside world as a total institution; it may pursue a task that subordinates sexuality yet is intensely physical; it may have a very clearly bureaucratic structure of labour and authority; and be single-sex, or perhaps mixed-sex with very clear internal sexual structuring. Alternatively, a company selling computer equipment may give considerable autonomy to sales persons to go 'into the field', may subordinate sexuality or exploit sexuality in the primary task of selling; have an organismic team structure; and be mixed-sex in a more integrated way.

Boundaries are important in permeable organisations though often they are facilitators of external contact rather than exclusion. Boundary roles may involve conflicting loyalties and pressures, difficulties in the role maintenance, as well as offering potential for innovation and autonomy. Similarly with the issue of sexuality, the boundaries of organisations may present difficulties for and constraints on the participants involved, as well as considerable opportunities for the expression of sexuality.

Where members travel across or beyond the boundaries, meetings between people from different organisations, as indeed from different departments, take a great variety of forms, depending partly on the autonomy of the respective members. These can also provide opportunities for less strictly monitored interactions than would be the case in 'home territories'. Like office parties, such meetings, perhaps on unfamiliar or neutral or extra-organisational ground (such as the 'business lunch'), can also be highly ambiguous, in being both on and off duty. Such ambiguities of work towards the organisation may interact with and become mirrored in ambiguities around the sexual significance of such meetings. Indeed work and organisational ambiguity may even have a sexual meaning, (and possibly vice versa) such as when a man invites a woman from another organisation for a working lunch, or to relax in an hotel (bed)room after business (Solomons and Cramer, 1985). In some instances sexuality may be used directly in securing inter-organisational relations as in the use of 'call girls' to assist business deals (Brenton, 1966, 79). This is also one obvious possible use of business 'slush funds' and thus the subject of numerous scandals and rumours in the world of commerce and government.[13]

Some business people and professionals have very high levels of autonomy in 'working' away from their 'home base', travelling freely, living in hotels, and attending conferences, and so on. These working conditions create the possibility for the 'business fling', sexual exploitation, the use of blue movies on pay televisions in hotel rooms. Similarly, the use of prostitutes by seamen, soldiers and other travelling workmen, has been long established, sometimes to the point of institutionalised (semi)-official facilities as with 'camp followers'. Organisational mobility and autonomy can be the means of creating opportunities for sexual liaisons—so that some workers can relatively easily include such possibilities within the 'working day'. Relatively autonomous workers like truckers can make use of their CB radio to 'eyeball' friends and lovers. According to one popular commentator ("J", 1969, 115–17), the greatest sexual potential is to be found in piano teachers and tuners, golf and tennis professionals, newspaper reporters, photographers, adult educators, landscape architects, academics, repairmen and delivery boys. Such sexualities may be organisationally constructed in reality or fantasy. Organisational sponsorship of access into peoples' homes is clearly very variable. This may lead to 'pre-emptive' strategies as in the case of a trainee cleric advised to sit in the window when visiting parishioners. Beyond this is the creation of vast realms of folklore around such 'visiting organisational members' as in 'Confessions of a Window Cleaner' etc. Similarly, places where workers transiently gather, such as motorway rest areas may be of interest for those seeking sexual liaisons (Corzine and Kirby, 1977).

On a broader scale organisational members are in some careers sent around the world, given 'bachelor' postings, 'distributed' along with spouses, family and marital home, and so on. Wives and sometimes husbands of prospective entrants are vetted, involved in company social arrangements (Kanter, 1977), and may define themselves in a complementary rather than a parallel way to their spouse. This is particularly important in 'greedy' organisational roles where people, often men, are never off duty—soldiers (Parker, 1985), police, clergy, diplomats (Callan, 1977), and many others (Finch, 1983). With such occupations and organisations there are considerable incentives in socialising, befriending, and being sexual with similar others. These organisations are as *social* total institutions.[14]

INTERNAL ORGANISATIONAL DIVISIONS

Organisations are characteristically structured and divided both horizontally, in terms of divisions of labour, and vertically, in terms of divisions of authority. These structures do not occur in any abstract way; they occur and are maintained through the social practices of particular people, most significantly for our purposes, people of similar or different genders and/or sexualities. Thus we can talk of 'sexual structuring' to refer to these features of organisational structures, in which organisations are continually divided by sex, and indeed sexualities. More precisely we can think of the organisational structuring of sexuality.

Divisions of labour and the labour division of sexuality
The gender division of labour between women and men is an entrenched reality both societally and in most organisations,

which in turn creates the labour division of sexuality. The broad tendencies for women to occupy less powerful, lower paid and lower status organisational positions, and for men to occupy more powerful, better paid and higher status positions is visible in both formal designations and informal roles (see Pollert, 1981). Gender divisions of labour represent the organisational expression of broader social structures, of paid over unpaid labour, of public over private, of productive over reproductive. Women remain with the weight and responsibility of unpaid, private and reproductive labours. Women and men are thus subject to dual labour markets, with many women acting as a 'reserve army of labour' (including sexual labour), performing dual or even triple roles, as paid workers, domestic child carers, and carers for the elderly and the infirm.

Although these (and other) divisions clearly create complex conditions in particular organisations, they all operate in one dominant direction—of men over women. Even atypical, established gender divisions of labour, for example, men chefs, derive from the promotion of skilled men in a predominantly female area rather than vice versa.[15]

Above all these organisational divisions create 'blocks' and 'groups' of workers differentiated by gender. Organisations are not neat, uniform asexual structures; they are more usually amalgamations of groups of women workers and groups of men workers, under the same control system of men. In mixed organisations where heterosexuality is dominant, this allocation in 'blocks' of women and men inevitably defines possible sex and love objects by means of job. Where one gender is in a minority, those few individuals are likely to receive greater attention in reality and/or in fantasy as *scarce*, potential objects.

These divisions are powerful determinants of gender roles, and of 'women' and 'men'. The social production of gender role includes numerous aspects of the person that bear on sexuality: appearance, dress, emotionality, desire for others. Managerial control of dress, through division of labour is particularly clear with aircraft cabin staff, nurses, shopworkers, amongst many others, especially women workers. More interesting still is the evaluation of 'appropriate' dress in the selection and training of women-dominated professions such as midwifery, teaching and social work.[16] Most mundane of all is the control of schoolchildren's dress, through uniform, banning of trousers for girls, and of make-up—the reproduction of the genders in action for all.

Divisions of labour also have clear effects upon the 'sex-ratios' of different organisations' membership. The differential valuation of labour, together with differential dynamics of sex-ratios, in turn affect the sexual behaviour and perceptions of participants. Gutek and Morasch (1982) have used the concept of 'sex-role spillover' to analyse such variable sexual behaviours, particularly between men and women, and particularly sexual harassment. They argue that women in what is traditionally 'men's work' tend to experience sex-role spillover as 'role deviates'—that is women may be treated by men as different from other (male) workers; are often aware of this differentiation; and tend to see it as directed at them *individually* rather than as role occupants. Women in predominantly 'women's work' tend to experience sex-role spillover by virtue of the presumed identity of 'work-role' and 'sex-role'. Thus such women in 'traditional jobs' may tend to under-report harassment and other sexually related behaviours, as the job itself is sexualised.

In the extreme case, in certain 'traditional' jobs, all women workers in a given organisation or job may be subject to equal sexual harassment. In contrast 'integrated' organisations, those with more equal sex-ratios, show very much lower levels of harassment, as seen below.

Social-sexual behaviour experienced on current job	Non-traditional (N = 89) %	Integrated (N = 40) %	Traditional (N = 100) %
Complimentary comments	74.2	46.2	57.6
Complimentary looks, gestures	66.3	56.8	63.0
Insulting comments	20.2	7.5	12.1
Insulting looks, gestures	13.5	5.0	16.0
Sexual touching	31.5	12.5	18.0
Required dating	6.7	0.0	2.0
Required sex	4.5	0.0	4.0

Figure 8: Experiences of social-sexual behaviour on current job

Source: after Gutek and Morasch (1982, 67)

Such interpretations of sex-ratios have to be treated with some caution, for as Gutek points out gender divisions occur at the level of occupation, job, and role-set, as well as for whole organisations as *combinations* thereof. Of these the role-set is of crucial and most immediate importance, as it is this that comprises face-to-face meetings between members of organisations.

According to such an analysis the Leeds TUCRIC (1983) survey's finding that 96 per cent of women working in non-traditional jobs reported sexual harassment as against 48 per cent in traditional, may obscure some under-reporting for the latter type of work. Similarly the finding of harassment by co-workers was twice as high as that by managers and supervisors, and could be interpreted in the light of the sex-role spillover approach. Harassment of women by co-workers in 'non-traditional' industries (for women) may be more recognisable as such than similar behaviour by managers and supervisors in 'traditional' situations. Thus the sexualisation of (usually women's) jobs 'as a whole', characteristically with male supervisors and managers, may increase the taken-for-grantedness of sexual harassment—as in institutionalised flirting relations between women boundary staff and men customers. The implicitness of this mundane sexualisation may be in tension with increased tendencies for harassment to be attributed, with increasing discrepancy in power between participants (see p. 37).

These broad divisions in the labour of women and men are, however, further complicated by the actual form of that labour, as a labour process. Labour process is the most concrete point of contact of members and their organisation. The work so performed can have a multitude of impacts upon the sexuality of those concerned.

Alienation of the labour process Labour processes and specifically alienating work are not just matters of economic exploitation, but have direct impacts upon the 'time-economy' and the 'emotional economy'—the 'subjective relations of practice' (Hales, 1980, 64–79). Social relationships at work are part of alienating work, and just as 'labour is *external* to the worker, i.e. does not belong to his essential being' (Marx, 1975, 326), so too is sexuality, accordingly objectified, at work.

Thus the particularly high levels (96 per cent in Leeds TUCRIC Survey, 1983) of sexual harassment by men of women working in industries that are not traditionally mixed or women's employers, occur in industries characterised by alienating work conditions, and lack of control of the product and act of production. Harassment could be interpreted as an attempt to create some human contact as part of or in reaction to this alienation, or just another alienated working act. In short, sexual harassment may be a *form of labour in which women become commodities for men*, as a 'reserve of sexual labour'. This represents a complementary explanation of harassment to the sex-role spillover approach referred to above. Some non-traditional jobs, such as journalism, combine relatively autonomous work with other alienations, from women and children, through long, inconvenient working hours, and disrupted home life. Some industries may however, combine the worst of both worlds. Police work, for example, often involves both very boring, repetitive, alienating work on the job and wider alienations from women, childcare and the whole system of reproduction through long, unpredictable hours and so on. It also provides some limited access to women co-workers, with men and women sometimes working alone, for example, in cars. The women police officers interviewed by TUCRIC reported high harassment levels, while one of the nastiest episodes of intensive harassment, with repeated direct propositioning, is described by Farley (1978, 54–60) in Washington DC Police Department's attempt to 'integrate' women in the early 1970s.[17]

Non-contact sexual harassment, such as female nude pin-ups, put up by men, seems particularly popular in men-only or near men-only organisations, with boring and sometimes dangerous work, such as the police, armed services, security, laboratory and portering work. A classic case was Arthur Scargill's and Maurice Jones' defence of the use of 'page three' pin-ups in *The Yorkshire Miner* in 1978 (Wilson, 1983, 13–14). According to Berlinguer (1985, 6), 'the fact that many workers read cheap pornographic magazines . . . can be explained not so much as . . . bad behaviour but rather as an escape from a reality which is both unattainable and unsatisfying at the same time'.

Many of these variations in labour process can be understood in terms of workers' variable relationship with technology and how that impinges on definitions of masculinity, femininity and sexuality. Technology has many well-established associations, both broadly generic and specifically sexual, both within and between genders. 'Hard' masculinity is often associated with heavy, skilled, dangerous, dirty, interesting, mobile machine processes; while 'femaleness' or 'soft' masculinity are associated with light, unskilled, less dangerous, clean, boring, immobile machinery (Game and Pringle, 1983, 28−32). These divisions are, however, subject to change and redefinition with the increasing introduction of automated and computerised technology. These may be both welcomed and seen as a possible threat for previous masculinities (Cockburn, 1983, 110, 117−18). Technological innovation also redesignates what is understood as predominantly 'female' work and accordingly redefines modes of femininity. Some men operating automated machinery may feel 'reduced' to the level of women, operating keyboards and video units, yet write off other men clerical workers as 'a bunch of poufters' (Cockburn, 1983, 139). In contrast Game and Pringle (1983, 86) report how men computer programmers look down upon the computer operators as 'sex-starved animals'. These authors suggest that:

as the job becomes more routine and limited the operators have projected an even stronger 'macho' style as some sort of compensation and expression of their identity. They have become as a group very isolated from other workers . . . locked in with the computer as effectively as other people are locked out.

(*ibid.*)

Rather similarly sexual horseplay, often routine 'homosexual' high jinks between heterosexual men, may increase with the introduction of new technological processes, that grant less personal responsibility for individuals. As described elsewhere (Hearn, 1985a, 124−6), horseplay increased with the replacement of an old technological system by an automated process in a chemical factory in which jobs were less interchangeable, where formerly men worked as a team and had to be aware of how others were getting on; and where there was even some degree of competition between men. Male independence and social bonding that could previously be shown and satisfied through the job and as part of the team were disrupted, and instead were transformed, by projection, into horseplay. Such expressive behaviour also acts as a means of fighting back against feelings of redundancy or near redundancy, as raised by working in a close relationship with automated processes. *Labour process hazards* Labour processes can also have more particular and tangible effects on organisational workers in the form of problems and diseases. Over and above the general alienation of labour processes there are specific technological hazards which merit special mention. The first malignant disease to be shown to have a clear relationship with a particular occupation was scrotal cancer, when its occurrence was described in chimney sweeps in 1775. In more recent times it has been associated with mule spinners in the cotton industry who were

most likely to contract [the] disease as their work of piecing together the broken threads of the mule caused them to lean over a faller bar which was covered with oil thrown off from the rapidly rotating spindles. The faller bar was at groin height and the mule spinner's clothing became soaked with oil which thus came into contact with his scrotum.

(Waldron, Waterhouse and Tesseme, 1984, 437)[18]

Many other chemicals, such as pesticides, radioactive materials, petrol and other hydrocarbons are liable to cause infertility, impotence, birth defects and child cancers to offspring (Fletcher, 1985). There are many other possible hazards to sexual and reproductive faculties in particular occupations and organisations. These include 'reduced libido, frigidity, changes in the gonads, an increased tendency towards miscarriage and premature births and an increase in perinatal mortality . . . [which may be] caused by chemical effects, noise, vibration and radiation' (Berlinguer, 1985, 5). Radiographers, especially those women who are pregnant, are one occupational group who face regular danger at work. Similarly, those suffering frequent exposure to anaesthetic gases increase risks of miscarriage and birth defects (Fletcher, 1985). Lesser but still significant hazards may affect those involved with VDUs, photocopiers and similar office equipment. Berlinguer (1985, 4) reports on workers' experiences in several furniture factories in the province of Pesaro, Italy, with the introduction of new and extremely rapid wood-bonding machines which emitted high-frequency electro-magnetic signals. Complaints of insomnia, fatigue and reduced libido followed, which eventually led to the machines' replacement after trade union intervention. In some countries, such as the German Democratic Republic, there were very stringent legal limits on doing paid work that may involve excessive vibration or similar hazards, because of the possible effects on reproductive capability.

Labour process stresses More subtle and less tangible effects of the labour process upon sexuality may derive from the timing, rhythm and stressfulness of the work. Overtime, night shift, and variable shift systems, such as Continental shifts, which alternate night working and day working, can all produce adverse effects on workers, both in terms of tiredness and disruption of body rhythms. Such working patterns can also be a source of stress, as can casualisation of work and unemployment, which in turn can damage people's emotional and sexual lives. To hark back to the early Human Relations school, shopfloor fatigue can include sexual fatigue; staff burnout may encompass sexual burnout; and managerial stress can extend to other 'hidden stresses' and a lack of interest in sex (Underwood, 1982).

Cooper and Cooper (1984) make the tentative suggestion that stress, as particularly experienced by high type-A women, may be a contributory factor in the onset of breast cancer. A Transport and General Workers Union study of stress at work among busworkers found a third of the wives of busworkers reported sexual relationships badly affected by the busworker's job (Shop Stewards T&GWU 9/12 Branch, 1981, 84−5). This all makes for a marked contrast with the frequently assumed association of success, power and sexuality, of which more will be said below. Indeed Berlinguer (1985, 5) suggests that 'If the work is alien and unsatisfying, more is often expected of the relationship with the partner and children in order to make up for the lack of satisfaction at work.'

This extra pressure from organisational work may itself become a source of worry so adding to domestic and organisational vicious circles. Important as this general insight is, it has to be treated with some caution. This way of analysing, particularly where it focuses upon the 'needs' of the 'hard pressed' and probably male individual worker, may rest on over-simple assumptions, such as a limited model of male sexual needs. Furthermore, in reality the interplay of organisational and domestic lives differs for people living alone, without sexual partners, or for two or more partners needing nurture, sexual or otherwise.

The basic problem seems to be that where the rhythms of labour dominate the rhythms of the body, which is probably the case in most organisations, work alienation may be accompanied by a sexual alienation. Indeed one novel way of conceptualising an organisation is as a social collectivity that does not take the rhythms of the body into account. It is perhaps partly for this reason that some workers will not choose to work night shifts despite the financial advantages. Indeed in September 1977 car workers at British Leyland refused night overtime on a new model because of disruption to family and sex lives. As the newspapers put it 'home comes first'.[19]

People work   In many organisations the labour process involves and may indeed comprise close working relations between people.[20] A particularly interesting set of organisations in this regard are what might be called 'people organisations', that engage in 'people work' (Stacey, 1981), 'people-processing', and especially 'people-changing' (Hasenfeld, 1972). In such organisations, such as those doing caring, nursing or social work, members may be put under considerable personal stress in coping with the distress of others. The emotional nature of the work thereby affects the emotional life of the organisations and its members. Responses to such conditions include the control of emotions through 'professionalism', 'institutional defences' and resort to a greater reliance on informal, group support. The heightening of the emotional life between organisational members can have various effects on imagined or actual sexual relations. Often increased emotional involvement will itself be highly ambiguous in sexual terms and liable to misunderstandings and misrepresentations. For example, a male social worker who comes to rely on women colleagues for emotional support in coping with job stress may develop relationships that are both ambiguous to the participants and, furthermore, understood as something different still by their partners. Similarly, sexual relationships outside work may be strongly influenced by the presumed expertise of the partner or partners already involved in 'people work'. This may be even more important for those workers seen as both professionally expert in personal relations and personally approachable.

In some organisational settings, fear and anxiety may increase sexual awareness and attraction to others (Dutton and Aron, 1974; Wilson and Nias, 1976). More generally, anxiety-arousing situations often lead to people seeking more contact with each other. These are well developed themes within the social psychological literature, even though still significant inconsistencies and contradictions remain in research material (Kendrick, Cialdini and Linder, 1979). Two possible avenues for research within organisational contexts are the impact of ambiguous fear-provoking situations (Morris *et al.*, 1976), such as 'routine' aircraft landings or medical surgery, supervision and appraisal sessions, revision and examinations; and the effect of shared emotional embarrassment on sexual arousal (Byrne *et al.*, 1975).

It should be added that in many 'people organisations' there is a clear gender division of labour with women tending to do the basic level work and men the middle and senior management. This is likely to be a major factor both facilitating and complicating sexual relationships and interactions.

The dimension within the gender division of labour may appear to be reduced by the more apparent emotional life of such organisations. In practice, however, this can be a further resource for the development of power relationships in these 'people organisations', for example the disclosure of personal feelings of stress about stressful situations in supervision sessions.[21] Yet again this characteristically takes place as power relations between women and men, and thereby reproduces and reinforces heterosexual ideology and practice.

Division of authority and the authority division of sexuality

In most organisations (gender) divisions of labour are reinforced by (gender) divisions of authority and power, as expressed through hierarchy, and vice versa. As with labour, authority is a major divider of sexuality. The preponderance of hierarchical organisations and the relative rarity of non-hierarchical organisations is both an instance and a product of general social and gender divisions within society. In turn hierarchical organisational structures make for hierarchical interpersonal, including sexual, relations between people in organisations. Hierarchical division of gender is rarely random, with men tending to occupy the higher and women the lower levels. In this fundamental way hierarchy, the gender division of hierarchy, interpersonal relations and sexuality are interrelated. As noted in chapter 4, sexuality is partly a question of power; power partly a question of sexuality. Both division by power and authority, and by types of work and labour may thus interrelate with gender divisions and divisions around sexuality.

The consequences of hierarchy or indeed lack of hierarchy are in some ways highly contradictory. Hierarchical organisations may be able to accommodate both a relatively high level of formality and even secrecy around personal relations and a relatively functional, and thereby tolerant, climate towards actual or potential intimacy. On the other hand, where sexual relationships become more established and perhaps threaten the ways of working in the organisation, reaction from those in the upper levels of the hierarchy can be intense, with threats, dismissals, reorganisations and other sanctions.

Less hierarchical, less bureaucratic organisations may display opposed tendencies. They may be both less able to accommodate closed, secret relationships and yet more *routinely* rigid in their reaction. In children's homes, communes or community organisations, sexuality is more obviously part of organisational life, and as such may invoke the whole range of *informal* reactions, social controls, ridicule and retributions. While life in the office may continue or appear to continue impersonally yet amicably, in an informal community organisation a sexual incident, actual or potential, may provoke a more immediate, extreme or even violent reaction.

These broad differences in and consequences of hierarchy are compounded by the distribution of the genders. The most common are mixed-gender hierarchies, with men managing women, or all-men hierarchies. All-women hierarchies may appear to exist in, say, girls' schools but these are often under the ultimate control of male governors, officials or councillors. 'Non-hierarchical' organisations, whether of men, women or both genders, are unusual. One of the most important ways in which organisations, and especially those that are hierarchical and bureaucratic, influence sexuality is through the creation of conditions of dependence and interdependence which themselves may provide the basis of romance (Huston and Cate, 1979). An organisational arena of dependence that deserves special mention and has indeed taken on almost legendary significance is the relationship between bosses and secretaries (McNally, 1979), with the latter often acting as 'office wives', protecting their charges from 'unnecessary' interference and strain, making tea, buying presents, even cleaning their bosses' false teeth (Miles, 1983, 199).

The valuation of men over women in mixed hierarchical organisations is paralleled in the tendency to value men's sexuality over women's sexuality. Men's sexuality tends to be associated with the properties of valued labour and hierarchy: control, activeness, physical power, freedom from constraint, intellectualism, coolness. These associations can account for contradictions between the gender structuring of organisations and sexuality, for both women and men. While women at work are frequently seen by men as 'sexualised' beings (MacKinnon, 1979), this can mean that they are both individually measured and assessed as such and generically, perhaps even collectively, under-valued, unvalued, as indeed sexuality itself might be. In contrast men may appear to each other as both asexual and yet also sexualised according to status, power and money in the organisation.

Thus one influential model of masculinity is the man manager dedicated (wedded?) to his job rather than to his gender or his sexuality. For him, grey, hard working, corporate:

the use of managerial time or other resources in pursuit of sexual ends is a violation of the primary code of the [managerial] culture. Not only is it a blatant assertion of idleness, it is a denial that the purpose of the manager is to make a profit for the company.

(Cleverley, 1973, 140)

It is the protestant work ethic personified.

In some ways an even stronger model of asexuality comes from the professions, especially the church, medicine, accountancy and the law. Such 'men workers are specifically "asexualised" in keeping with their supposed neutrality and the supposed neutral competence of masculinity presented' (Hearn, 1983, 14).

This supposed asexuality co-exists alongside its apparent opposite, whereby success and career become indicators of men's masculinity and sexuality. For example, Gould (1974, 97 − 8) in 'Measuring masculinity by the size of a paycheck' notes how, 'There are many phenomenally wealthy men in the public eye who are physically unattractive by traditional criteria; yet they are surrounded by beautiful women and an aura of sexiness and virility.'[22] Gould argues that, in contrast, a 'woman in the same financial position loses in attractiveness. . .; she poses a threat to a man's sense of masculinity . . . men are unsexed by failure'. While there are obvious exceptions for powerful women in the media and entertainment world, for those women in managerial and comparable positions they may be perceived by men to lose their sexual power subtly, indirectly or intermittently.

Men managers with women subordinates may use sexuality, sexual harassment, sexual joking and sexual abuse as a routine means of maintaining authority. This may be thoroughly embedded in the taken-for-granted culture of the organisation. On the other hand, real differences in power and authority do make perception of sexual harassment for specific types of behaviour more likely. Thus the authority division of sexuality (usually of men over women) may involve a subtle dialectic between the ignoring of the (ab)use of sexuality as in 'normal culture' and its patent ever presence. Authority (of men) over sexualised work (of women) is thus itself sexualised, but in a dialectical way, shifting in the space created between 'normal culture' and patriarchal power.

These characteristic features of male-dominated hierarchies are complicated significantly with the entry of women into management. There may be considerable pressure for such women to 'learn to become managers'. Women managers may be seen as even offering 'potential' for a more sophisticated, more sensitive model of management (Jacklin and Maccoby,

1975). However, women managers may also present a considerable sexual threat to men–either by undermining men's presumed confidence and capability (Mayes, 1979) or as possible and thereby disruptive sexual partners for male managers (Loring and Wells, 1972; Bradford, Sargent and Sprague, 1975). There are some women managers who may even be able to trade on male insecurity in developing their *local* power base through the use of clothes, furniture, decor and so on to manipulate male colleagues and subordinates (Korda, 1976, ch. 8). A number of alternative styles may therefore be available to women managers, for example, the emulation of men managers or the cultivation and elaboration of a distinct female style. Some women managers may react to such pressures by devoting themselves more completely to the job than their male colleagues (Cooper and Davidson, 1982). Such orientations represent considerable threats to male homosociability (Lipman-Blumen, 1976).

An important yet little explored area is the nature of men's homosocial or potentially homosexual relationships in mixed organisations. While many men may prefer other men's company this is coupled with a profound fear of intimacy with men, homophobia, often reinforced by hierarchy. Accordingly male–male relationships can easily become ritualised, with physical contact being limited to 'hearty' slaps and hugs rather than tender intimacies.

Compulsory heterosexuality These sexual divisions, by authority and labour occur in most organisations *through* and in association with a characteristic form of sexuality, namely heterosexuality. The power of certain labours, of hierarchies, of men, are in practice enmeshed with the power of heterosexuality. The dominant concrete form that heterosexuality takes in this society is an hierarchical one, and the concrete form that hierarchy[23] takes is a heterosexual one. Thus a major, and perhaps the central, feature of the sexual 'normality' of organisations is a powerful heterosexual bias: a form of 'compulsory heterosexuality' (Rich, 1980). This entails degrees of men's domination and oppression of women, in intricate relation with the domination and oppression of homosexuality, lesbianism and other sexualities perceived as 'other'. Furthermore, the particular form that compulsory heterosexuality takes in most organisations is the domination of men's heterosexuality over women's heterosexuality or over a more egalitarian heterosexuality.

It is important to emphasise that although compulsory heterosexuality is continued through dominant ideologies and assumptions, it actually takes place in organisations through particular concrete, social practices. These range from managerial policies and powers, through to everyday informal conversations, as well as more occasional incidents, such as legal or tribunal rulings. (Men) managers often have the power to routinely 'buy in' women, sexuality, heterosexuality, through the hiring and assessment of workers; through the portrayal of images of women in promotion and advertising of products and other published material, such as 'girlie calendars'; as well as through the 'more occasional' acquisition of sexual slaves or women to 'facilitate' business deals. The recruitment, selection and hiring of outsiders is an important field for investigation, in relation to physical attraction, presentation and other aspects of sexuality (Schuler and Berger, 1979; Rose and Andiappon, 1978). Potential members and other strangers are obliged to negotiate their way through such novel situations as interviews, to display themselves and allow the members to present a particular public image of the organisation. In extreme cases sexual harassment, sexual favours, and even prolonged liaisons may be the condition of gaining jobs, promotion, recommendation.

Even though most managements will not indulge in all the practices and policies mentioned above, and may specifically decide not to use them, they remain *available* for use at times deemed appropriate by management. Even organisations that adopt specific anti-discrimination policies may persist in such practices as the use of heterosexual images and stereotypes in promotional literature. Men managements are characteristically reservoirs of heterosexual power: they have a repertoire of practices available to conspicuously display and promote compulsory heterosexuality.

Interstices

The internal division of organisations, by both labour and authority, both frequently sexually structured, together with external organisational form, have controlling effects on the proximity of organisational members to each other. It has been noted how the degree of closure and openness creates conditions of dependence and autonomy for members, sometimes to the points of annihilation or travel throughout the world. Proximity within organisations remains one of the major determinants of the development of sexual relationships, and especially more socially accepted heterosexual relationships (Quinn, 1977; Gutek and Nakamura, 1982). However, the very organisational structures, typically formally sanctioned, that produce proximities, of which the most obvious is the placing of members by managements in specific places, offices, factory floors, within specified or assumed degrees of movement away from 'base' are also the sites of greatest managerial control.

Because of the degree of control of space and members within spaces, it is often the interstices, the spaces between spaces, that are less directly controlled by management, and thus can provide further opportunities for meeting, intimacy, and various sexual behaviours. These spaces can be physical spaces, such as corridors, staircases, lifts, kitchens, passageways, entrance ways, 'cubby holes', anywhere that people 'bump into' each other.[24] This is so much so that, in some schools, corridors, playgrounds and stairways can be places of high harassment risk, so that girls, and sometimes boys, adopt avoidance strategies, such as arriving late at lessons (Mahony, 1985, 49). These spaces can be of particular importance in total institutions and other organisations subject to planned regimes.

Interstices also occur in time, and indeed in the social intercourse that takes place *between* people from different departments, sections, and organisations (Hearn, 1985a). Thus we may note the importance of tea breaks, lunchtimes, and drinks ('one for the road'), as well as the more occasional office party, Christmas 'do' and summer outings, in the sexual culture of many organisations. Roy's (1960) classic study of 'Banana time' is illustrative of the significance of 'gaps' in work culture, the opportunities so provided for contact not prescribed by management are often intensely felt, whether sexual or not. The office party has passed into the folklore of many organisations, and needs to be understood in terms both of actual happenings and of perceived meanings, typically of surprise liaisons from past parties. These may be talked about as times when 'anything goes', though in fact they may often have a highly ritualistic character, especially in hierarchical organisations, with clear rules about how people should behave. Cleverley (1973) sees them primarily as tension-releasing mechanisms in the face of the taboos that operate throughout 'normal working life'. Korda (1976) demonstrates the intricate relation of status and spatial movements at office parties that may serve to illustrate and *reinforce* the power of members. Thus even within these 'social interstices', the formality of authority and other aspects of organisational relations may remain. In order to explore the complexity of these and other ambiguous sexualities, part visible, part invisible, we need to focus on the impact of sexuality upon organisational life. This is examined in the following chapter. The external form and internal divisions of organisations may be powerful determinants of sexuality, but in isolation they provide rather less than half a story.

6 The Sexual Construction of Organisations

Having analysed the various ways in which organisations construct sexuality, we now move on to examine how sexuality constructs organisations, thereby exemplifying the dialectical relationship of sexuality and organisational life. This proceeds by way of a series of powerful, yet characteristically elusive, impacts of sexuality within and upon organisational life. We thus outline how sexuality is apparent, is kept less than apparent or remains unapparent within organisations. This entails reviewing material, some qualitative, some similar to that in the previous chapter, yet here the focus is upon sexuality and categories describing that sexuality. What is at issue is the power of sexuality, sexual labour-power, within organisations in addition, and sometimes in reaction to the power of organisations already discussed.

In some organisations, such as those that explicitly exploit sexuality, sexuality has an obvious presence, and is a major determinant of the organisational dynamics. There are, however, many more where the impact of sexuality is altogether more subtle. There is a widespread tendency in organisations to exclude sexuality or, rather more precisely, to attempt, appear or pretend to exclude sexuality. Many organisational managements refrain from admitting the presence of sexuality at all, let alone its influence upon organisational life and underlife.

This frequent 'denial' of sexuality compounds the more general methodological difficulties of studying sexuality. For example, the general problem of interpretation which pervades research into sexuality is of special significance in investigating the mixture of meanings within the sexual underlife of organisations—with their rumour, gossip, taboos, collusions and innuendoes. Furthermore, as discussed in chapter 3, what may appear as 'problems' in the pursuit of a particular social science methodology may be better understood as examples of organisational processes within the organisation in question.

Having detailed the structural determinants of and constraints on sexuality, this chapter is thus concerned with the *qualitative* nature of sexuality, at each determination of the organisation. For example, even where sexuality is obviously organisationally constructed, as in initiation or degradation ceremonies of a sexual nature, these events are likely to have a multiplicity of meanings and qualities. It is as if whatever the quantitative determinants of sexuality, sexuality itself (almost) always has a multi-levelled nature, a series of levels of meaning. This should not be seen, however, as mere qualitative detailing within a quantitative or structured framework, for the qualitative nature of sexuality itself often constructs organisations, through a process of equal power. With this in mind, we have found it useful to conceptualise the sexual construction of organisations in terms of a series of 'fronts', albeit of different types.

The concept 'front' has a double and somewhat contradictory meaning: on the one hand, that which is 'at the front', as in 'in the front line' of organisations; on the other hand, that which obscures or even deceives, as in the 'front region', obscuring the 'back region' of organisations. Accordingly, organisations are constructed in the form of a variety of 'fronts' that both exhibit and obscure sexuality and its power. Some of these 'fronts' are not immediately recognisable as such; indeed such processes as secrecy and unseenness are, in these terms, just as much 'fronts', obscuring sexuality, as those 'fronts' that explicitly display sexuality.[1]

Four major 'fronts' are examined in this chapter: *visible*, *secret*, *unseen*, and overarching all of these, the *elusive*. These fronts are related to each other as shown in figure 9.

These 'fronts' themselves have a dialectical form. They incorporate not only particular types of sexuality (visible, secret, unseen and elusive), but also parallel qualitites of sexuality namely the visibility, secrecy, unseenness and elusiveness of sexuality respectively.[2] Arguably the less visible they are,

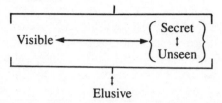

Elusive

Figure 9: 'Fronts' of sexuality in organisations

paradoxically the more powerful they become; as with clandestine and total institutions, the power of sexuality often increases in its attempted exclusion.

These 'fronts' typically are ways of defending organisations against the power of sexuality, of denying that sexuality is present within the organisation both to members themselves and others outside. Together these 'fronts' comprise the sexual construction of organisations.

THE VISIBILITY OF SEXUALITY: VISIBLE SEXUALITY

Attending both to how sexuality becomes visible and to the visible aspects of sexuality involves looking at the media through which it is open, observable, tangible and noticeable. By visibility we refer to the possibility of direct observation either by an outside observer or by most organisational members. The main types of visibility are considered: visible behaviour and actions such as touch and speech; and visible traces such as dress and written records. Visible actions and behaviours include occasional sexual acts; officially or managerially sanctioned sexualisation; unofficial 'secondary adjustments'; explicit sexual advances and stances from organisational members; open and/or mutual sexual relationships; sexual harassment, both contact and non-contact.

Open sexual acts
Organisations as part of the public world are usually not seen as fit places for observable full sexual acts. The major exceptions to this are the performance of sexual acts as part of the sexual purposes of the organisation as in some live sex shows or various pornographic and voyeuristic enterprises.

Sexual acts such as sexual intercourse, masturbation, sexual abuse and rape may also be performed openly and visibly within some closed institutions such as prisons and boarding schools. These may be kept secret from the officials of the organisation but are an open and accepted part of the underlife and communal life. Total and closed institutions can indirectly facilitate sexual acts and indeed assaults for various reasons including the 'total' twenty-four-hour nature of such institutional living, lack of privacy, resistance to authority, sharing of sleeping accommodation. Such acts have a variety of impacts: as a form of power relations and cohesion amongst residents; as a threat to official regimes, sometimes bringing powerful reactions following 'discovery'. Sanctions such as expulsion from the army or boarding schools for homosexuality illustrate how organisations are forced to officially recognise sexual activity which may be constant and visible to a majority of the people living there. The extent of this sexual life would probably not be apparent to outsiders, and only be acknowledged by those looking beyond the organisational front through first-hand accounts from residents or former residents, such as Curb and Manahan's (1985) on lesbianism in convents.

In non-total institutions, open sexual acts may take place in a more limited way such as at office parties. The works 'do' observed in a large hospital not uncommonly involved such observable pairings making blatant use of the premises, both cubby holes and semi-public 'back regions'. Their impacts on the organisation may appear negligible; may cause disruption of relationships with management, especially if the latter are involved; can give rise to sanctions such as dismissal, transfer and occasionally to extortion; affect promotional opportunities; or restructure longer term, informal working relationships.

Open sexual liaisons

According to Quinn, the author of a study of 130 'romantic relationships' in organisations, 'organisations are a natural [sic] environment for the emergence of romantic relationships' (1977, 30). The visibility of such liaisons depends on many factors, including the relative status of those involved and the culture of the organisation. Quinn found that almost a third were recognisable through them 'sometimes physically [displaying] their affections at work'. The other major signs of such relationships were being seen together away from work (78 per cent); spending unusual amounts of work time chatting (57 per cent); taking long lunches (47 per cent); and having long discussions behind closed doors (42 per cent).

The impact of these relationships on the participants was variable, including behavioural changes around positive organisational performance, such as greater productivity; loss of competence, such as arriving late and/or leaving early; and power changes, such as promoting the other person. Perhaps most important were the showing of favouritism (72 per cent male to female; 60 per cent female to male); the establishment of guaranteed channels of communication between the pair; and (for a third of both women and men) the loss of respect from other members. Sexual liaisons are liable to lead to confusion, gossip, worry amongst colleagues and in some cases more direct intervention from management by transfers or even dismissal. In Quinn's study women were more than twice as likely to lose their job; men usually being in a higher position, tended to be seen as less dispensable, that is in the eyes of other men.

Display, harassment and other explicit sexual behaviour
Apart from sexual acts and liaisons, explicit sexual behaviour in organisations can take many forms: sexual display, the exploitation of sexuality (Hearn, 1985a, 117–19), sexual advances, conspicuous sexuality in body movement and posture, sexual harassment and sexual horseplay. In addition these behaviours may be attentional or requiring a response, physical or non-physical, verbal or non-verbal (Gutek and Nakamura, 1982, 196–7).

Sexual display is a frequent element in the definition of organisational boundaries, in advertising, promotion, 'public relations' and so on. Secretaries, receptionists, television 'hostesses', salespersons in boutiques are predominantly women, and involve the selling of sexuality as part of labour-power (Bland *et al.*, 1978). Sexuality is thus both officially incorporated and literally marginalised. Sometimes this process takes bizarre forms, such as the use of ranks of models to flank the presenting of prizes at some male sporting championships, such as snooker. Such displays of sexuality at the margin contrast with the supposed 'asexuality' of male management (Parkin and Hearn, 1987; Hearn and Parkin, 1986–7). An interesting contrast is the way workers, usually men, on building sites have unofficial contact with the public, through peeping, voyeurism (Feigelman, 1974) or display. Their sometimes raucous sexuality is *not* part of their labour-power, but rather is often expressed in defiance of a lack of autonomy within the gaze of the public. An interesting example, in November 1985, of this phenomenon was men building workers at the new parliamentary buildings at Canberra, Australia, wolf-whistling Princess Diana on her 'royal tour'.[3]

Sexual display is, however, not just for outsiders, clients and members of the public. In some organisations explicit sexual forms of behaviour become part of the organisational culture, emphasising structured gender divisions, sexual tensions, and possible protests to (male) authority. Ardener (1974, 704) has described the practice of 'mooning', predominantly by young women, that developed in the United States in the 1950s and 60s.

In the autumn of 1966, in a college in Iowa, the girls and boys both lived in one three-storey H-shaped building. A block of rooms of girls was on one side, and a block of boys on the other, joined across the middle by single-storied common rooms. Twelve girls' rooms each with a large, plate-glass window, faced those of the boys opposite.

The following account was collected from one of the female residents:

At night, after we were locked in [*sic*] at midnight, stripping and dancing in the windows took place, to tease the boys. Normally this never went beyond bra and pants. One night when the ringleaders were happy-drunk, instead of a peep or strip show, it was decided to do a 'mass moon'. In each room, one girl was ready in the dark, standing on a chair bending over with her bottom pressed against the window. Another girl flicked the light on for a few seconds. It was like a dare . . . considered wicked and naughty.

This activity is known as 'pressing a ham' or 'hamming'. Ardener's informant also stressed that 'the girls at the college were normally considered to be "very moral" and little sexual intercourse took place—for one thing . . . there was no opportunity'. Sexuality is explicit and in use as part of a defiance by women to the fact these men could come and go freely, while they were locked in.

Sexual harassment, despite the problems of definition (see pp. 43–4), is a pervasive form of explicit sexual behaviour in many organisations. It is performed by management on workers and vice versa, by peers, by organisational members on clients, and vice versa, and so on. However, to see harassment as a *process*, rather than just as specific actions, is important because it forms such a significant part of the *visible routine* of many organisations. A series of incidents observed on a bus illustrates this.

A woman (age c. 50) gets on the bus and has difficulty in putting her season ticket in the automatic punching machine. The male conductor (c. 25) winks at a male passenger, indicating superiority to the woman, and says 'put it in slowly'.

A few minutes later the conductor goes up to a young female passenger (c. 20) and exchanges a few pleasant words.

Shortly after, he sits down opposite another female passenger (c. 30) and gives her change (presumably not given earlier), which she accepts gratefully. He then, without asking, takes the woman's newspaper she was reading, flips through it, hardly reading, finds an item of interest, leans forward to comment on it to the woman, and immediately returns the paper with his left hand and slaps the woman on the side of her knees with his right, then goes off.

He returns to his 'post' by the exit, exchanging pleasantries, smiling and eyeing up and down young female passengers, and ignoring older female passengers, as they leave the bus.

Harassment of this sort also poses a problem for management, subject to both legal and economic pressures to respond, at least in terms of official policy on equal opportunities. Policies and grievance procedures are often designed to deal with the more blatant forms of harassment, that are persistent and more easily verifiable, and that are between organisational members. As harassment becomes 'less blatant', 'more ordinary' and regular, yet less persistent with a single recipient or with non-organisational members in occasional contact, official policy becomes less easy to formulate and less effective.

Implicit sexual behaviour
A wide range of behaviour in organisations is visible, sexually

related, yet less explicitly sexual. This includes, firstly, the use of the eyes: gazing, scanning, eyeing from a distance. Secondly, it may involve movement in relation to each other, and use of touch. Thus touching or proximity can be welcomed and is therefore not harassment, but it can also simultaneously be a means to exerting or accepting authority, especially where the contact is conspicuous. The powerfulness of touch and the frequently associated strong feelings are fully exploited by *The One Minute Manager* (Blanchard and Johnson, 1983, 94–5), in what amounts to a behavioural modification prescription for managers. Perhaps the interesting point is that whereas unwelcome touch is likely to be sexual harassment, welcomed touch can be either sexual or non-sexual or ambiguous. Additionally, movement also often involves structured avoidances. This may be because of the lack of sexual attraction (or even feelings of repulsion), attraction but awareness of differences in power and status, ritual distancing from the desired 'object of affection' at meetings, office parties and other social occasions, or sexual sublimation.

The ambiguity of touch in organisational settings is explored by Solomons and Cramer (1985) in terms of the presence of various 'comfort zones', and the discomfort caused to many men by women's socially accepted variability in clothing and appearance. They suggest that assimilation of women into male groups involves issues of trust, dependability and touching; and that the question 'Can I touch you?' 'represents the *social* hurdle'. They note two contrasting types of ambiguity surrounding touch, firstly in relation to mutuality and achievement, and secondly in relation to harassment and business and association.

In many corporate settings there is usually little physical contact between colleagues apart from shaking hands, occasional slaps on the back or, perhaps, an arm around a shoulder. But even this kind of ordinarily accepted physical contact between male managers often cannot be spontaneously expressed when one of the managers is female. One of us was with a group of male colleagues when some good news arrived related to a difficult decision the group had made. There was much cheering and jollity. The men slapped each other and hugged and made a lot of noise. One of the men came to the woman, held out his arms and then stopped. 'May I hug you?' he asked.

Some men do *not* ask permission. When this occurs it can be very awkward. A woman consultant was shocked when a new client, durin₂ a business discussion over lunch with her and three other female managers from his company, placed his hand on her knee and when she left gave her an extremely ardent hug. In this case, the other people at the table were also subjected to a great deal of embarrassment observing their boss's clearly inappropriate behaviour without knowing what they could do to stop it. The consultant wanted very much to tell him clearly that his behaviour was inappropriate, but felt the need to be careful less she lose an important contract.

(Solomons and Cramer, 1985, 166)

The second example clearly shows that what may be sexually implicit or ambiguous behaviour in the eyes of some participants may be sexual harassment for others; and that such behaviours therefore blur with those harassments considered in the previous section. A similar complex relationship of the implicit, the ambiguous and the harassing is applicable to some speech and joking in organisations as discussed below. Implicit sexual behaviour often *underwrites* explicit sexual behaviour by providing the taken-for-granted routine of organisational life, which itself is more explicitly sexual at certain times in the form of harassment, display and so on.

We have already noted in the previous chapter how much work is alienating. Accordingly, speech in organisations is characteristically about things other than the organisational and thus a form of implicit sexuality:

Conversations in offices are invariably personalised. . . . Not surprisingly, . . . conversations rarely concern the subject matter of the things [being typed]—it is quite difficult to construct a conversation around an invoice. Rather conversations centre around personal, domestic concerns, such as families, weddings, children, cooking, knitting, marriage, boyfriends and clothes etc.   (Barker and Downing, 1980, 83)

Everyday speech is also a major vehicle for the perpetuation of heterosexuality in organisational life, as exemplified by the sustained usage of talk about heterosexual sex acts in many male conversational cultures in organisations (Collinson, 1981, 223).

In her study of a Bristol tobacco factory, Pollert (1981, 142) describes how:

on top of . . . the discipline of work and of factory rules . . . as women, they were exposed to constant sexual patronization, not just from the charge-hands and foreman, but from any men who worked around them: 'Hey, gorgeous', 'Do us a favour, love', 'Come here, sexy'—all are familiar forms of address for women.

A similar study by Webb (1982) of a department store has showed how heterosexist banter and practices were the language of authority. She points out that 'when [shop] assistants joined in with managers' jokes, allowed themselves to be petted and flattered and even initiated teasing it was always on the men's terms. . .'. Compulsory heterosexuality is not just ideas and policies, it is specific speech, interactions.[4]

What is perhaps most significant in all these examples, is the way that the 'terms of reference' are set by heterosexual men in most organisations. This is so much so that lesbians may be expected to express 'the "fun of flirting" with their male colleagues, as well as the importance of using "charm" in business transactions' (Finkelstein, 1981, 194).

Dress and appearance

Dress and (sexual) appearance are explicit and unspoken ways in which sexuality is visible, even though often by engendering an association with something other than itself. Dress and appearance are thus both obvious and subtle, such that the categories of 'women' and 'men' are to a large extent made visible and substained through them. This is partly a matter of managerial control as already noted (pp. 82–3); however, official rules on dress are not one-way—there is a dialectic of control (Giddens, 1979). Firstly, although controlling, managerial rules also *acknowledge* the importance and power of dress and sexuality; they are in effect officially sanctioned sexualities. Secondly, dress, rules about dress, and deviations, minor, major and blatant, are ways of showing sexuality. No wonder a family with 'a long history of honourable membership of the police force . . . felt . . . indignation . . . when [they] became aware of a policeman in his early 20s in uniform . . . wearing a gold earring' (J. Miles, 1985). School pupils remain experts in this field of subtle redefinition. Thirdly, it would be wrong to see conditions of dress as simply imposed upon different workers. As a female radiographer reported, they can be issues of complex negotiation:

a new superintendent [radiographer] . . . decided that a confirmation of uniform was needed, with which all staff agreed. A consensus was held as to what colour option for shoes and cardigans. When it was realised that red was in the lead those who had chosen black, which was the least popular joined forces with those who had chosen blue so that blue was the decided colour. Another issue that radiographers had a decided say—in the end—was the acquisition of cardigans. The superintendent had chosen jackets without prior consultation with staff. When this was realised a deputation of all the radiographers was able to alter that decision.

Because of the established social relationship of cultural definition of dress and gender division, these intricate relationships of dress and sexuality within organisations are characteristically invested with a power dimension. Although there may appear greater variability, more options and more decisions for women than men in their dress, for women entering power positions there may be few role models available for dress and appearance (Solomons and Cramer, 1985). In reaction to this there are now well established 'image consultants' (Streich, 1985) and 'clothing consultants' (Brampton, 1984) to aid the development of 'executive dressing' and 'power dressing', particularly for women, once again as if they are some kind of anomaly, paradoxically affirming them as such.

The written and the recorded
Evidence of the official stance of organisation and management towards sexuality is readily available through recruitment, policies on promotion, transfer and relocation, and official rules on sexual conduct. Advertisements vary from 'Attractive female escorts wanted for international clients . . . No experience necessary' to 'Management couple. . .responsible couple. . .sought to provide a housekeeping and catering service to the Lord Mayor and Lady Mayoress at their official residence in Cardiff'.[5]

The policies of many organisations are based on traditional marriage patterns (Loring and Wells, 1972, 117). The official policy of a large Japanese bank studied in 1968–9 was that 'Women must resign from the bank at the time they marry. This rule is as old as the bank and has no exceptions' (Rohlen, 1974, 78). Even though organisational policies on promotion and transfer are changing, due *inter alia* to changing marriage patterns, 'bachelor postings' and 'postings with wives' persist. Indeed there is a sense in which the more 'broad-minded' and sympathetic organisations are to the person's total situation, including their domestic arrangements, the more the private and sexual aspects of people's lives become a *legitimate concern* of organisations in the public domain.[6]

Official rules on sexual conduct cover visiting arrangements in prisons and other total institutions; professional prohibitions on relations with patients and other clients for doctors and other medical and welfare workers; public policies against sexual harassment adopted by trade unions and managements. Often these remain as written statements in codes of conduct, grievance procedures and company policy. For example the BBC rule book states:

> In principle, no member of staff should be directly or indirectly in authority over a relative or *someone with whom they have close personal ties* . . . . Subject to this rule, which is strictly observed in the case of close relationships, e.g. . . . . husband or wife, . . . common-law spouse, there will be normally no objection to relatives working in the same department.
> (Our emphasis) (Cited in Harrison and Lee, 1986)

In addition there are occasionally more particular and precise memos such as that below, which was produced by a British local authority.

> Lewd and Offensive Calendars, Posters, etc.
> The Council now has a clear policy that lewd and offensive calendars, posters, etc. should not be displayed in Council premises.
> Whilst discussions take place with Unions about the wider aspects of Sexual Harassment please ensure that as a first step all calendars, posters, etc. depicting the male or female form in various stages of undress or nudity are removed.

—or the British army internal memorandum 'Female homosexuality in the army', in which lesbianism is specific grounds for dismissal (see p. 76).

Explicit discriminations and actions against gay people have been reported and recorded in many other organisations. Sometimes discrimination and dismissal have led to Industrial Tribunal proceedings, although there have been many more informal harassments of gay men and lesbians. Frequently these concern teachers, youth workers, social workers and others with welfare responsibility for other, perhaps younger, people (Ferris, 1977). But others have involved a trainee manager, insurance clerk, handyman at a youth camp, a chef in a police canteen, a chief executive of a local authority and so on (Campaign for Homosexual Equality, 1981; Cohen *et al.*, 1978; Beer, Jeffery and Munyard, 1983; Taylor, 1986). A particularly interesting Industrial Tribunal in Leeds in 1975 considered the case of a gay bus driver who had appealed against dismissal and lost. The Tribunal ruled that: 'There would be an understandable concern in the minds of the public who are aware of this conviction, if they had to put their children on the bus, including girls' (Cohen *et al.*, 1978, 54−5). The assumption here is that gay people want to assault others, including members of the opposite sex.

Industrial Tribunals remain an important source of written information on sexuality in organisations. Although their evidence is certainly a more partial view of reality than their legalistic tone might suggest, they do show the official face of organisations at its most public.

THE SECRECY OF SEXUALITY: SECRET SEXUALITY

The sexual construction of organisations is necessarily most obviously seen in visible sexuality and its impact. Organisations are also sexually constructed in equally important though less obvious and visible ways. Through the actions of specific organisational members and organisational processes, sexuality is often kept secret, rather than being unseen as such. The secrecy that surrounds sexuality is reinforced by the fact that organisations are often, and perhaps characteristically, sites of secrecy. Closed or bureaucratic organisations represent particular 'concentrations' of secrecy, with accompanying problems for research and researchers (Sjoberg and Miller, 1973; *Urban Life*, 1980). For example, 'leaks' and even 'official leaks' from government departments ostensibly allow the public to participate in certain organisational 'secrets'; however such leaks are often cynically used to pre-empt an unfavourable reaction to policy or divert attention from other secret aspects of the organisation. The fury at genuine 'leaks' such as those by Clive Ponting and Sarah Tisdall in the British Civil Service demonstrates the extent of protection of policies that exist routinely in organisations.

The state of secrecy in organisations is also subject to many other social, political and technological factors. The development of information technology and computerised systems of record keeping clearly increases the potential for organisational secrecy, particularly about personal information, including that concerning sexuality. On the other hand, computerisation has indirectly increased awareness of the political nature of information handling, and thus legal constraints in this area have been introduced. Even so, severe doubts must exist on the ability of both state and private organisations to hold sensitive information on individuals accurately and confidentially. Such problems of secrecy are compounded by the qualitative nature of sexuality and it being seen as inappropriate in the public world of organisations. To assess the often powerful impact of secrecy, especially that around sexuality, within organisations necessitates ingenious research strategies, as in conflict methodologies (Lehmann and Young, 1974; Lundman and McFarlane, 1976).

Furthermore, the concept of 'secrecy' is itself a curious one. The so-called 'irony of secrecy' refers to the notion that possessors of secrets can only make them known by their abolition through partial or total disclosure (Adler, 1980). A secret exposed is no longer a secret and even by referring to a 'secret area' one is already acknowledging and partly eroding the 'secret'. Secrecy and secret sexuality in organisations may also form part of the underlife or may refer to aspects of organisational rules that seek to deny the existence of sexuality as a facet of organisational life. This process takes several different forms, and includes the secrecy of unwritten managerial rules and policies, as well as clandestine relationships and hidden hierarchies amongst the organisational members.

Secret records, rules and policies

Most organisations have some system of formal rules, policies and records, that are recorded, yet inaccessible, and usually controlled by men. Where they are concerned with sexuality, their inaccessibility may parallel, reinforce and even collude with the inaccessibility and secrecy that often surrounds sexuality itself. This is seen most obviously in the use of files and records on individuals and families within personnel departments, medical and social work, education, the police and many other agencies. Both their existence and their contents, including intimate details of sexualities, real or imagined, may be secret.[7] Such information may be used as a means of power by the controller of records, such as by professionals against members of the public. For example, a male G.P., on noticing that a female 'patient' had attended National Health Service psycho-sexual counselling, arranged by another G.P., remarked to her whilst 'treating' her for a stomach complaint 'Good grief, how can I look at something like that in five minutes. Look at the number of cards you've got. You've even been to a psycho-sexual clinic.'

The scale of 'official' record keeping is difficult to appreciate. The National Police Computer at Hendon has a capacity of 40 million entries (one for every adult member of the British population) and is claimed to be 'the largest data retrieval system of its kind in Europe' (Aubrey, 1981, 78).

In December 1985 internal police documents were leaked to *The Observer* newspaper indicating that an elaborate system of local street information existed in some police forces (Davies and Foster, 1985). In the Lothian and Borders force, for example, beat officers are told 'to secure the services of at least one informant in every street . . . someone who knows the inhabitants and is inquisitive enough to find out what is going on'. As a result of such information gathering, personal reports are compiled of which the following two are examples: 'Miss G. (full name, address and date of birth) is now residing with her parents at (full address). She is about three months pregnant.' The woman had no criminal record and is not alleged to be involved in any offence. 'After the arrest of a man for "exposing his posterior" outside a house in Edinburgh, a report states that the man ". . . stated that the house concerned is being used by homosexuals. Both occupants are obviously so inclined." The full address of the house is recorded.' One collator of such information described his work as follows: 'It used to be a question of recording criminal activity in your area, but the new breed of collator takes down everything.'

The analysis of secret or partially secret organisational rules and policies is even more complex than the unearthing of records and files. Rules and policies may be overt, kept secret by formal managerial decision, informally secret, or even 'secret' by default only being known in reaction to a crisis or unexpected series of events. More commonly rules and policies that are unwritten, and at least to some extent hidden, represent features of a managerial consensus rather than a deliberate deception.

In most residential institutions, such as prisons, halls of residence, army quarters and so on, there is rigorous segregation by sex that expresses unwritten rules on sexuality. For example the arrangement of dormitories in an education centre was explained as follows:

Staff member: We put the girls on the top two floors and the boys on the floor below. We do that so that the boys don't have to go past the girls' doors!
Visitor: Not the other way round?
Staff member: (laughing) Oh no, its commonsense. Its natural . . . .

In addition, the extension of anti-discrimination laws and codes may lead to the development of further covert policies on sexuality, that may well remain discriminatory. Either way such rules are not easily scrutinised or compared between organisations. Discovering these policies and rules is usually a matter of 'decoding' other information, of using clues from rules about other aspects of organisational life. For example, firms that insist on interviewing prospective employees' wives may have covert policies of favouring married men in executive positions or of not employing homosexuals.

Some informal managerial practices that are partially covert, are, however, far more complex in that they may be used to discriminate against people, usually women, on grounds of appearance, either through 'attractiveness' or 'lack of attractiveness'. This is graphically illustrated by the following account, provided by a personnel manager, of policies for the employment of nurses:

Some years ago I was involved in recruiting nurses in the United Kingdom for a newly built hospital for oil staff at Kirkuk in Iraq.

Most nurses, in my experience, are pretty, and the four we selected were no exception. Their arrival was regarded as a staff benefit by the romance-starved bachelors of the oil company. Within six months all four nurses were wedded and busy producing families.

John Skliros, managing director of the Iraq Petroleum Company at that time, took us to task for this lack of foresight in sending out such pretty young ladies. We duly interviewed more nurses and flew out four of the plainest we could find. Within six months all four were wedded and producing. Kirkuk is very isolated. After a visit to the oil field, John Skliros sent for Crawford Clarke, the staff manager, and said he had never seen such ugly wives and, since we were evidently acting as a matrimonial agency for our bachelor staff, the least we could do was to send out attractive nurses. Thereafter, recruitment was much more fun.

(Included in Harrison and Lee, 1986)

A modified version of these potentially double discriminations was reported by a publisher's editor who expressed doubts about the wisdom of appointing a 'very pretty' female representative yet had, despite this, persisted with the appointment.

A further category of unwritten rules and policies are secret simply because they are *not known* and only appear *reactively*, often in a *crisis* situation. An example from residential social work was where a worker in a hostel for the mentally ill was sacked for having an affair with a resident. The worker said:

The philosophy of the hostel was that we treated residents as equals and it was encouraged that we should develop personal relationships there. *But there was absolutely no code of guidance from management as to how far these relationships should go.*

(Our emphasis) (Quoted in Sharron, 1983)

In this case a staff petition stated that the resident was in no danger of being exploited and that the social worker in question was a worker of the highest calibre who frequently interrupted her private life to give residents extra support and assistance. An area manager said:

The department's code of conduct did not specify behaviour concerning personal relationships but that whether the people involved are adults or children they are in the care of the department and we expect social workers to behave in a controlled professional manner.

In another case (Boseley, 1983) an officer in charge of a progressive home for physically handicapped adults was sacked for failing to put a stop to a love affair between a 23-year-old medical secretary who could only move on crutches or in a wheelchair, and a care assistant at the hostel where she was staying temporarily. In both these examples there was no formulated policy and the reaction to the 'crisis' of the discovered relationships was to cite professionalism and the dependent nature of the client.[8] In the first example the partner in the affair was sacked but in the second one the officer in charge was held responsible. The policy on sexual relationships could not have been discovered in either case as it was not merely hidden in the sense of not being available but it was not formulated until after the event.

Other similar instances of unwritten policies arose, firstly, in the police force when a male and female traffic officer were demoted for allegedly becoming 'too friendly' when patrolling together;[9] secondly, in the company Skyrail Oceanic Limited which, in 1978, sacked a woman booking clerk the day after she had married an employee from a rival London travel firm;[10] and thirdly, with the sacking of a nurse after topless pictures of her had appeared in a magazine.[11]

A final example arises from interviewing two people who went abroad as partners rather than as a married couple and where the man was working for a clothing company. The firm had no rule to deal with partners. Everything was an 'off-the-cuff' ruling by a senior manager and his decision was that the man should be treated as a bachelor for all practical purposes. This deprived them of the more spacious married accommodation, and enforced rigorous division of bills for travel, medicine and insurances, lower grants for furniture and other commodities. Moreover, in these locations it was more acceptable that married men spent their weekends with women other than their wives, rather than for these two people to be unmarried and not seeking other sexual partners.

Secret sexual relationships

The most conscious perception of hidden sexuality is, in many organisations, that of clandestine relationships, real or imagined. Although by definition hidden, and indeed kept secret, they form an important part of public awareness of the impact of sexuality in organisations, as in the 'downfall' of public figures through affairs or sexual orientation. The fact that such 'secrets' become headline news exemplifies the 'irony of secrecy' on a massive scale. The power of such affairs was seen when Sarah Keays alleged that Cecil Parkinson told her secrets of the Falklands War in the course of their relationship. Commander Michael Trestrail was required to resign as the Queen's bodyguard when a male prostitute, with whom he had had an affair, gave information to the press. In addition, an important part of the impact of clandestine relationships in politics and public arenas is the power of the threat of 'telling', as, for example, in the Rita Jenrette case in the United States. As the estranged wife of a congressman, she threatened to expose many congressmen, state governors and others involved in drugs, drinks and sexual affairs (Blundy, 1981).

The high publicity given to these sorts of relationships is reproduced within more local 'news networks' within individual organisations. They have a similar variety of, and often major, repercussions upon organisational life. Many of these relationships in organisations are 'open secrets'. They may be comparatively easy to discern within gossip and rumour. Participants often continue to act as if the relationship was secret and members continue to collude as if they were unaware of it (Quinn, 1977). A survey of six theatre clubs demonstrated at least one extra-marital affair was going on in each, known and relished by club members, but unknown to the husband and wife of the lovers (Reid, 1981).

Such affairs have a whole variety of organisational impacts including favouritism or punishment. For example, in a hospital the quality of conference lunches strictly correlated with position in the organisational hierarchy with one glaring exception. The explanation given was that the man's superior had ordered the lunch but gossip and rumour was that the man's sexual relationship with the catering officer was the deciding factor. In contrast, a small organisation's newsletter was critical of a woman who, unknown to the editor, was having an affair with one of his superiors. She used her power to have him demoted and disciplined but the reasons given were for a minor contravention of organisational rules.

It is difficult to briefly describe the complexities and convolutions of organisational dynamics that affairs can engender. They can be a sign of both power and, if not powerlessness, then at least vulnerability. Furthermore, the power of the affair can itself become entangled with organisational power. Certain organisational members may indeed be 'tolerant' of others' affairs, only to subsequently use that information against them to ensure organisational conformity. The Labour Party MP, Joe Ashton, in his play 'The Majority of One' about the 1976 British Parliament, has described how the party whips threatened to tell wives or 'girlfriends' if Members of Parliament did not vote as suggested. As he put it, in a radio interview ('The Week in Westminster' BBC Radio 4, 14 June 1986), the whips exhorted members: 'Get in [the voting lobby], you bugger [*sic*]' . . . or else.

The multifarious and sometimes contradictory implications of affairs are also to be seen from the Esther Rantzen-Desmond Wilcox affair described in Leapman's (1986) recent history of the BBC. The liaison between the television personality and her own department head was both semi-secret and semi-public. The privileged access of the one to the other certainly irritated some colleagues on her programme and in his department. However, Rantzen's programme, 'That's Life', was itself perhaps the success story of the BBC at that time in the mid-seventies. Their personal relationship, the success of the programme, and the internal politics of the BBC, developed together in a shifting interrelation, at different times affirming and undermining organisational roles and power, and eventually following their marriage and child, leading indirectly to Wilcox's departure to freelance journalism.

The impact of clandestine relationships in an individual local organisation and at national or even international level may often cause the '*post hoc*' rewriting of organisational histories by those with the power to do so.

THE UNSEENNESS OF SEXUALITY: UNSEEN SEXUALITY

Sexuality is not only kept deliberately secret in organisations, but remains hidden, partially or totally, in another linked, but conceptually distinct way. Sexuality in several important respects remains unseen by virtue of sexual taboos that persist about it within organisations, as with the general taboo on the expression of personal feelings within organisational life. Although conversations in organisations may be personalised, the expression of personal feelings, and moreover sexual feelings, is more problematic. Accordingly, sexuality has an invisible quality, and furthermore, certain aspects of sexuality are invisible. Invisible sexualities include a variety of bodily and mental processes, of which sexual states, perceptions, desires and fantasies are particularly important. Although some of these processes are primarily diagnosed as bodily or mental, the relationship between body and mind is inextricable, as exemplified in sexual arousal.

Sexual states

While some taboos may be in the process of being eroded, it is still uncommon for such everday female states such as pre-menstrual tension, dysmenorrhœa, menopause or early pregnancy to be acknowledged, let alone discussed in most organisations. Similarly, at the institutional level, health service provision for specific health problems of women, such as breast cancer screening and testing for cervical cancer has been vastly under-resourced and under threat. The women's health movement has responded by bringing these issues to the fore, creating self-help groups and building alternative organisations such as well-woman clinics. These, in turn, have met their own, usually male, resistances. Well-woman clinics reflect the difficulty that women face in having their specific states taken seriously. The overlap between women's health and sexuality would appear to be a source of anxiety to men as exemplified by the reaction to a Scottish Health Education group's booklet on women's health care. This was censored by Government officials and medical officers as 'too strident to be a Government document and over-concerned with sexuality' (Veitch, 1983).

The pre-menstrual syndrome is rarely taken seriously within organisational life, and is merely seen as having 'nuisance value'. This is reflected in the literature on management theory. An unusual example is Cardwell's (1985, 198—9) discussion of such states in his commentary on 'managing women'.

When growing up my mother used to refer in hushed voice to specific illnesses which beset my female aunts as 'women's problems'. These illnesses affected the female reproductive organs. The hushed reverence and confidentiality with which my mother described such maladies led me to a state of blissful ignorance as to how this subject should be treated by men and women who are not related. Unfortunately in the office subjects like this involve those with a right to know and those with a duty to tell because they affect work. My first major experience of this indicates the problem and how ill-equipped I was to handle it. My immediate second-in-command was a woman who had some simple gynaecological problems . . . . The woman eventually had to enter hospital for a minor exploratory operation. Realizing my inexperience in such matters, she sought to confide in my immediate superior. However, she still had to seek my approval for sick leave.

We faced each other as if we had never met before. . . . My blushing was matched only by hers . . . . She left after five minutes. In that time I had managed to look at my desk to avoid looking at her and had listened to nothing she had said. . . . I had failed her as a manager and as a friend. It transpired that everything went well from her point of view [regarding the operation]. Again this information came by hints, nods and winks.[12]

The embarrassment generated by women's bodily states can lead to real difficulty in obtaining sick leave for fear of being stigmatised. The inability of men to deal with these states leads to an over-emphasis on them as a problem for women in organisations. Alternatively it leads to women feeling it unwise to discuss the real source of their distress and pain, with strong group collusion often necessary to protect the person from management's attention. For example a professional woman in a demanding job was suffering severe problems during menopause exacerbated by her widowhood and childlessness. Her behaviour was having an impact on the organisation but strenuously hidden by other female colleagues who sought to protect her in the work place. While these bodily states may seem to be hidden and not explicitly sexual, their social connotations clearly are, for women and men in different ways. A particularly explicit and offensive example is provided by Laws (1985, 19−20) from an interview with a man, telling of his boss in a hospital laboratory:

there was a female toilet [sic] just outside the lab so we could always see the women going to the toilet and he actually used to time them and if they were taking a long time he used to say 'Oh well they've got the rags up, there's no point in chatting her up.'

Sexual perceptions and desires

Alongside the organisational process of sexual states are a wide range of sexual perceptions of organisational members. Firstly, we have already noted how sexual assessments may be made by those in formal authority positions in organisations, usually men, as in, for example, interviewing for prospective posts. Where these are not translated into action and behaviour they remain invisible, unless elicited in informal conversation or research inquiry. Secondly, sexual assessments may be made by those in organisations, yet largely outside formal organisational roles, as part of the organisational culture—this may be in terms of who is 'fancied', even though again this is not translated into action. This may blur into a more diffuse process of sexual 'secret ranking' (Zetterberg, 1966), by which people are given status according to sexual and other forms of attraction or attractiveness. Such 'rankings' may be maintained as secret by processes of group collusion between members of organisational cultures. Because of the practical *interrelation* of such 'hierarchies' with organisational hierarchies, this form of perception and emotion is further discussed in the next chapter.

Thirdly, there are more focused sexual desires, with the actual or possible development of sexual liaison, love or sexual arousal.

Another aspect of the invisible are the sexual desires and feelings experienced by men and women whether reciprocated or not. If the object of the desires and feelings is in the same work setting then the impact can range from increased organisational performance (Gutek and Nakamura, 1982, 184–5), to working over to attract the attention of the other, through to sexual harassment. The desires may be attainable but against organisational written policy, as with homosexuality in the army. They may run counter to unwritten policies and rules, for example, in the case of people with learning difficulties.

This appears to be one of the most neglected aspects of sexuality and indeed invisible sexuality. Feelings and desires do not exist in isolation, they blur into fantasies and into less emotionally involved perceptions and assessments as in hidden hierarchies.

The theme is further pursued in the next chapter in focusing on feelings and emotions as part of both sexuality and organisations. Finally it is necessary to stress the ordinariness and ubiquity of feelings and desires, as well as states, making the neglect all the more remarkable. Organisational life is constructed in a very everyday way by the impact of sexual feelings as in the following example. 'When I was first at work, I was a bit coy. And this chappie, he was a bit shy as well. He was in the next department. And I knew he cared for me, but he never said anything. I just knew.'

Sexual fantasies

Whereas sexual states are designated primarily as bodily and perceptions designated primarily as mental constructions of extra-personal reality, fantasies are both perceptual and intrapsychic realities. Sexual fantasies can be directed at particular individuals, personalised or impersonal imaginings.

Fantasies take place in the imagination and are distinguished from sexual desires and feelings by their unattainability. Yet these can become an exercise of power because, though not based in reality, the person may act as if they are. The archetypal example of this is in fantasies about boss–secretary relationships. For example, the following fantasy was reported by a male local government worker:

I don't know what it is but this woman, a secretary, still [after ten years] sometimes comes back in fantasy. It's not that I liked her or that she was particularly attractive. She wasn't. I think it was partly to do with her being a secretary and married to one of the architects [in the same organisation]. She also got drunk at a party that I didn't go to and is supposed to have started loving everybody. I suppose that's why she still figures in my fantasies. She also had big breasts. I can't even remember her name or anything else about her.

This is an area for mythology of outlandish proportions. In the blatantly sexist *A Programmed Guide to Office Warfare*, the following case for choosing the 'best-looking' secretary as against the most competent is presented:

First it will make your life more pleasant. Secondly, she will excite the envy of your colleagues. Thirdly, she can be deployed . . . to disarm the opposition. . . . suppose you have a favour to ask of another department, you send your beautiful secretary, for who could resist such charm? If you have bad news to impart, again you send the ravishing beauty to calm the savage beast.
(Burton, 1971, 67)

The possibility of a sexual relationship as part of the boss–secretary relationship is well established in this culture and society. This fantasy persists and can have powerful impacts within organisations, however unlikely this may be in reality. The continued feeding of such fantasies can be recognised in terms of recruitment and job descriptions. An extreme example is the following advert:

LEGAL SEX
£7,500
Correction!
LEGAL SECS

A slightly more subtle example is to be found in a British Telecom advertisement on British television. The advertisement depicts a boss and secretary with the secretary dark-haired, 30ish, slightly plump and bespectacled. She deals with her boss's administrative difficulty through the use of the telephone. She is next depicted imagining herself romping through waves on a palm-fringed beach in the company of her boss. Reality intervenes again when the boss thanks her for her help and departs, leaving her with her fantasies.

In addition there are fantasies about the fantasies of the opposite sex, as exemplified in an article in *The Surveyor*: 'Susceptible males can be encouraged by the provocative behaviour of female colleagues; less well-endowed female staff can imagine sexual harassment—wishful thinking perhaps! —when it doesn't occur.' Furthermore, these misperceptions may be internalised by their recipients. Following new policies to reduce sexual harassment in a local authority, the 'ladies from one department' as they signed themselves, sent the following 'poem' to their trade union news-sheet.

> With great amusement in your paper,
> We read about the casanova caper.
> In offices and corridors over all,
> In our treasured City Hall!
>
> Please, let us know why we missed out?
> We work too hard, without any doubt!
> Tell us, where we have to go to share the fun?
> We, the much deprived will quickly run,
> To all the lovely bosses there!
> Get cuddles, kisses and promotion? now be fair,
> How lucky can you really get? I Care!

A pity it does not happen at all,
To us hard workers at City Hall.
The under-privileged!

Fantasy can be innocuous or a powerful determinant of behaviour, the more so for being internalised and thus not obvious. Unseen sexuality, and above all sexual fantasy, stands in clear contrast to the visible 'front' of the organisation. Sexual fantasy is the most inaccessible aspect of invisible sexuality, in both research terms and in practical organisational situations. Locked into the person's mind, it resides in the receptacle of the private. All manner of denials and obscuring of sexuality in the public world of organisations (of which more are discussed below) facilitate its development in the private mind, which itself reinhabits and impacts upon the public and the organisational.[13]

THE ELUSIVENESS OF SEXUALITY: ELUSIVE SEXUALITY

All that has been said so far in this chapter, on the visible, the secret and the unseen 'fronts' of sexuality is itself subject to a further 'front', namely the elusive. The elusiveness of sexuality both encompasses and reinforces the impact of sexuality on organisational life, whether it is visible, secret or unseen. Elusiveness refers here to the fact that sexuality is open to multiple, different interpretations; to the difficulty of producing accounts of sexuality; and to the way in which sexuality often only appears by reference and allusion. Elusiveness also refers to the shortcomings of the written word, the attempt to capture the impossible on paper. Research difficulties and the shortcomings of traditional research methods, such as the ordered collection of empirical evidence, follow from the persistence of elusiveness. On the one hand, we have discovered the 'ever-presentness' of sexuality in organisations and the ways it can permeate, influence and be powerful; on the other, sexuality almost always remains 'one step removed' from being pinned down, measured and researched unambiguously. Instead elusiveness led us to have to contend constantly with ambiguities, subtleties, collusion, rumour, gossip, joking, innuendo and allusion, as well as using them as research resources.

Innuendo and allusion are commonplace within organisations, with 'whispers, winks and asides' used to draw attention to sensitive issues and areas. Instances of allusion may be particularly useful when researching sexuality, as clues to look further, either to a particular event or broader issues such as the impact of sexuality. For example the contradiction of sexuality and work may itself be only alluded to in an organisational setting because of its incongruity. Innuendo is often reserved for occasions when it can exert most effect, and yet can be disclaimed as meaning nothing or having another meaning. It can be retracted but an event has been alluded to and this remains. Additionally innuendo is a clue to the exercise of power and authority in organisations. It tends to point the finger where power is being or could be exercised but only hints at the source of the power. At the same time it can itself be an exercise of power between people with a reference to 'something', such as sexuality, which 'shouldn't' be there, pointing to an area of conflict but giving an ambiguous statement about it. In such ways information is passed on and/or authority is reinforced but the ambiguity of the statement ensures that the perpetrator can disclaim and the recipient ignore it. The contradiction is perpetuated and resolved at the same time.

One example is person X, well-known for having sexual affairs, sometimes arising in the workplace and causing some disruption of organisational life. Rumour speculated about the latest person involved, gossip confirmed it but innuendo was used to say that 'Person X gets themselves into some "pickles" but this latest one "takes the biscuit".' Allusion and innuendo, linked with gossip and rumour pointed to a clandestine affair but was sufficiently ambiguous to be interpreted as meaning that person X is disorganised in some other facet of organisational life.

A further example was observed in a coffee break taken by five male academic staff in the middle of a three-hour university meeting. The break was taken in the small office of a secretary in the department of one of the men, as there was a coffee machine there.

Lecturer A: Have you got an ashtray here?

Lecturer B: (on home territory). Oh yes, there's one here.
                Susie smokes non-stop.
Lecturer A: But it's empty.
Lecturer B: She's off today. Geraldine doesn't smoke. She
                hasn't any vices, have you Geraldine?
                (laughter all round)

The point here is that this took place in Geraldine's office during an 'invasion' by five men. It is hard to imagine Geraldine speaking in this way to Lecturer B; if she had she might be called 'brazen'. This emphasises how we see that sexual innuendo in fact has a *differential impact* on organisational life and members depending whether the recipients are female or male. Such variable impact was noted when candidates for a head of department position underwent an interview from their prospective subordinates, in addition to a formal panel interview from higher management. One question sought the candidates' (all men) opinion as to whether gender issues were an important consideration within the organisation. Several candidates paid lip service to its importance but their jokes, accompanied by 'nods and winks' revealed stereotyped and discriminatory views about women. The jokes contradicted the 'straight' replies, and trivialised the issue. Yet it could be argued that jokes are jokes and not to be taken seriously. However, at this interview, some of the men present were amused but the women were furious!

Such innuendoes, with their double or more meanings, exemplify the elusiveness of sexuality. It can be seen not only as a clue to the existence of the power of sexuality, but also as an organisational process used to deny its existence. Innuendo, allusion and joking are ambiguous processes which illustrate the elusiveness and power of sexuality in organisational life, but power may occur many times over as one can get rumour and innuendo upon innuendo upon innuendo . . .. Innuendo has new triple meanings, however it is used, but involves further problems of interpretation when it concerns sexuality.

The multiple meanings of innuendo and allusion in individual transactions apply also to the more collective use of innuendo, as in gossip and rumour about supposed or actual sexual events. The question of the ambiguity of the supposedness or actuality (of sexuality) is indeed a defining part of rumour and gossip.

The truth-value of such events is not at issue. As in psychoanalysis and symbolic interactionism, if an event appears real, it is real in its consequences. Gossip, rumour, as well as the telling of scandals, may often tell more about the *teller* of the gossip, or their organisational context than the object of the gossip. For example, a rumoured case of a sexual encounter between a male professional worker and a female client in a large public organisation was rumoured by another male professional to have been subject of a complaint to the trade union. This piece of gossip could be interpreted either as a probable sexual incident or an indication of some other tension or disharmony within the organisation that happened to be expressed in sexual terms.

Rumour and gossip, like innuendo, provide numerous opportunities for action without responsibility; and in organisational terms, opportunities for dealing, or rather partly dealing, with areas of difficulty, insecurity, change and even crisis (cf. Shibutani, 1966). The tension that they refer to may be primarily sexual, or a projection of another tension on to the sexual, or perhaps more likely and ambiguously further, both.

The elusiveness of the sexual is also to be seen in conversational joking and practical joking within many organisational cultures. Sexual references are available for maintaining social contact between workers, for affirming status, and authority differentials, for ridiculing and coping with management, enlivening dull work, expressing interests in and anxieties about sex, and much more. They bring elusive sexuality from the private into the public, and thus comprise a powerful material of organisational life. Like the story of the 'new lad with . . . Diplomas Galore' who came to the shop floor of an engineering factory and '. . . had a french letter on his back by ten o'clock' (Collinson, 1981, 219), the significance of the sexual lies in its amenability to telling, retelling and further elaboration. The elaboration itself has several facets: over time; in terms of truth, falsehood and myth; and in terms of how the sexual links with authority, education, initiation, youth, maleness, masculinity, work, contraception, ridicule, underlife and so on. Patently, even these elaborations may be perceived differently and given different meanings by different participants—a further facet of elusiveness.

Finally, in this chapter it is necessary to highlight an important practical and conceptual difficulty. The elusiveness of sexuality, as it impacts upon organisational life, arises largely from the elusiveness and ambiguity that besets sexuality in this society. Sexuality is that which is most displayed, flaunted, exploited; and yet that which is most unknown, mystified and kept from public discourse. It is that which is most one's own, the body and its desires and yet which is most taken away (MacKinnon, 1982). Elusiveness in a hundred and one forms expresses those contradictions. However, elusiveness also arises from a second source, namely the continued contradiction and interaction of sexuality and organisations, their simultaneous and ambiguous presence and occurrence.

Part Three
Organisation Sexuality

7 Organisation Sexuality: A Paradox

Organisations construct sexuality, and yet contradictorily sexuality constructs organisations. The organisational construction of sexuality and the power of sexuality to reconstruct organisations exist in dialectical relationships. This analysis has, however, been to some extent based on an artificial division, for the reality is that in specific instances sexuality and organisational life are *one*. Organisational life is not sexual in one department or on one shift, and not-sexual in the next; likewise, sexuality does not occur separately from the organisational workers and members, and social processes between them.

To say this is to seek to describe a material reality of organisations in its complexity, not just the 'bits' reserved for industrial sociology or organisation theory. To say this also raises an immediate problem of expression in language. This is particularly so in that the very categories 'sexuality' and 'organisation' or 'organisational life' refuse to refer to the other. Terms such as 'organisational sexuality' or 'sexuality in organisations' or even 'organised sexuality' suggest themselves, but all give too much independence to the category 'sexuality' which is then qualified to become 'organisational' or 'organised'.

It would be more accurate to speak of this reality happening as one and accordingly labelled singly as 'sexanisation' or 'orgexuality'. Alternatively we recognise the term 'organisational-sexual reality' to be somewhat cumbersome and somewhat misleading. To dissolve the hyphen[1] necessitates coining a new phrase to articulate a new concept, 'organisation sexuality',[2] itself a paradox of material reality, whereby organisational life and sexuality occur simultaneously. Not only do organisations construct sexuality, as does sexuality construct organisations, but more importantly, the very occurrence of 'organisation' invokes 'sexuality', and the very occurrence of 'sexuality' in the public domain at least, frequently invokes 'organisations', so they are no longer separable. Additionally, it has to be recognised that the public domain incorporates activities not in organisations, but 'in the street', including open spaces, meeting places, public transport, and streets themselves. This therefore suggests that an equally important phenomenon within the public domain as organisation sexuality is 'street sexuality', occurring in crowds, queues, street corners, parks, alleyways and so on.[3]

Generic powers, predominantly patriarchal, include the power of men over women, the public realm over the private, production over reproduction, and heterosexuality over other sexualities (see p. 60), all of which subject and control sexuality in different ways. These powers are maintained, reinforced and indeed contested through the processes of organisation sexuality, though its significance and effect is clearly variable for different powers. This is to be seen in the way harassment in organisations by heterosexual men reinforces the power of men over women's bodies, paid jobs, reproductive labour and sexualities. Secondly, and less obviously, the obscuring and lack of recognition of organisation sexuality subtly reinforces the range of generic powers. For example the sexual construction of boss—secretary relationships are usually seen as irrelevant to the 'functioning' and 'performance' of organisations. Thirdly, 'organisational-sexual reality' or organisation sexuality has many interrelated elements: physical movement and proximity of people; feelings and desires; ideology and consciousness; and language and imagery. It is through these media that generic powers are maintained and contested. Thus generic powers are perpetuated and challenged through these physical, emotional, conscious and symbolic media. Organisation sexuality made up of these elements is itself a dominant medium of generic powers.

Thus, for example, the power of men and men's sexuality, and especially heterosexuality, is maintained and resisted through the use of physical space between each other by men and women; the valuing of men's feelings and desires over women's; the male domination of ideology and consciousness; and the development of patriarchal language and imagery in organisations. Furthermore all these media operate simultaneously and in relation to each other. Although it is analytically convenient to separate out the various elements for discussion, they too occur as one in specific instances.

ORGANISATION SEXUALITY AS MOVEMENT AND PROXIMITY

The organisational control of spatial movement, the impacts of touch and indeed of avoidance of contact upon organisations have already been described. However, as noted, this separation is false, for both organisations and sexuality are combinations and discriminations of movement and proximity. Thus changes in movements and proximity potentially *produce* both organisation and sexuality. For instance, in Bolton School there is an 'apocryphal school rule' that in lower forms *all girls* should keep three feet apart from all boys (Neville, 1985, 25). In Sweden, some women's organisations have campaigned for the creation of 'no sexual behaviour' areas in organisations, rather like 'no smoking' areas. A mundane, yet more complicated example, is the gender segregation of and control of time spent in toilets in most organisations. These 'rules' both imply and produce organisation and sexuality, with their respective controls upon each other.[4]

This important general point may become clearer if we consider in addition to proximity between people, the maintenance of perhaps more distant physical relations by, for example, eye contact, either one-way, mutual or multi-directional. Organisations are frequently zones of relatively high-density gaze. For example, heterosexual men may use them as sites for scanning and searching, for evaluation of women in terms of sexual attractiveness. They may be arenas for looking, giving the 'look', leering behind backs, and so on. On the street, women may learn to avert the eyes for protection, and men may do likewise, to avoid appearing aggressive or seductive (Henley, 1977, ch. 9). In contrast, in many, if not most, organisations avoidance of gaze as on the street is more difficult and even socially unacceptable. The meaning of gaze and its avoidance in organisations is further complicated by their size and structure. Expectations for varieties of gaze and its avoidance, with their differing sexual connotations, are an integral part of organisational life, with their different degrees of physical, social, and particularly hierarchical, proximity. For example, such variations are likely to occur in different organisational contexts, from face-to-face role-sets to occasional, even random, proximity with (relative) strangers, each varying by gender segregation (see Gutek and Morasch, 1982, 60–2).

Organisational membership typically involves a degree of sociability and politeness. For certain sorts of workers, especially women, such as secretaries and personal assistants, politeness as implicit sexuality is part of the job, part of labour-powers sold. Higher status members can be grumpy; secretaries are expected to be pleasant. Worse still, organisations can be places of relative captivity: women workers are often not expected to roam throughout the workplace; they may be literally targets, virtual captives, for men's sexual harassment through control of movement (Seddon, 1983).

The significance of gaze, touch, proximity within organisations is that they can be arranged and managed to both ignore and take account of sexual connotations at the same time.[5] Perhaps the most obvious example of this is to be seen in medical organisations where certain members, usually doctors and nurses, have permission to touch and gaze 'clinically' (Foucault, 1973) at others, usually patients. Professional and organisational regulations proscribe the extension of gaze and touch to explicitly sexual behaviour, yet in doing so such rules *confirm* their sexual connotations. This applies all the more so in medical, gynaecological work, where formal proscriptions are considerably elaborated through all manner of micro interpersonal cues (Emerson, 1970; Henslin and Biggs, 1978). However, in addition the organisation sexuality of medical relations operates through staff relations and their movements and proximities. A stunning description of this is provided by the Australian sociologists, Game and Pringle (1983, 108–9):

Doctors exercise not only the power of the father but direct sexual power over nurses. Medical dominance is reaffirmed by sexual domination.
   Playing the doctor–nurse game — you have to play the hierarchy all the

time and the sexual component is pretty central; doctors expect you to flirt with them and find them attractive. (M)
That the work involved touching people's bodies exacerbates this. Thus the sexualisation of power relations is most pronounced in operating theatres.
There's this kind of flirtation thing going on all the time . . .'and what have you got for us now sister'. (F)
For a start you're all running around in things like pyjamas. There are expanses of exposed thighs. Doctors hitch their jockettes up over their hipbone . . . the surgeon will say 'nurse, I've got an itchy thigh'—and of course they're gowned and gloved and you have to go and scratch them—or wipe their brow when there's no sweat. . .. It's so grossly humiliating but you can't refuse to do it. (G)
A surgeon has the power to enforce sexual contact on nurses, particular junior ones, as part of their nursing duties. Obedience to doctors can include sexual obedience.

In organisational settings that do not involve the exposure of bodies or parts of bodies, similar relations occur in more subtle ways. Organisational spaces are peopled, generically and sexually structured. 'The boss may freely walk into lesser [*sic*] employees' offices and desk areas, but the subordinates don't have the same privilege of entering the boss's office' (Henley, 1977, 31): this is an invasion of territory, with sexual connotations. 'Every woman as she walks through her environment sees, whether aware of it or not, the images of a boss dictating while the secretary writes, head bent. . .' (Henley, 1977, 59): this is a dominance of body posture, also with sexual connotations.

Organisational-sexual reality involves a relatively high density of gaze and potential sexual contact, frequently watched over by the overarching, one-way sexual gaze of the manager, supervisor, overlooker or other male voyeur.[6] Such patterns are patriarchally legitimate.

ORGANISATION SEXUALITY AS FEELINGS AND EMOTIONS

Both organisations and sexuality are patterns of feelings and emotions; both rest on emotional presence and involvement to survive. Though the instrumentality of organisations may be contrasted with the expressiveness of sexuality (see chapter 1), the reality is that organisations are places of emotion, ranging from anger to joy to sorrow, from love to hate, with characteristic emotional climates and cultures. Though sexual feelings may appear as residing other than in the social (MacKinnon, 1982, 2), and thus the organisation, this is mere appearance. Organisation sexuality is in part feelings and emotions that are both organisational and sexual.

This simultaneous patterning of affect is perhaps illustrated most clearly in the possibility of sexual attraction, liaison and fantasy between members of organisations. The organisational context creates differences between participants in terms of hierarchy, role, status, job description, mobility, that form part of and comprise the person. Heterosexual liaisons are particularly complicated by the unlikelihood of the parties being peers or colleagues, 'partly because organizations often define women and men differently in the first place, even when they do similar jobs' (Hearn, 1985a, 115). Ros Miles puts this more starkly as follows: 'women rarely fall for their equal at work, we're [women] conditioned to look for men who are older, richer and more successful than we are' (1985, 112). Because of these complexities of power, she suggests that women should be positive about what or who they want, be selective and be in control, avoid bosses (Nelson, 1980, 131) and married men, as lovers, at work. Organisation sexuality comprises in part a complex pattern of sexual-emotional dependence and independence (Huston and Cate, 1979), so that people 'fancy' and fall in love with others with whom they are organisationally 'thrown together' or from whom differentiated, or who are organisationally beyond their reach (Goodison, 1983).

This raises the question of the sexual aspects of the broader pattern of emotional relationships that exist within organisations. These include elements of randomness of people being 'thrown together' as well as 'secret rankings', 'hidden hierarchies', and other more established patterns of feelings. In contrast to closely knit family relationships, people enter most organisations on a limited contractual basis, as apparently free agents, with the implication that their sexuality remains free-floating and anonymous. This personal anonymity may give to the emotional life of organisations and its unknownness a sexual potential, and even thrill. On the other hand the pattern of feelings in organisations may be well structured informally. In many organisations there is, as Zetterberg (1966) suggests, a well-defined 'erotic ranking' in which status and power derive partly from physical attraction between individuals although this is rarely explicitly acknowledged. This ranking may, but probably will not, coincide with the formal hierarchy of the organisation with important repercussions either way.

Another dimension of organisation sexuality is that feelings and emotions themselves are often subject to a process of sexualisation. This might be more obvious with some emotions than others especially where vulnerability can be inferred, for example anxiety and distress. Furthermore, the interpretation and impact of emotions varies according to gender and organisational context and position.

ORGANISATION SEXUALITY AS IDEOLOGY AND CONSCIOUSNESS

Organisations and sexuality are forms of ideology and consciousness in terms of domination of the construction of reality. In considering organisation sexuality in this way we are not concerned with organisational ideology in a general way but the place of sexuality within ideology. This is in many, if not most cases, overwhelmingly patriarchal, and specifically heterosexual. While heterosexual ideology is not necessarily patriarchal, it is this form that patriarchal ideology usually takes in this society, in managerial assumptions, organisational sub-cultures, harassments. However, heterosexual ideologies can also incorporate within them major contradictions: between women and men; between oppressive and non- (or less-) oppressive heterosexuality; between harassment and reciprocal pleasure. Perhaps the most important, yet still neglected, contradiction of men's heterosexuality in mixed-sex organisations is their clear preference for men and men's company.[7] For example, men's use of *heterosexist* language and joking to maintain solidarity on the shopfloor (Willis, 1977; Cockburn, 1983) may be coupled with horseplay between men and 'homosexual' high jinks, all performed by supposedly heterosexual men, sometimes as a parody of homosexuality (Hearn, 1985a, 124−6). Collinson (1981) has explored this theme in more detail, noting the way in which sexist joking, 'having a laff' and so on appear to sustain a fragile and contradictory reality. It is as if without this constant fetishism of the heterosexual joke, this constant *reminding* of heterosexuality, the reality of men's 'intimacy' with each other would become 'awfully' clear. In such situations, heterosexuality is ideology indeed.

These contradictions may become even sharper in single-sex organisations that are *both* oppressive of homosexuality, as in the police, armed services, some churches, and yet obvious places for gay men to seek other gays. For example, some monastic orders or dioceses have become well known for their gay fraternities despite official disavowal of gayness.

Less patriarchal or apparently non-patriarchal sexual ideologies are less usual but exist in certain organisations. There is, however, no simple correlation between the prevalence of male homosexual ideology and the lessening of men's oppression within organisational ideology (Stanley and Wise, 1979). A stronger case might be made for a bisexual ideology by definition being less patriarchal, though the fact remains that there appear to be very few organisations with a clear bisexual ideology apart from those set up specifically by and for bisexuals, such as SIGMA. A bisexual ideology might suggest that there is no, at least overt, discrimination on the grounds of sexual preference, but this is not the end of the argument. Men may continue to dominate a 'bisexual organisation' and more subtly may use such possibilities to oppress women, especially those left on the boundaries of the organisation as partners or friends of men members.

The most obvious examples of less or non-patriarchal sexual ideologies would appear to be feminist and women's movement organisations. Despite certain difficulties in reporting, especially for separatist organisations, there are now a number of accounts of the impact of organisational ideology in such situations ranging from local organising, to national political organising. A special word must, however, be added on the relationship of feminism and organising in general terms. While there is a growing number of feminist studies providing critical commentaries of particular organisations, one major strand of feminist theory and practice is critical of the dominant form of organising. According to this, the formal, hierarchical, bureaucratic organisation is seen as patriarchal in itself and alternative, less hierarchical, small-group and network structures of organising are preferred. In this sense the form of an organisation can itself implicitly represent or reinforce a particular sexual ideology. The substance of a sexual ideology can be displayed not only in events in the life of the organisation, but in the form of the organisation in the first place.

Finally, sexual ideologies vary in the manner of their articulations, in both their *explicitness and observability*, and in their (self-) *consciousness*. There are relatively few organisations, such as sex shops, with a completely explicit ideology with regard to sexuality. For most, articulation is less explicit and as already noted predominantly and implicitly heterosexual. Articulation of ideology also increases with consciousness, and specifically gender consciousness, of that ideology. In other words in some, though relatively few, organisations, the explicitness of the sexual ideology will be increased through a specific consciousness of gender. This is most obviously the case in women's movement organisations and all the more so in lesbian organisations. Such all-women organisations may thereby have a more explicit sexual ideology and are to be clearly distinguished from other single-sex organisations where consciousness of gender is obscured, for example, some parent-teacher associations and some women's voluntary organisations which remain dependent on male-dominated organisations. Thus not only is there a clear distinction between sexual preference and sexism, but also between the distribution of genders and consciousness of gender.

ORGANISATION SEXUALITY AS LANGUAGE AND IMAGERY

Organisation sexuality not only exists in movements, feelings and ideas, but also at a mediative and symbolic level, in language and imagery. These are one element of the complex of organisation sexuality, and moreover the media through which other social processes occur, the means of their perpetuation.

Language and imagery have various significances for an understanding of sexuality and organisations. Both organisations and sexuality are themselves in part forms of language and imagery. Organisations produce language and images, and are produced by them. In a somewhat different way sexuality is frequently expressed through language and imagery, and language and imagery can certainly produce forms of sexuality. Organisation sexuality consists of that simultaneous interplay of language and imagery. Similarly, members use language in organisations to convey meanings around organisation sexuality, and members are used in the language of organisation sexuality, often in discriminating ways (cf. Lakoff, 1975, 4): current language is largely 'man made' (Spender, 1980).

Imagery, and particularly sexual imagery, operates in a way that is comparable to language though less easily defined. Images both produce and are produced, use and are used. Sexual, and other gendered images used in organisations derive from a great variety of sources, such as advertising, newspapers, television, films and pornography. Feminist and sympathetic male scholarship has achieved much in recent years in demonstrating the discriminatory way women are frequently portrayed in such media. These displays are explicitly oppressive in the case of pornography and the use of naked women on business calendars; romantic fiction creates more subtle images through the continued replay of the masterful man and submissive woman; most children's literature and comics reinforce the gender roles of men at paid work and women in the home, men as dominant and aggressive, women as passive; on television quiz shows it is taken for granted that the male compère is accompanied by women, there to be his 'hostesses', and 'rewarded' by a pat on the bottom or comments on their 'glamorous' appearance; and so on.

Such images are themselves the product of organisations, especially those concerned with culture and communication. They, in their designs, phone-ins, chat shows and other displays are usually compulsorily heterosexual. There are, in Britain at least, no radio requests for gay or bisexual lovers.[8] Images from these organisations are frequently adapted and produced 'afresh' in other organisations, not specifically concerned with image manufacture.

Furthermore, language and imagery are themselves frequently interrelated with each other, so that meanings in one sphere suggest meanings in the other, and vice versa. This can be seen most clearly in organisations where symbolism is well elaborated, be it through established historical traditions, as in many religious organisations, or relatively recent developments, as in advertising agencies. The combined power of image and language in dominating and defining women as 'pure' and 'submissive' is to be seen on entering many Christian churches, in the physical fabric and sculpted figures, in hymn and service books. These uses of the symbolic in image and language are reiterated and given human articulation in the conduct of some services, as in virtually all-male processionals and other liturgical practices.

In the world of advertising sex and sexuality are oppressively and heavily implicit through the repeated use and impact of imagery and language. The mutual reinforcement of language and imagery is the medium by which symbols arranged by advertising organisations are brought into peoples' homes, lives and psyches. In the search for the 'striking visual image' and the 'hard-hitting slogan', anything that is legal is acceptable. Sexuality is taken for granted as an essential part of these searches as characterised by the creation of an illusory sexual environment around any product whatsoever. The *How to Advertise* (Roman and Maas, 1979) manual notes that 'Liquid diet products were originally sold to men on a health positioning. Sales took off when *advertising told women* that these diet aids could make them stay thin and sexy' (our emphasis) (p. 26); and 'Emotional commercials for Final Touch fabric softener show husbands praising their wives for putting "so much love into everything". That campaign doubled Final Touch Sales' (p. 27).

There is such a multitude of uses and abuses of sexuality in advertisements, it is difficult to know which particular examples to cite. They range from the obvious, as in cosmetics, perfumes, soaps, clothing, through to other less obvious applications, such as cars, food, household appliances, finance and computers. Frequently this involves the reference to and reinforcement of sex and sexual stereotyping (Courtney and Whipple, 1983).

The construction of advertisements is one of the most important, complex, and subtle aspects of organisation sexuality; it is also an area attracting continuing attention of feminist and other critical analysis, often informed by semiotics (e.g. Goffman, 1979; Dyer, 1982). Williamson (1978, 20–39) has elaborated one scheme demonstrating how advertisements exist within a currency of signs, in varying degrees of complexity— in terms of products being signified a meaning; acting as signifiers of meaning; generating further meaning, being a meaning; and/or interchangeability with meaning. Some of these complexities are illustrated in the following semiotic analysis:

An ad for Renault cars . . . sets up a correspondence between the car and a woman through the content and form of the signifiers. The woman is made synonymous with the car through the shiny dress she is wearing and through its colours, and in addition through the formal techniques of cinematic dissolves and the montage of images. The silk-clad, slinky, fashionable model lies in a sensuous horizontal position in the first frame of the commercial. Her image dissolves slowly into the image of a car in the next few frames, the curves of her body forming the outline of the car. Subsequent frames show the fragmented parts of a woman; her hands, head, torso, etc. are juxtaposed with, dissolved into or made to stand instead of the car's instruments, headlights and reclining seats. Elongated fingers and manicured, painted nails sensuously touch and caress the control panel and the car's phallic-looking locking mechanism. Woman as a sign, shaped and moulded like a car, displays herself to be looked at by men. She is made into a decorative, passive object available and controllable like the car. She is moulded in the form that men desire; she is controlled by the gaze of the absent man and is represented by the imagined fetishes which men are supposed to respond to. She adorns and caresses the car and men are invited to caress their cars/women. The images are misty and the music throbs. This kind of ad expresses women's sexuality in men's terms; it invites the signified voyeurism and sexual power and control through the forms of the signifiers.
(Dyer, 1982, 120, 123)

Dyer continues to note that even such complex significations exist within further systems of signs, so that '"chains" of signification and signifieds can become signifiers for further chains of signification. . .'. An eighties Fiat advert refers back to the 'sexual woman' theme so dominant in car advertisements; but this time by juxtaposing a young, attractive (presumably Italian, Catholic) nun alongside the rear of a car, the rear window of which has stained glass, behind which we were told is a 'far-from-spartan bed'. A particularly subtle genre is advertisements for airlines, particularly international ones. These frequently invite the potential passenger to 'fly', 'float' or even 'fly me', so producing a 'new experience'. A TWA advertisement showed a picture of a smiling man, apparently floating above his seat, and gazing at and extending his hand towards a female member of the cabin staff. She, resembling an adult school girl in appearance (short stature, white shirt, with tie, gym slip style dress, long girlish hair pinned back), returns his gaze smiling into his eyes. Their hands almost meet around a glass she holds and hover over a folded newspaper covering the man's legs. She is reaching down further than would be expected; his hand remains lower, about six inches immediately above his groin. The slogan above reads 'More like *floating* when you're flying' and that below, 'T.W.A's new Ambassador Class seats are a new experience.'

A Pan Am full double-page newspaper advertisement was headed, across both pages, 'The Bigger Experience'. Sub-headings are 'Bigger on the inside', 'Little things make us bigger', 'Big around the U.S. and the world' and 'Big in the Apple'. There are five pictures: a jumbo jet; a scene in the Clipper Class section; a blonde, conventionally glamorous, female member of the cabin staff with bow tie; a silver coffee pot; and a helicopter. The nose of the jumbo jet points towards the 'Experience' of the headline. The eyes of the cabin staff member gaze straight at the reader,[9] whilst holding a tray of food. This picture is cut off, in a straight line, at the bottom of her thighs and the capital 'A' in Pan Am is positioned centrally and immediately below. The whole advertisement is completed, in the bottom right-hand corner with 'You Can't Beat the Experience'.

The interplay of imagery and language is particularly apparent in the process of sexual stereotyping, in both advertising and other organisational contexts. Stereotyping is one routine way in which language and imagery are combined to categorise organisational relationships and roles. Though grossly inaccurate, they are not simple fictions but crude simplifications of complex issues, often with far-reaching effects. Bradford, Sargent and Sprague (1975) have shown how sexual stereotypes in organisations 'give rise to expectations regarding values, interests, aptitudes and abilities of a person just because the other happens to be male or female'. Stereotypes are used to portray and attempt to make sense of particular people, for example, young women, *in the simplest of terms*, as dumb blondes, tragic maidens, sophisticated manipulators, victims, and so on. Frequently stereotypes have a sexual element or imply sexual parody. They also often occur in 'heterosexual' pairings, such as macho/seductress, chivalrous knight/helpless maiden, possessive father/pet, tough warrior/nurturant mother (Kanter, 1975). Although these depictions derive from various sources, such as romantic literature, family mythology and comedy, they are not separate from or outside organisations: the crudeness of the language and presentation masks the subtlety of their influence on organisational life.

Sexual stereotypes may be particularly important in organisational boundary functions, public relations, recruitment, and so on. For example, the Health Education Council, an organisation known for its progressive stance on health, produced an advice booklet *Stay Fit in the Office* (n.d.). This portrays men thirty-three times as conscientious, asexual black-suited bosses, and women eight times as subservient, stupid, fantasising, making mistakes and in office roles reflecting home roles. All this is presented in the cause of improving health!

Two further examples of sexual parody, especially of women, are barworkers and nurses.

As Hey (1986, 43) suggests:

If we think of the popular cultural imagery that attaches itself to the role of a barmaid, we construct an image of a sexually provocative, friendly, sympathetic, and 'mature', experienced woman . . . . Barmaids do a lot more than serve drinks! Barmaids are classic token women. A perfect construction of male fantasies - the maternal *and* sexual.

Involved though the barmaid stereotype is, it is less complicated than the sexual parodying of nurses:

The angel and the dragon are old favourites, but in the last 20 years they have been joined by a third stereotype which has become the most popular of all - the nurse as sex symbol. Barbara Windsor in the *Carry On* films is perhaps the best known (and her sexy nurse is interchangeable with all the other dumb blonde characters she portrays), but there are many other examples of the feather-brained female who wears black stockings and whose main interest is flirting with the houseman. Newspapers love pin-ups of nurses in bikinis, captioned 'What the doctor ordered. . .', and the busty nurse is a favourite subject of seaside joke postcards, get well cards and even, one year, the trade union COHSE's Christmas card. Just a bit of fun? These images are the most acceptable end of a spectrum extending to pornographic films which have nurses as the focus of male erotic interest. *Naughty night nurses* and similarly titled films are often to be seen in the cinema clubs of Soho. (Salvage, 1985, 22).

The secretary is perhaps the archetype of the organisational sexual stereotype, as discussed earlier, both obscuring and parodying the issue of sexuality. This exemplifies the paradox of organisation sexuality, denying the existence of sexuality whilst permeated by sexual stereotypes and making use of them in employment practices. The parody of sexual reality in stereotyping allows organisations to handle the contradiction by appearing to acknowledge that there is an issue and that it has been dealt with all at the same time, so that the reality of organisational life with its powerful sexuality is further obscured.

Most organisations are havens of sexist language. There are continual assaults usually by men upon women by such words as 'chairman', 'manpower', 'statesman', 'manning levels', 'spokesman', 'workmanship', 'master plan/file/key', 'fellowship' and so on and on. In short, language of this sort *is* sexual harassment. Imagine how offensive and harassing to a black person all the above words would be if they were routinely changed to read 'whitepower',[10] 'chairwhite', 'stateswhite' etc. An 'offensive compliment' was paid to the female author of this book when a male colleague said her feedback in a training session had been 'absolutely masterly'!

Such oppressions are often further exacerbated by their lack of recognition by those men using such language and imagery, a resort to joking and ridicule, and outright refusal to acknowledge any need for change. For example, 'the inevitable nubile pin-up over well-worked machinery, heavy sexual references and jokes . . . are . . . accepted as the *natural* form of shopfloor life' (Collinson, 1981, 196). An up-market institutionalisation of such practices is in the very name of the 'Playboy' organisation, which might suggest a child's game, *not to be taken seriously*, rather than a magazine and enterprise exploitative of women.[11] Increasingly these meanings are being made conscious, recognised as oppressive, and challenged. This political process of changing organisations is likely to be difficult and uneven.

These struggles, despite the complications already mentioned, usually remain at the level of explicit meaning, for example, attempts to introduce non-gendered language like 'chair' or 'chairperson' into organisations. Language and imagery, however, also operate at a much more implicit level, in ways that are less easily confronted and altered by 'policy decisions'. Indeed sexist language and imagery provide the basis for a more specific *sexuality of language* in organisations.

Inquiry at this level of meaning is assisted by recent developments in structural linguistics and semiology, particularly the processes by which said meanings are naturalised, and conflicts hidden behind 'marks of floating signifiers'. Poster (1984, 28−9) has summarised some of this work, drawing, *inter alia*, on Barthes and Baudrillard, as follows

In advanced capitalism signifiers (words) are split off from signifieds (meanings) and referents (things), . . . The predominant linguistic form in advanced capitalism is not the symbol but the signal. Since the linguistic elements are fragmented, signifiers are able to 'float' as it were in the space of social practice and be combined with signifieds and referents at will. . . . Qualities that are desired by the population (success, self-confidence) are attributed to commodities irrespective of their functionality or material utility. Thus shaving creams promise sex appeal; deodorants guarantee self-confidence, automobiles are a means to an active social life; soft drinks are the key to community, love, popularity; and so forth. . . . The mechanism of the signal, whereby signifiers are attached to commodities, ensures an immediate if unconscious response by the receivers of a message.

The transfer from symbol to signal is crucial in the construction for understanding organisation sexuality. Organisations are in part constructors of signs and in part themselves systems of signs, about things, commodities, members, and so on. Organisations consist of routine separations and segmentations of tasks, roles, functions and people; between skills and parts of people; between sexuality and people. The taken-for-granted segmentation and fetishism of sexuality from (other aspects of) the person is thus daily reinforced.

It is this process of segmentation of persons, parts of persons, and indeed sexuality that reproduces (the significance of) the concept of signs, within capitalism, and moreover patriarchy. Indeed the sign is characteristic of patriarchy, referring, as it does, genders, 'bits' of people, appearances, to qualities in a manner that is part arbitrary and part apparently arbitrary. This building up of multi-layered patriarchal meanings can be deconstructed through the interpretation of these signs, to display patriarchy in terms of the process of mystification of material powers.

This process has direct relevance for the sexuality of language and imagery in a number of important ways. Signifiers link with meanings and things, which themselves have further links with other signifiers, both verbal and visual, powerfully and determinantly. The supposedly anomalous position of women in organisations (MacKinnon, 1979, 216) makes women into signs and information for men, with numerous associations with sexuality. This is perhaps most easily seen in the cultural meaning of 'secretary' as word and image. The multiple meanings of men's 'possession' of secretaries, and indeed of women in 'liaison' roles and as assistants to men mirror the widespread possession of women by men in language (Lakoff, 1975, 29–31). The word 'secretary' produces a host of signifiers—the possibility of task definition, as well as the sayings of 'women', 'office wife', 'subservient', 'attractive', 'sexually available', 'prim', 'efficient', 'neat', 'pert', and so on. For most men 'having' a secretary is a sign of sexual power, however implicit, as in the power to 'appoint', 'promote', 'sponsor' and 'assign' others, especially women, to jobs and roles. Once 'appointed', some women, particularly secretaries, are involved in keeping the 'appointments book', usually for individual men, for the perpetuation of this process for men. Women exist in the spaces created by men in the routine separation made in organisations between tasks, roles, functions and organisational members, between separate skills and parts of people, between sexuality and people. In this organisational world women do not fully exist: woman is 'that sex that is not one' (Irigaray, 1978), and 'is valuable in so far as she permits man to fulfill his being as man' (Leclerc, 1981, 79).

Men's domination of sexual associations is, however, much more pervasive than the signification of women workers. The sexuality of language includes formal organisational references to 'policy thrusts', 'promotion drives', 'market penetration', and all manner of 'special projects' and 'projections'. Words like 'tools', 'equipment' and 'instruments' can refer to the necessary materials for undertaking a piece of work and can have attached additional sexual meanings. Similarly, compromise and co-operation can become 'limpness'; supposedly incompent or lazy workers can be labelled 'wankers'; and competitors, tired workers and alienated work objects may all be 'fucked'. Furthermore, formal organisational structures and plans may also closely parallel the structure of the 'male sexual narrative' (Dyer, 1985): the setting of goals, the determination of targets, the drive to achieve ratings, the mastery of tasks, the need to score, to meet the planned organisational climax.

The process of sexual association outlined above blurs with a more arbitrary control of signs. In many organisations a complex of meanings exists whereby everything sexless may become sexualised. Whole organisations, parts of organisations, types of work, objects, commodities, people, furniture, may take on sexual meanings, positively or negatively. These knowledges are rarely recorded: a magazine survey suggested customs officers, bank managers, and car mechanics are 'sexy', while social workers, VAT inspectors and salesmen are not; and that floors and blinds have sexual connotations, where fluourescent lights and curtains have not (Pascall, 1984). This is a wholesale patriarchal imperialism of the definition of (organisational) reality. Organisations persist as fusions of people, objects, furniture etc., with interlocking sexual meanings attached, mostly patriarchally defined.

Not only are women the objects of sexual imagery in pin-up calendars, the recipients of sexual harassment, physically and in sexist language, they are yet further oppressed by the male sexist ethos, assumptions and methods of most organisations, whereby dominant language, maleness and imagery work in mutual reinforcement.

Finally, organisation sexuality also operates at a much deeper psychological level in *confirming through their apparent opposition and otherness* what organisation and sexuality are. In short 'things' and people can become sexual by being and appearing as organisational, and so 'not sexual'. Their 'non-sexual-ness' may paradoxically increase their sexual appeal, by virtue of difference, emphasised contrast, challenge. Much of the power of sexuality in organisational contexts arises out of an ambiguous interplay with the supposedly 'desexualised' world of organisations and 'work'. The possibility of sexual labour-power in the organisational context sits uneasily alongside the trappings of organisational life. This unspoken contradiction serves only to increase the allure of that sexuality, as in the sexuality of office parties, and the idea and practice of 'sex on the premises'.

This 'creative' tension is used and exploited in fantasy, in advertising, in films, in comedy, in pornography, for the benefit of men at least, in the 'male sexual narrative' of the British 'Carry On' film series. Another example of this genre is the 1960 Wilder-Diamond film, 'The Apartment', in which the central *comedy* theme is a bureaucrat's regular loan of his flat to his boss for the latter's extra-marital affairs, so that he has to leave his own flat even in the middle of the night. The employee's dedication, the ambiguous triumph of organisation sexuality over his sexuality is the point of the film. Other elaborations on this theme are exploited in pornography:

One of the commonest settings for work-place pornography is the office. The frequency of its appearance as a setting indicates its importance for the consumers of porn. In solid office scenes with desks, chairs, typewriters, even bulging in-trays, girls [*sic*] are shown studiously taking dictation in owlish glasses and severe hairstyles, quite unconscious that their neat white blouse is completely open down the front and the boss is absently playing with their breasts. Office girls cannot open a filing cabinet without revealing that they have nothing on under their respectable grey skirts—nor can they go shopping in their lunch-hour without feeling compelled to model the see-through bra, suspender belt and black stockings for the boss in the afternoon.

(Miles, 1983, 34–5)

Two particular features are worthy of further comment here. Firstly, there is the association in many men's eyes of uniforms and 'severe' formal clothing, and sado-masochism; this may in part be related to a repressed homosexuality aroused from military and other similar, all-male, aggressive organisations. Secondly, there is the ambiguous sexual wearing of glasses, especially by women. Dorothy Parker's quip that men seldom make passes at women who wear glasses gains its poignancy from the sexual connotations of glasses, especially when removed, as a veil.

The use of the 'non-organisation-ness' of sexuality often confirms a sense of organisation, as when sexual presentation of organisational members is *incorporated* to 'demonstrate' organisational efficiency and briskness. The patriarchal archetype of this is the placing of women in uniforms, often with a combination of meanings around 'smartness', 'femininity' and *reference to men's uniforms*—signs once and for all that women's sexuality has been 'organised'; and this is therefore a 'complete' organisation. When men remark of women in uniform, 'Doesn't she look smart', they usually mean 'Doesn't she look sexy'. It is a form of verbal undressing made possible by the contrast of the impersonal uniform and the imagined body, all 'dreamed up' in 'impersonal' language.

As suggested by Barthes the attachment of signifiers evokes an unconscious response from the receiver of the signal already conditioned to equate certain meanings to certain words without needing to check their validity. By developing the concept of organisation sexuality we have attempted to 'bring to the surface' part of men's unconscious world. The comparison of the unconsciousness of organisation sexuality with the unconscious psychodynamic processes of the human personality is difficult to avoid. In recognising unconscious reinforcements through the signifiers of language and imagery we attempt to bring such issues towards consciousness where they can be acknowledged, dealt with, challenged and changed.

8 Narrative: History, Experience and Change

Male sexual narrative exists. Bizarre as this may sound, this repeatedly is what we have found in analysing sexuality and organisational life. This is so in 'acceptable' research methods; in dominant, linear forms of writing; in patriarchal and hierarchical organisations; and in organisation sexuality. The dominant constructions of each of these are male-dominated stories that refer to events that are themselves part real, part supposed. The male sexual narrative is thus a real story about real events; but it is also a very selective account of research, organisational, sexual and other realities, ignoring as it does huge areas of life–experience, relations, contradictions, oppressions. Noticing this incessant regularity has meant that a questioning of the dominant male sexual narrative has become for us inevitable. However, in saying this we do not see the way out as a simple switch to a purely reactive 'female sexual narrative'. This is for a number of reasons, particularly that this might be seen as a patronising tokenism that could be appropriated as a comfort to men, allowing them/us to look no further. Additionally, simple 'resort' to alternative narratives, in this case the 'female', may well leave unchanged issues of power relations, and the fact that all these renegotiations take place within and are currently circumscribed by patriarchal society. Instead of escaping into simple 'either/or' 'solutions', with their danger of *defining* the Other (here the 'female') as being not-male, and thus *pre-defining* it by the 'desirable' or 'undesirable' qualities of its Other (the 'male'), it is necessary to recognise and work from the contradictory experiences of present power structures.

It is important to understand these issues within an historical context. The male sexual narrative, although dominant, has clearly been subject to historical change in its particular form. Patriarchy is not an historical monolith. It has developed from the private power of the father, to the public 'works' and 'politics' of men, the growth of male public 'selfhood' and its 'fall', the capitalist extravaganzas, imperialisms and extensions of power, to present patriarchal forms: the search for the individual, the self, the body, *in the individual* in utter tension with its *reorganisation* in public institutions. Indeed one of the comparatively recent changes in the structuring of patriarchy, despite the long establishment of the power of the public world over the private (O'Brien, 1981), is the 'publicisation' of specific patriarchal forms, contracts and institutions. Most obviously this has involved over the last century or more a huge transfer of power from the multitude of 'private' fathers to the 'collective' power of the state (Burstyn, 1983) and other organisations. Other historical changes have taken place in the non-organisational parts of the public domain, 'in the street'.

It is within this historical context that the making of sexuality more explicit, and the more conscious recognition of sexuality within organisations (that this study is itself party to) takes place. This inevitably contributes to a developing change in the relationship of the public and private worlds. The placing and even the incorporation of sexuality into the public stands in contrast to historical processes of desexualisation in organisations. This resexualisation is itself a profoundly contradictory phenomenon: (i) it may represent a development of the sexualisation that has been long established in certain parts of the public realm, and particularly in certain jobs and occupations traditionally performed by women; (ii) it may in contrast be an indirect means of separating the sexual from the asexual, of splitting previously blurred fusions. It may also be (iii) part of a much longer-term means of transcending sexuality/asexuality.

The making public of sexuality, like the move from fatherhood to state and other organisations, is in one sense a mere surface alteration of social relations; on the other hand, it does hold out the *possibility* of a more fundamental redefinition of the public and the private, the possibility of making *private oppressions known*, and so undermining patriarchy. This giant stasis and revolutionary fluidity are simultaneously what changing relations of sexuality and organisational life are concerned with, in this patriarchal 'order'.

Organisation sexuality derives from this process, as an *unstable* relation not just a conceptual bridge. The appearance of organisation sexuality is a conjunction of the supposedly pure, isolated individual, striving against alienation from selfhood and individual sexuality, and against increasingly public patriarchal organisational forms. Patriarchal organisations characteristically *re*-incorporate this isolated individual; more precisely, they re-incorporate parts of the person, including sexuality, segmented from each other by organisational definition and redefinition in roles, tasks and job descriptions. The way in which sexuality is constructed as a separable and *defining* characteristic of women, and in a different way of men, is both an instance and a root of patriarchy.

These very publicisations of patriarchy and of sexuality bring with them powers and shifts in power. The supposed or pretended exclusion of sexuality from organisations, and its further re-incorporation into organisations as above, themselves in turn become available for public contesting. Increasing public debates around sexuality and patriarchy, for example, around the existence and level of sexism and sexual harassment, have become more possible. It is these that provide the historical backcloth to this study. They enable us to 'speak the unspoken', and so continue those debates already begun. And, as in any debate, the consumer/reader/participant is able to accept or reject what is suggested here, and so continue these debates and material changes further. The presence and process of such debate has certainly made for difficulties in the writing and ordering of a 'completed' piece of work. The excitement of breaking out of traditional research methods has been counterbalanced by that of breaking into the serious academic analysis of unlikely material. At times it has appeared that we have been researching the unresearchable, trying to put into words that which demands faithful attention and description lest it vanish (or nearly so) in the words expressed. Above all it has meant enjoying the research process in its own right rather than as a means to an end; combining fun and a continuous anti-patriarchal critique.

Our researching and writing about sexuality and organisational life have not derived from a discrete decision taken at a particular time. The 'topic' has surfaced from a metaphorical unconscious in writing about the more general relationship of gender and organisation. The matter of sexuality and organisational life has since become obvious in its absence; once recognised there is indeed an (over)abundance of relevant material, in published, observable and inferable forms. In gathering and analysing this material, we have attempted to contribute to the more conscious recognition of an important area of both personal experience and academic study.

In doing this we have raised many questions around the relationship of sexuality and organisational life. Many of these have been given only brief attention and partial answers; many more defy simple answering. Although this study has overviewed the topic, it has done so in an exploratory way. Some issues such as the frequent implicitness of many sexual and sexually-related policies in organisations; the connections between hierarchy and the development of heterosexuality and heterosexual relations; the differential forms of presentation of sexualities within single-sex and mixed-sex organisations; and the differential experience and oppression of those whose sexual preference does not conform organisationally, deserve much more detailed research attention. In saying this we would be very wary of massive empirical studies by disinterested and prying researchers. Instead we suggest more focused research attention by those committed to what Rubin (1984, 275) calls 'a radical theory of sex' against sexual oppression. This raises many possibilities, ranging from specific research for specific sexual interests, such as research by lesbians on anti-lesbian discrimination in organisations (Taylor, 1986), to furthering of awareness of the relevance of organisation sexuality within organisational analysis. To be precise, the almost total non-recognition of sexuality by organisation theorists is another aspect of their sexism. Recognising the importance and impact of sexuality is a first step in producing change to a less entrenched situation.

Changing research in these, and similar directions, is itself clearly one aspect of more general social change around sexuality and organisational life. Research is virtually always an organisational and, therefore, a sexual phenomenon. The usual models both of hierarchical research and of male-dominated research are implicitly, and sometimes explicitly, sexual, in an hierarchical and male-dominated way: a further instance of male sexual narrative. Democratic research that reduces hierarchy and recognises the interrelationship between hierarchy and gender divisions is more valid as a model of research and more likely to produce more valid research especially, but not only, in researching organisation sexuality. If oppressed by hierarchy it is unlikely a person would be able to research this or its impact upon research.

Similar issues arise in terms of changing relationships between individual researchers and their employing or comparable organisational base. Employing organisations are rich sources of material even though turning one's attention to one's own organisation can accentuate the personal, ethical and political problems of research. If what we, or others, are saying about sexuality in organisations has no relation to experience, this is probably not saying much of value. This in turn may generate an impetus for bringing about change in organisations away from sexual oppression.

Organisation sexuality is in the public domain, and yet at the intersection of the public and the private; the spoken and the unspoken; it is subject to the range of social powers, patriarchal, capitalist, yet has power itself, in particular acting as a medium in the reproduction of gender power. Organisation sexuality is thus of significance in the continuing debate between marxism and feminism, gender class and economic class. 'Reconciling' these is often through placing gender class within economic class analysis, so that the 'gender dimension' is explored in terms of the sexual division of labour at (paid) work or in the domestic sphere, as in the domestic labour debate. Thus most marxist feminisms incorporate feminism within the categories of marxism.

Located in this context, the study of organisation sexuality may assist the placing of economic class within gender class analysis, even placing marxism within feminism. As MacKinnon (1982, 30) states, 'feminism stands in relation to marxism as marxism does to classical political economy: its final conclusion and ultimate critique'. The category 'organisation sexuality' is the exact opposite and complement of the category of 'domestic labour' and needs equally close scrutiny.

We are in no doubt that gender, sexuality, women and men can no longer be avoided in the study of organisations and other public forms of life, as 'in the street'. Street sexuality appears to be equally as pervasive as organisation sexuality; and though also neglected, is an integral part of sexuality in the public domain, justifying further research and political attention. Genderless, asexual 'hierarchised' categories, so long accepted, need to be questioned, modified and recast. While such asexual categories persist they remain subject to critique as logocentrism/phallocentrism: the reduction and subordination of all to a 'masculine order'. Indeed as Cixous (1980, 92–3) suggests:

What would become of logocentrism, of the great philosophical systems, of world order in general if the rock upon which they founded their church were to crumble?

If it were to come out in a new day that the logocentric project had always been, undeniably, to *found* (fund) phallocentrism, to insure for masculine order a rationale equal to history itself?

Then all the stories would have to be told differently, the future would be incalculable, the historical forces would, will change hands, bodies; another thinking as yet not thinkable will transform the functioning of all society.

Whereas sexuality in its public representations at least is often a form of organisation, organisations are always implicitly and frequently explicitly forms of sexuality.

This text, including the conclusion above, has been a collaborative venture. This has involved a process of debates, different ways of seeing, attempts at understanding each other, agreement and disagreement. As the text has progressed the clearest differences between us have emerged, partly due to our different genders, and partly our individual interpretations in the light of the different powers of women and men. For these reasons we conclude separately, with a focus on our own genders in relation to organisation sexuality.

ON MEN AND MEN'S SEXUALITY–by Jeff Hearn

The set of practices and relations that we have conceptualised as organisation sexuality, though material, have different significances and implications for women and men. More to the point, this exploration of the relationship of sexuality and organisational life has not been for me a disinterested study; it has created ripples, not just in one but in a number of ponds. The issues and questions raised have changed my understanding of men as a collectivity, men's sexuality, men in organisations, as well as of men's sexuality in organisations. They have also changed my own self-understanding. Such information is not a series of snapshots but derives from active engagement in the world, 'practical, sensuous activities'. In this end section, I focus on men and men's sexuality, and thus my active engagement, my 'practical, sensuous activity'.

Indeed, to be quite precise, it is the attempt to understand and change myself and other men that has increasingly become the motivation for completing this study. Although we have worked collaboratively I have seen my prime and legitimate concern as the understanding of men, within the complex interaction of sexuality and organisational life. This is what I and men know most about and what we (men) have primarily to attend to in opposing sexism and supporting feminism.[1]

It has to be first stated that what we have collaboratively discovered represents a major indictment of the dominant state of men, men's practice and men's sexuality in organisations. As such it invites critique. Men have constructed in organisations, through our own agency and the social structures within which we act, many terrible things in the name of 'sexuality'. Some of these practices, like gazes and laughs and sneers, may appear innocuous, even innocent, but that apparent 'naivety' is itself part of their 'ordinary' (male) power.

Typically men's sexuality in organisations is ·a shifting combination of an easily accessible homosociability and an hierarchic, and often explicitly oppressive, heterosexuality. Organisations provide for men available pools of other men to join and become part of, often preferring the company of their own gender, yet also heterosexist in ideology and culture. Alongside this social bonding is the near ubiquity of the association of hierarchy and heterosexuality. As already noted, heterosexuality in this society and culture is predominantly hierarchical. The hierarchy of organisations is the most frequent and visible form that hierarchy takes in the public domain. Such hierarchies may be formal and/or informal, as contrasted with the formless hierarchies of power 'in the street'. The hierarchy of organisations both constructs hierarchic heterosexuality, and is thereby constructed. Hierarchy in organisations is the most obvious social and formally structured expression of the hierarchic power relations of heterosexuality between men and women.

Organisation sexuality is for men characteristically a mixture of homosociability, latent homosexuality, homophobia and heterosexual phallocentrism, given structured form. Thus men's sexuality towards women has to be seen in the context of, in relation to, and even as the result of men's sexuality with each other. Accordingly, an understanding of supposedly 'normal', straight male heterosexuality, in organisations at least, necessitates a consideration of the relevance of homosexuality and homosexual desire amongst men, both as a constituent part of that 'heterosexuality' and as something often feared. Women are in these ways 'somewhat incidental' for men's sexual presence: as sexual 'others', outsiders; as signs of and subject to men's hierarchic power; and as members of the 'desired' 'opposite sex', who are usually effectively avoided for most organisational time. Furthermore, men's relations towards women, whether sexual, intimate, social or violent, may include projections of or deflections from feelings, sexual or otherwise, towards other men, and fear of those feelings. This can involve men 'proving' their manhood by violence, objectification of women, sexual feeling towards and 'falling in love' with women, as well as the range of organisational oppressions. These 'proofs' may stand in place of accepting such feelings.

Within and around this dominant male 'organisation heterosexuality', men act in a variety of ways towards other men. These range from the centring of organisational experience around the repeated reference to 'fuck' and 'fucking'; to an ever-ready, and 'respectable', almost polite, willingness to notice sexual innuendo of organisational situations, jokes, words; to genuine, internal uncertainty and doubt about dealing sexually with other organisational members of any gender; to articulation of a willingness to act against sexual oppression by, say, removing offensive female pin-ups from 'public' spaces. Such practices are not alternatives, and may be performed in various permutations by individual men.

Furthermore, men's sexuality towards each other is often complex and contradictory. Men who are supposedly asexual, priests, wear dresses;[2] men who are supposedly heterosexually 'macho' indulge in 'homosexual' high jinks and horseplay; men who may appear the most sexually disinterested may underwrite the sexuality of others, as in, say, managers' condonement of other men's sexual harassment. Such contradictions illustrate the fact that for men (our) sexuality is often a question mark, an unspoken disturbing presence, in everyday organisational reality.

Thus men have created a public world of organisations, where, although often physically gathered together, we men also remain distant emotionally and sexually from each other. This circumstance is not only an academic or theoretical issue but one of immediate practice, at least for those of us who are members of organisations. Practice in this context refers to how we act sexually in organisations, including whether we explicitly harass, implicitly support harassment, oppose harassment, and so on and on. Unfortunately much of men's sexuality in the organisations we have created is desperate, uncomfortable, ritualised, ambiguous, however much we would like to reach out and embrace other men. Above all is the repressed wish of men to recognise all other men as brothers, who happen to meet and be met, and comprise (parts of) organisations, not just be mere carriers of organisational role.

There is an urgent need for new ways of behaving between men in organisations. If intimacy, sexual or social, between men was normal there; if there was, for example, no bar on men kissing in public spaces, especially in organisations, current definitions of male power, and indeed the public–private divide, would be threatened. The potential for peaceful and intimate brotherhood between men seems to exist in almost all organisations. Indeed even if one considers that most segmented, ritualised and regimented of organisations, where men may be insulted as 'bunches of girls' or 'old women', where homosexuality is the most persecuted—that is, the military—such possibilities persist there. Interestingly, fleeting references to such possible intimacy are to be found from as far apart as a serving British tank commander—who claims that in the tank is the love of fellow men 'in the best sense of the word'[3]—to an American men's anti-sexist movement spokesperson, 'There's something about that all male contact [in the army] that was beautiful for me'[4] (my insertion). If these generous feelings can occur in the most patriarchal and oppressive of organisations, it seems possible that similar intimacy is realisable in other organisations. Facilitating intimacy, and indeed homosexuality, in the army might also lead to seeing potential enemies as less threatening, with their own potential for intimacy, social or sexual.

Men's traditional male solidarity, bonding and class culture needs to be transcended by a solidarity of intimacy. Men's fear of each other, 'nurtured' from the earliest encouragements of aggression, the terror of hurting others of the same gender and of being hurt, stands in the way, abstractly solidified into organisational structures, roles and hierarchies. Organisations routinely provide reinforcements of that terror (as we step into the public world), and it is that which we need to overcome by gentle, vigorous steps.

ORGANISATION SEXUALITY: A WOMAN'S VIEWPOINT–by Wendy Parkin

The concept of organisation sexuality has evolved during our joint research with mutual recognition of the interrelatedness of organisational life and sexuality, and how this reinforces patriarchy through the perpetuation of the male sexual narrative. We both recognised that what were initially perceived as methodological difficulties in the study of organisation sexuality were, at the same time, organisational processes effectively obscuring the impact of sexuality on organisational life. Neither of us subscribe to a 'sex differences' approach in which inherent, specific and exclusive characteristics for women and men are used to justify and perpetuate a division of labour within hierarchical, heterosexual organisations. Such organisations promote a 'maleness' of power, authority and leadership as a dominant orthodoxy of functionalist theory (cf. Burrell and Morgan, 1979). These main areas of agreement cannot, however, avoid the paradox of a man and a woman writing jointly in this field of research. Mutual acknowledgement and analysis of the way organisation sexuality reinforces male generic powers also carried with it an exclusive experience for each of us. The gender roles attributed to women by our society determine that the woman's experience is predominantly that of oppression though this is not recognised by all women or experienced uniformly. Thus, although there has been broad agreement in analysis, there has been a fundamental difference in the impact of the research experience depending on whether one is a woman or a man: one cannot disagree with the other's experience. Jeff Hearn's account of the impact of the research for him parallels mine in the way that the development of the research has also been a development in awareness; mine has been a developing awareness of the depth, intricacy, complexity and enormity of the oppression of the male sexual narrative.

Resistance to male oppression is through the different strands of feminist theory and practice. One strand of this resistance is an anti-organisational stance which recognises the institutionalisation and embodiment of male power in hierarchical organisations. Thus, all-female co-operative alternatives, such as women's peace camps, are set up as a protest. This is not to argue that women are intrinsically peaceful or that we organise ourselves co-operatively and non-hierarchically, for some women successfully gain status and power in hierarchical organisations, a few achieve powerful leadership positions, and war is still seen as justified by many women. This anti-organisational stance is used by feminists as a statement of the way gender roles ascribed to women in our society can be used as a powerful and threatening political challenge to male supremacy, especially with regard to the control and power over the weapons of war. Similarly, many black people are unwilling to reinforce white supremacy by 'entering' white-dominated organisations, preferring to set up their own radical alternatives.

There are advocates of women-only writing and research as being the only way in which women's experiences and oppressions can be effectively explored, preferably outside the constraints of male-dominated, hierarchical organisations. This again parallels the experience of some black people who feel the need to produce their own literature and research as a common experience of racism.

With organisation sexuality I have recognised the inextricable link between male oppression and male sexual oppression with one continually reinforcing the other. For this reason, there are women who see the only alternative to the violence within male sexuality in the formation of women-only relationships, whether sexual or not. Further to this is the advocacy of the development of a female sexual theory, as Hollibaugh and Moraga (1984, 413) suggest:

We believe that women must create sexual theory in the same way we created feminist theory. We simply need to get together in places where people agree to suspend their sexual values, so that each of us can feel free to say what we do sexually or want to do or have done to us.

This is a recognition that the male sexual narrative *is* and a further recognition that an essential component of feminist theory therefore must be a feminist sexual theory. This again would be a political stance against male sexuality, and the way masculinity, generic powers and sexuality are inextricable. Such politicisation is essential in the face of the variety of oppressions of the phallocentric male sexual narrative. Sometimes these are powerfully displayed, as when military men gaze admiringly at huge phallic shaped atomic warheads.

Another dimension of the political challenge of feminist theories is the development of women-only consciousness-raising groups, where the impact of the male sexual narrative can be explored. Such groups would facilitate sharing experiences, for example, of rape or sexual harassment in organisational settings, and offer support and strategies for countering and resisting. Further still, and very important to me, is the recognition of the positive experience of intimacy and sisterhood amongst women, starkly contrasting with fear of intimacy amongst men and male exploitation of (their) heterosexuality.

For me the research has revealed a profound further dimension of male power with my developing and increasing recognition of the male sexual narrative within the work ethic; within organisational structures and goals; in dominant orthodoxies as to how research should be conducted; and in the ignorance, disregard and trivialisation of women's sexuality and sexual states. Furthermore, I have recognised the domination of the public domain over the private domain and the way the public domain has taken over the private experiences of women and our sexuality, and redefined both publicly.

A further profound revelation has been the growing awareness of the extent of sexual harassment through imagery, symbolism and language. Again there are parallels with racism. Some black people have shared with me their feelings that blatant racist statements can be easier to tackle than the constant perpetuation of negative connotations and images of blackness and black people in language and the media. Similarly, pornography, though extremely offensive, is more obviously open to attack than the day-to-day harassment of sexist and sexual language and imagery. Some attention is being paid to altering sexist language with 'best person for the job', replacing 'best man for the job' and so on. These alternatives continue to attract a high level of ridicule and dismissiveness with accusations of 'awkwardness', 'crankiness', even paranoia. More subtle and possibly more powerful is *sexualist*[5] language and imagery. This can be in 'girlie' calendars on the wall; in romantic fiction perpetuating stereotypes; in advertisements giving sexual connotations to everyday objects; in the sex-role stereotyping of secretaries; and in the media presentation of women as in some quiz shows. In addition there is the ubiquity of the male sexual language of 'masterly', 'virility', 'thrusting', 'rising to the challenge', 'punchiness' and a whole variety of jokings, sneerings, and innuendoes as part and parcel of organisational life. It is insidious but, once recognised, is a permanent day-by-day harassment. For me, this issue of male sexual organisational language has been the major revelation of the research, the awareness and consciousness of which has developed as the research has progressed. I see it as underpinning the dominant heterosexual, hierarchical orthodoxy. It is a widespread and continuous onslaught which is personally harassing and which I perceive as harassing for all women, whether recognised or not. Thus in being a woman I have experienced oppression, particularly through language and imagery; in being white I become the oppressor: for both these reasons I see the need for fundamental change.

This prevalence of the harassment of language and imagery for me, suggests one focus for change. I now recognise the maintenance and reinforcement of male generic powers through organisation sexuality and thus the continued male sexual domination of ideology, consciousness, imagery and language. Recognising this, and especially the need to change the subtleties of sexual language, to attempt to change perceptions, is another strand of feminist strategy and practice. This is not to argue for female alternatives to male sexual language, for seeking female alternatives to words such as 'virility' is not the same as seeking their abolition altogether. From my viewpoint, as a woman, one of the means for challenging the power of the male sexual narrative is to recognise its embodiment in language. For many men this could be perceived as 'emasculation' of their manhood whereas such change would be liberating for men and women. This would therefore probably reduce men's acting out of their 'manhood' again and again and again in ways destructive to women.

The current asymmetry of power between women and men leads to a necessary asymmetry in prescription for change for women and men. Men can only prescribe for themselves; women can prescribe for both themselves and men. Only women, experiencing as we do this inequality, can say what is wanted from men and for women ourselves. Women's resistance to and challenge of the oppression of the male sexual narrative is an undermining of the genderism[6] of patriarchy.

Postscript to the Revised Edition: Updating Theory and Practice

Since the first publication of *'Sex' at 'Work'* in 1987, in which the relationship of sexuality, gender and power in organisations was analysed, there have been further major advances and consolidations in the recognition of sexuality and gender in organisational analysis. One aspect of this process that has been of interest to us is how our work has been variably interpreted by readers and researchers. The general response has been to see the first edition as a way of promoting and progressing the analysis of sexuality, gender and organisations. In some interpretations there have been attempts to locate and categorise our work within different existing theoretical frameworks, and occasionally we have found these readings to be problematic. Some of these issues are addressed later in the postscript.

Paradoxically, there are also a number of continuing silences from the mainstream(s) as well as a variety of social connections and social divisions within these critical studies. This postscript now re-visits debates and analyses in the context of local, national and global changes as well as substantial theoretical developments. The postscript comprises discussion of the changing context of sexuality and organisations; recent research and literature; current debates and controversies; and future issues for practice and theory.

THE CHANGING CONTEXT OF SEXUALITY AND ORGANISATIONS

Before identifying and exploring the substantive theoretical and political debates on sexuality it is important to recognise the importance of the changing national and global contexts. There has been a rise in religious fundamentalisms, New Right familialism and nationalistic racisms, along with various responses to HIV/AIDS. In addition to increasing sexual scandals in residential child care settings, continuing recognition of child sexual abuse with setting up of Childline along with research and practice in profiling perpetrators, there has been a growth of international information technologies for the transmission of sexual imagery, the creation of virtual sexual realities, the further development of sex tourism, and an apparent widespread acceptance of sexual violence and sexually explicit behaviour on television and film. Forms of state control of sexuality are various and encompass Section 28 of the Local Government Act (1990) and sex education in schools.

In this context, a complex interchange has developed between governments, international corporations, the media, and indeed feminism and sexual social movements that has made sexuality both a *legitimate* area of public attention and interest, and at the same time a subject that is deeply *problematic*. Indeed, in some ways this book and the preceding first edition have contributed to this. More precisely, there is a continuing tension between the apparent ordinariness and ubiquity of sexuality and the various ways in which sexuality and power are obscured—as if it can now be said 'we have dealt with it'. This includes a continuing avoidance of the full horror of sexual violence and sexual terror.

RECENT RESEARCH AND LITERATURE

This section summarises some of the literature that was omitted from the first edition or has been published since.[1]

The gendering of organisations

Recent research and literature on the gendering of organisations has been strongly influenced by debates in and around feminism. During the 1970s and 1980s, the two most prolific feminist or feminist-influenced sets of literature on gender and organisations have come from Marxist and socialist feminism;

and writing on 'women in management', especially from North America. As already noted (p. 36), sexuality was not generally the central focus of interest of these studies. More recently, there have been increasing numbers of feminist studies on gender, and on particular divisions of labour in organisations, which in turn address sexuality to a greater or lesser extent (for example, Walby, 1990; Witz, 1992; Savage and Witz, 1992; Mills and Tancred, 1992; Reskin and Padavic, 1994; MacEwen Scott, 1994; Due Billing and Alvesson, 1994). Furthermore, in some radical and anarchist feminism the very idea of organisation is held to be dominated by men, and so subject to critical theory and practice. Ferguson's (1984) *The Feminist Case Against Bureaucracy*, a classic text in this debate, has been subject to further feminist critique by Due Billing (1994).

Heterosexual harassment
There is a continuing development of research and literature on heterosexual harassment in the workplace which is part of the broader concerns of women against male violence and objectification in its various forms (Kelly, 1988). Sexual harassment as an issue has been taken up in workplace, and other organisational campaigns, by trade unions and by women's groups. These campaigns and groups have often, but by no means exclusively, been led by women office workers and public sector trade union sections and committees.

This has led on to more detailed analyses of the factors that appear to affect either level or perception of harassment. Academic work on sexual harassment has developed from two major directions. First, there are psychological and social psychological studies, sometimes employing the 'imagined situation' as means to the analysis of differential evaluations of and responses to harassment. 'Many of these studies use similar research designs, all classic analyses of variance designs, in which students, employees or managers are asked to rate one or more scenarios' (Gutek and Dunwoody, 1987).

Second, there is the increased concern of industrial sociologists and sociologists of work and workplaces with sexuality and sexual harassment, as a necessary development of a general concern with gender relations and power. The major example of this approach, has, not surprisingly, been developed through feminist studies of industrial organisations (for example, Pollert, 1981; Cockburn, 1983). These two approaches are usually somewhat separate, but on occasions, their insights converge. Nancy DiTomaso (1989) brings them together by using the frameworks of both sexual harassment and sexual discrimination to analyse workers' perceptions in three different organisations. (Also compare Gutek and Morasch's 1982 research, and the Leeds TUCRIC 1983 survey; also see pp. 83–5.)

The bringing together of heterosexual harassment and heterosexual relationships is found in MacKinnon's (1979) work and in the collection by Neugarten and Shafritz (1980), *Sexuality in Organizations*, on policy-related material and academic papers on 'romantic and coercive behaviours at work'. This theme has also been elaborated more recently by Thomas and Kitzinger (1994).

To illustrate the development of this political activity, action research and social survey, we may note that the Alliance Against Sexual Coercion, based in Cambridge, Massachusetts, published an annotated list of 171, mainly American, publications on sexual harassment to that date, including ten surveys (1980); while the trade union organisation Leeds TUCRIC's (1983) study of sexual harassment included a bibliography of 73, mainly British, publications and 11 British trade union publications. In addition, in 1987, the Ministry of Social Affairs and Health in Finland published an excellent review, research and biographic text, giving details of 341 publications and ten bibliographies on sexual harassment, with particularly useful information on Scandinavian and German sources (Hogbacka *et al.*, 1987). Studies have also been produced of harassment in African organisations (Hollway and Mukurasi, 1994).

There is increasing research evidence of both incidence and variety of forms of sexual harassment in national and cross-national studies demonstrating both the persistence of harassment and the cultural differences in the perception and responses which in some contexts includes the use of tribunals and other legal remedies. In the light of this, there is increasing interest in the extent to which sexual harassment can or should be understood as a unified phenomenon or be critically interrogated in terms of local discourses and thus countered through local political practices (Brant and Too, 1994).

Lesbians and gay men in organisations
Most organisations remain highly complicated and embedded structures, indeed archives, of heterosexuality and hetero-sexism. Most are dominated by groups of heterosexual men. On the other hand, such men, as managers or workers, may often be socially defined as heterosexual, yet be at the least homosocial, and possibly homo-erotic in their relations with each other: there is a characteristic and routine homosociality of heterosexual men in organisational situations. In addition, most organisations are arenas for the development of 'hetero-sexual complementarity' between women and men (Cockburn, 1988). Such heterosexual hegemony tends to construct lesbians and gay men as isolated exceptions, so that they and their sexuality come to be seen, by many heterosexuals at least, as private and individual, even as personal 'problems'.

Recent gay politics and organising has been transformed with the onset of HIV/AIDS. Relevant changes include the development of organisations for prevention, support and campaigning, and in some cases their subsequent 'de-gaying'. There has also been continuing concern with the extent to which lesbians and gay men are united or divided through same sex desire, the relations of 'homosexuality' and 'heterosexuality', and the primacy of gender or sexuality (Edwards, 1994).

There now exists a considerable number of empirical surveys and analyses of discrimination against lesbians and gay men and their treatment in organisations, often initially produced as small-case studies and pamphlets (for example, Campaign for Homosexual Equality, 1981; Beer *et al.*, 1983; Greater London Council, 1985; Labour Research Department, 1992). Some of the reports and surveys of this type have collected information on combined samples of lesbians and gay men, 'making it difficult to determine whether the problem [of employment discrimination] operates differently for the two populations' (Levine and Leonard, 1984, 701). A valuable review of the literature on employment discrimination against gay men is Levine's (1979) survey in the *International Review of Modern Sociology*. There have been relatively few studies specifically concerned with lesbians in organisations. *All in a Day's Work*, produced by the Lesbian Employment Rights in London (Taylor, 1986), is the only British survey of its type that we know

of, and an example of research that deals with both unemployment and employment. Levine and Leonard (1984) identify five
empirical studies (Saghir and Robins, 1973; Chafetz *et al.*, 1974;
Bell and Weinberg, 1978; Brooks, 1981; Schneider, 1981), plus
their own, which give some information on lesbian job
discrimination. Apart from the finding of relatively high levels
of anticipated and experienced discrimination, they offer some
tentative conclusions that discrimination is greater in the private
sector than in public sector organisations, and in medium or
large than in small organisations. This may partly be due to
strategies of self-employment or specialisation in particular
areas of work in, both of which may involve work in small
organisations. Organisations are often hostile places for
lesbians to live and work in. Hall (1989) has analysed in depth
the complex interpersonal strategies developed by lesbians for
maintaining personal integrity, in the face of double oppression.
The private experiences of lesbians and gay men in the public
domains of heterosexually dominated organisations might
suggest that a kind of 'social total institution' is in operation.
On the other hand, there is some particularly interesting
research by Schneider (1984) which suggests that, for some
lesbians, organisations can be places for more positive
relationships than for many heterosexual women.

In contrast, some organisations do operate with an explicit
and conscious ideology, working assumptions and practices,
that are not based on heterosexuality. Sometimes this may be
an important element in the actual foundation of the organisation, as, for example, with gay switchboards and gay advice
services. In other cases, non-heterosexual ideology and practice
may develop over time with changes in the membership of an
organisation, and the sexual orientation of the membership.
Weston and Rofel's (1985) case study of 'Amazon Auto
Repair', a small business of lesbian owners and lesbian workers,
is a very informative illustration of the complex interrelation of
sexuality and work, the possibilities for and limitations on
reformulating dominant divisions of people's public and private
worlds. Perhaps, above all, it shows up the fact that sexual
culture and economic class structure cannot easily be separated;
each is formed on the basis of the other. While sexuality can
be conceptualised as consumption (Lippert, 1977), it is also

production; while the politics of sexuality can be practised as struggles over the control of the body, they are also more variable encounters, in which control is not necessarily the prime strategic issue (Diamond and Quinby, 1984).

Sexuality and gender in organisations

The considerable variety of sources and approaches that are now recognised has prompted concern with the complexity of the interactions of sexuality and gender in organisations. While the recognition of the importance of interrelations between sexuality and gender, and especially gender divisions of work and authority is not new (see, for example, Hearn and Parkin, 1983), focused studies on those connections have followed on the earlier studies of harassment, discrimination and sexual relationships noted above.

The Sexuality of Organization (Hearn *et al.*, 1989) is a diverse and international collection which represents one attempt to move the debate to consider the various connections of sexuality and gender. It explores through both theoretical over-views and empirical case studies the intimate overlaps between sexuality, gender and organisations. In different ways, the contributors place sexuality as a very important element in the understanding of gendered organisational process(es), and not just something that is added on to the analysis. Thus, for example, Sheppard (1989, 142) argues that the notion of organi-sational structure as an objective, empirical and genderless reality is itself a gendered notion. One major reason for this is the presence of sexuality and sexual(ised) processes in organisa-tions. In particular, the pervasive dominance of heterosexuality in most organisations is emphasised. Theoretical reviews include those by Mills (1989) and Tancred-Sheriff (1989). The first shows the relevance of a wide variety of organisational liter-ature for the consideration of gender and sexuality, especially the production and reproduction of gendered identities. The second both critiques and develops labour process theory to analyse the relationship between the control function in organisations and the construction of gender and sexuality. Case studies presented in this collection include those on resi-dential care organisations (Parkin, 1989), lesbians in organisa-tions (Hall, 1989), and women managers (Sheppard, 1989).

A number of other writers have taken up these theories. Adkins (1992a, 1992b, 1995) has focused on the structuring of sexual labour in the service industries. Collinson and Collinson (1989; Collinson, 1992; Collinson *et al.*, 1990) have researched both men's sexuality on the shopfloor and in the finance sector, and in recruitment and selection processes. Cockburn's (1983, 1989, 1990, 1991) work is wide-ranging in considering the variety of ways that men maintain and reproduce power over women in organisations. This variety extends to the place of sexual domination and alongside and in relation to, say, labour market domination; the interrelations of different oppressions and social divisions; and the diversity of actions and interests of different groups of men, for example, by class, age, race and sexuality. She has, for example, analysed the sexual regimes of a large retail company, in terms of the power of two managerial forms: one controlled by traditionalist men 'at best gentlemanly, at worst, they saw women as fitted only for kitchen and nursery'; the other controlled by newer modernist men, in which women were expected to 'tolerate, join in, enjoy and retaliate in kind when sexual innuendo and jokes, the stock-in-trade of modern management, were employed' (Cockburn, 1991).

Pringle (1989a, 1989b, 1993) makes her prime focus gender and sexuality, particularly in bureaucracies and boss–secretary relationships there. She is insistent on the need to record the extent of gender and sexual power and domination in organisations, and she is also especially concerned to analyse the pervasiveness and complexity of power. In doing so, she draws critically on poststructuralist theory to chart the ways in which gender/sexual power relations operate in multiple directions and may be only understood more fully by attention to psychoanalytic, unconscious and fantasy processes. One potential difficulty of this kind of development is that the analysis of complexities and power can be interpreted, we would argue, falsely, as diluting power analysis.

What is particularly interesting is the way in which research on sexuality and gender in organisations is now developing internationally. This is both re-affirming the basic themes found in earlier work, and is developing new dimensions both through comparative studies and further theorising. Following Konecki's (1990) study of 'worker flirting' in a radio-electrical plant,

Haavio-Mannila has explored cross-cultural differences between attitudes to erotic relations (1994) and their consequences
(1995) in Denmark, Estonia, Finland, Russia and Sweden.
These latter two studies are not only cross-national but also
compare differences between flirting, falling in love and sexual
harassment, and between engineers, teachers and workers. In
particular they point to marked differences in organisational
environments in terms of both the amount of erotic signals and
cues, and the dominant attitudes, negative or positive, to erotic
interactions. The intersection of such elements can produce
organisational environments that are 'erotically peaceful',
'erotically tense', 'sexually harassing' and so on. Such studies
provide a framework for further complex comparative analyses
covering additional dimensions and locations.

In addition, two recent textbooks, one on organisational
behaviour and gender (Wilson, 1995), the other on critical
perspectives on organisational theory (Mills and Simmons,
1995) have recognised the importance of sexuality in organisations. These may assist further in making it more difficult to
exclude sexuality from future organisational analysis and
theoretical development.

CURRENT DEBATES AND CONTROVERSIES[2]

This section reviews a wide range of interrelated current
debates and controversies around sexuality both in general and
in respect of organisations.

Material oppressions and discursive constructions

One of the most general set of debates that has arisen from
much of the literature on organisations, gender and sexuality is
that two sub-perspectives may be recognised, often in some
kind of tension–however, this is a tension that may be seen not
as a problem but rather as dynamic and (re)productive. These
two sub-perspectives may be characterised as, firstly, that which
focuses on *material oppressions* and secondly, that which
focuses on *discursive constructions*. These two are sometimes
seen as in opposition as in some current debates 'between'
modernism and postmodernism or they may, however, be seen

as converging. Material oppressions are being understood in increasingly complex, differentiated and multiple ways, just as the (re)production of discourse and discursive constructions is a material accomplishment, and indeed an organisational and technological one too in present contexts.

To take the second approach first, perhaps the main lesson of the discursive perspective is the need to look beyond and to deconstruct the obvious, the dominant taken-for-granted, by which organisations are constructed and indeed analysed. In particular, this entails the deconstruction of those perspectives that hold, or seek to hold, dominant control within organisations, often the domination of the modernist project(s) and paradigm(s). In doing so, emphasis is shifted to the subtexts of organisations. Sexuality, or certain forms of sexual process, are examples of such subtexts. Discourses of and around organisations are themselves sexually-encoded.

In the sub-perspective focusing on material oppressions, organisations are sites and structures of oppression. To say that is not to demonise organisations, nor is it to ignore the positive or facilitative or creative aspects of organisations (see Giddens, 1979, on structure, as both constraining and facilitating agency). 'Creativity' can, of course, be accompanied by or even facilitate oppression.

One way of understanding oppression is to conceptualise it as a shorthand for series of *social processes*, by and through which *particular* dominant groups and classes oppress others in a wide variety of ways. It is difficult, for example, to reduce oppression by men to one single explanation. In speaking of the oppressed and oppression, we are referring to the way certain constructions or categories of people may be relatively consistently treated in ways that denigrate or undervalue or hurt or proscribe more favoured courses of action for them as individuals and/or collectivities. The variety of ways and arenas in and through which men (may) oppress include biological reproduction and the capacity to reproduce; sexuality; caring and nurturing; and violences. These can be thought of as types of reproduction of social life (other forms include paid employment and cultural forms). The forms that oppression may take range from direct violence and force to the indirect use of violence through hierarchy and the unfair allocation of resources, as is the case in most organisations. Thus for this pattern of oppression to continue, men also oppress *each other*– in the making of 'men', especially when as boys and young men engage in competition, in violence, in resistance, in oppressing themselves.

Accordingly, in both sub-perspectives, organisations can be understood as structured, gendered/sexualed, sexually-encoded (though not necessarily sexualised), reproductions. Thus organisations may be analysed in terms of cultural reproductive materialism, that is simultaneously discursive and material (Hearn, 1992, 1993).

What is sexuality?
A second significant question in the study of sexuality and organisations is what is meant by sexuality in the first place. Though few would restrict 'sexuality' to physical sexual contact or even to sexual-social relations, some commentators tend to limit sexuality to social practices relating to desire whereas others hardly distinguish sexuality from gender. A further dimension is the question of whether sexuality is understood primarily in conscious or even intentional terms or in less conscious or even unconscious terms. This in turn suggests different models of organisations–as action-based structures or sub-structures of unconscious processes. We have accordingly re-examined the meaning of sexuality which we introduced in the first edition (see pp. 53–8).

We now suggest the following definition of our use of sexuality. The term sexuality is used to refer to the social expression of or social relations or social references to physical, bodily desire or desires. These desires can be real or imagined, as in imagining the desires of others. They can be by or for others or for oneself. Others can be of the same or different sex, or even occasionally of indeterminate gender. In addition, Stone remarks that 'Despite appearances, human sex takes place mostly in the head' (1977, 483); indeed imagined or fantasised sexual relations may be as important a part of sexuality as observable sexual practices. Sexual practices may range from mild flirtation to sexual acts, perhaps with enclosure and/or penetration. While such acts may be accomplished willingly, unwillingly or forcibly by those involved, the notion of consent needs to be viewed with caution. It is important to emphasise that sexuality may include references to narcissistic, bisexual, homosexual, heterosexual and various other sexual preferences and practices, even though the notion of individual preference remains problematic. It should be added that a major focus of attention will be heterosexuality, necessitated by its dominance of most organisations. This emphasis should not be interpreted as a commentary on 'normality' or 'naturalness' in sexual relations or preferences. Sexuality is best seen as both a specific, and a wide-ranging, necessarily open-ended topic.

In addition to the question of desires within sexuality, there is a range of other relevant bodily states and experiences that relate to these desires, including puberty, pre-menstruation, pregnancy and menopause. Thus, to summarise, the definition of sexuality used here is the social expression of social relations to and social reference to bodily desire or desires, real or imagined, by or for others or for oneself, together with the related bodily states and experiences.

Sexuality is thus a specific set of phenomena and practices, as defined above; but it is also diverse. To reduce this broad range of powers, actions, thoughts and feelings just to sexual acts is likely to give an inaccurate, even sexist, view of sexual realities. Sexuality is no monolith; it includes and refers to the body and touch, emotion and desire, thought and fantasy, image and appearance.

Thus sexuality is a very broad category that can include numerous material, discursive elements and practices–sex, sexual relations, sexual relationships, sexual acts, sexual behaviours, sexual activity, sexual feelings, sexual orientations, sexual desires, sexual identities, sexual practices, sexual violences, sexual harassment, sexual fantasies, sexual experience(s), sexual domination, sexual abuse, sexualities. And furthermore, sexuality is not separable but is constructed, as in gender, *in relation to* sensuality, the body, birth, motherhood, fatherhood, violence, and much more. Gender and sexuality do not exist in isolation, but in their *specific* conjunctures with such divisions as age, ethnicity, class and bodily facility. And furthermore, the relationships of sexuality and sex, and gender and sex, are problematic, as are their popularization in certain discourses (Keller, 1987).

The study of sexuality, gender and organisations
These debates about the relationship of sexuality, sex and gender are not just matters of definition of the topics, they are also important for the very definition and development of the academic study of these topics.

Witz and Savage (1992) suggest that there is danger that an emerging 'sexuality paradigm' will obscure and deflect from the gender paradigm in organisations. Clearly, *'Sex' at 'Work'* covered at length the neglect of sexuality in organisations as did *The Sexuality of Organization* (Hearn *et al.*, 1989), in an attempt to rectify the omission. There was, however, no intention of establishing a separate field of sexuality and organisation or a secondary paradigm in competition with the analysis of gendered power relations (also see Hearn and Parkin, 1983, 1986–7, 1988). Both books developed analyses around the integral power relationships between gender, (hetero)sexuality and organisation. Nevertheless there is a paradox between the increasing focus on sexuality and not creating a separate object of analysis.

Furthermore, sexuality can be understood as *both* a foundation of gender (MacKinnon, 1982) and a focused aspect of gender relations. We would argue there is no necessary connection between studying sexuality and anti-modernism/postmodernism or between studying gender and modernism. Our own view is that sexuality is a fundamental aspect of the reproduction of patriarchies and patriachal relations.

A parallel issue that has been identified by Pringle (1989a, b), Bologh (1987, 1990) and others, is the way in which gender and sexuality may be 'added on' to previous non-gendered, non-sexualed analyses such as supposedly impersonal models of bureaucracy, Weberian or otherwise. 'Adding on' sexuality and gender is unsatisfactory (Sheppard, 1989). Organisational analyses, concepts and models need to speak directly of sexuality and gender, and not as an afterthought.

Feminist theories and sexuality
Recent feminist research and literature on sexuality has emphasised a number of different themes. First, it is important to recognise the international and cultural dimensions of feminist theory and practice including black feminism, feminism of

women, of colour and feminist perspectives on disability and age. From all these sources issues of sexuality, gender and power are raised even though there are differing social practices and social relations in the way in which sexuality is politicised in relation to women's lives. Second, there is the continuing concern with the intersection of sexuality and violence. While this connection is clearest in the cases of sexual assault, rape, pornography, prostitution, and child sexual abuse, what has been equally significant has been the exploration of this connection and continuum into coercive sex, pressurised sex and the eroticisation of dominance more generally (MacKinnon, 1982; Kelly, 1988). This perspective raises the question of the similarity and differences between women who are formally 'sex workers' and women who are not (Delacoste and Alexander, 1988). This focus leads to a third theme–critique of 'normal' male sexuality (Coveney *et al.*, 1984; Itzin, 1992) and 'normal' sexual relations, and in particular heterosexuality. One of the indirect effects of the scale of HIV/AIDS has been the intervention of governmental, medical and health agencies in the creation of official discourses around 'heterosexuality'. In the United Kingdom in particular there has been a considerable feminist debate around heterosexuality, and equally women's heterosexuality and heterosexual women. (*Feminism and Psychology*, 1992; Wilkinson and Kitzinger, 1993). Some of this is revisiting ground that was prominent at the beginnings of Second Wave feminism; some is attempting to develop accounts of sexual relations and sexual experiences that are not reductive to monolithic power structures or individual psychology.

This theme links with another focus of attention–that on women's pleasure and danger (for example, Vance, 1984). In substantive terms, this concerns both the general question of the relation of pleasure and desire for women, and the particular issue of women's relation to violence, pornography and sado-masochism (for example, Ardill and O'Sullivan, 1986). In more theoretical terms, these debates entail analysis of the relation-ship of sexual representation, sexual actions, sexual experience and the theorising of desire (Kristeva, 1980; Davies, 1990).

Feminism and Foucault

One favoured theoretical area for discussion has been around the tensions between feminism and Foucault (Ramazanglu, 1994; McNay, 1992; Sawicki, 1991; Diamond and Quinby, 1986). Since the publication of the first edition of this book, there has been a considerable increase in interest in the relationship of feminist theorising and Foucauldian theorising. We have already observed (pp. 56, 169) how Foucault's work has profound shortcomings in terms of his lack of engagement with sexual/gendered experience, and particularly in that which is painful and violating. He is not centrally concerned with gendered and sexualed categories like 'women' and 'men'. These shortcomings remain.

More generally, it can be argued that Foucault's perspective undermines or at least can be used to undermine feminism. However, to say that might be to assume that it is possible to speak of feminism in the singular. If one addresses feminisms, including those that are diverse and those that are themselves influenced by poststructuralism, then any such tension is more complex.

Whilst recognising these deficiencies and dangers, we see Foucault's work as of interest in a number of ways. First, and perhaps most importantly, he was expert at raising questions, not least about sexuality. Second, he addresses the contradictory relation of speech and silence in discourse, and specifically discourses on sexuality. This leads to a third insight that power is both productive and ubiquitous rather than repressive and confined to power-specific structures or processes. This is also especially significant with regard to sexuality. Indeed we think it is appropriate to speak of the power/sexuality relation paralleling the power/knowledge relation. He conceptualises sex and sexuality as effects of power rather than simply being pre-existing essences that are then constructed through power relations. Fourth, Foucault not only de-essentialises sex and sexuality, but cuts across the many theoretical debates on sexuality which have been cast in dichotomous terms–between essentialist and social constructionist accounts, between naturalistic and political accounts, between material and discursive accounts.

On the other hand, we see Foucault's work as potentially dangerous in taking the gender out of sexuality, in reducing sexuality to arbitrarinesses, and perhaps most significantly in justifying the sexual libertarianism of the some at the expense of the sexual domination of the others. This last theme–of the attempts to move beyond identity defined through sexuality and beyond social classification made by sexuality–has resources with his own life's projects, as recently explored in recent biographies (Eribon, 1992; Miller, 1993; Macey, 1993).

The critique of heterosexuality

In much of our own and others' work on sexuality, gender and organisations, a central theme has been the question of heterosexuality, and the attempt to move the debate away from essentialised and naturalised views of heterosexuality (for example, Hearn *et al.*, 1989). In a variety of texts, we have addressed heterosexuality and particularly men's heterosexuality, as the dominant form of sexuality; and subjected compulsory heterosexuality to critique. These critiques have been developed more fully elsewhere (for example Hearn *et al.*, 1989; Hearn, 1992). We have also developed an analysis of what is meant by sexual harassment to a wide range of sexualised activities including unwanted touch, joking, invasion of space, noise, all of which we seen as problematising heterosexuality. More generally, is it necessary to say that we see heterosexuality as problematic beyond its manifestation as overt coercion recognising it as an unequal social relationship which in turn structures most organisations. This all questions heterosexuality and recognises the range of its manifestations in terms of the wielding of power in organisations, both in interpersonal relations and organisational structuring.

In addition, these critiques of heterosexuality lead to the consideration of questions of the relation of surface/appearance and reality/knowledge–whether this is in terms of the specifics of the sexuality of dress (see pp. 149–50; Sheppard, 1989) or the general epistemological significance of looks and appearance for the analysis of gender (Hearn, 1987, pp. 11–15).

Capitalist labour market processes, sexuality and sexual harassment

Linked closely to these general theoretical debates is that around the status of 'the economic', and specifically capitalism in the possible construction of sexuality and sexual harassment. In our view 'organisation sexuality' (not 'organisational sexuality

ity' which is a term we especially criticise as unsatisfactory, as it privileges one term over the other) is not a specific product of capitalist labour market processes, though they are, along with many other processes of course, relevant. It is important to emphasise that sexual harassment cannot be 'explained' by capitalist labour market processes. In the first edition of this book we discuss in one section (see pp. 84–9) of chapter 5 ways in which dominant (patriarchal) constructions and themes of organisations could be said to construct sexuality. This included the extension of capitalist labour process theories in that direction. This is followed by a counter argument that sexuality can be understood as constructing organisations, or, put another way, that organisations are constructed by sexuality. These two chapters were followed by a further chapter on 'organisation sexuality', by which we mean the simultaneous operation of organisations and sexuality. In both the succeeding chapters, sexual harassment is discussed again. Sexuality, sexual harassment and organisation sexuality are thus analysed in a complex way that builds an argument step by step. We do not argue that sexuality and sexual harassment are primarily or exclusively the product of capitalism or capitalist social relations, as has been suggested (Adkins, 1992). Such an argument is one interpretation of our work which we do not accept, as we have written previously (Hearn and Parkin, 1994). This reading appears to be based on taking one part out of context of a wider analysis, and assuming that this partial analysis is the whole story of the first edition.

The dominant framework for understanding all of this is *patriarchal* social relations: capitalist labour market processes are *one instance* of patriarchal relations, not the explanation of organisation sexuality, be they sexual harassment or otherwise. Or to put this slightly differently, 'production relations, including capitalist ones, are after all also forms and matters of sexuality, procreation, nurture and violence' (Hearn, 1987, 101). Capitalism is one form of patriarchy.

These arguments are given further weight by recent cross-cultural and international research on sexual harassment and 'erotic relations' in organisations (see p. 172) both in terms of the persistence of patriarchal relations and the importance of cultural variation and difference.

The concept of sexual work in organisations

A related contentious issue is the relationship of work/labour to sexuality. Rather than just seeing work as something that can be sexualised, we prefer to argue that a much closer relationship between work and sexuality is possible. This entails the very definition of what sexuality and work are. Thus, in some contexts, it may be useful to think of sexuality in organisations, and indeed elsewhere, as a form of work. A slightly different approach is to see organisations as arenas of sexual labour, just as they are for emotional labour and other forms of labour. Accordingly, an important concept in much of our own and others' work is that of sexual work/labour and sexual labour power (see pp. 61, 98, 102–3, 148–9 and elsewhere). These concepts are also developed elsewhere (for example, Hearn, 1987). For this we are indebted to Bland and her colleagues (1978) who had previously written on the selling of sexuality as part of labour-power. As we say 'sexuality is thus both officially incorporated (in the body) and literally marginalised (p. 102). Furthermore, it is necessary to reiterate that in our reference to the 'reserve of sexual labour' in the first edition (p. 85), we are *not* referring to the 'reserve army of labour' under capitalism as used by Beechey (1978, 1982) and Bruegel (1982); rather we are referring, as elsewhere, to the 'reserve' of women's sexual labour that can be brought into direct and indirect appropriation and exploitation under patriarchy and patriarchal relations–or as we put it earlier 'sexual harassment may be a *form of labour in which women become commodities for men*' (p. 85).

Patriarchy and sexuality

Our approach in this book, whilst acknowledging the importance of discourse, discursive constructions and discursive practices, fundamentally builds upon materialist, particularly feminist materialist, theories of sexuality. In saying this, we are not referring to those materialisms in which the material is defined on an equivalent to or a direct product of employed work in production. Rather the materialism in question is that which privileges the existence of the body and the gendered control of bodies. In such a materialistic view, it is through the powers, constructions and controls of and on the body as sexuality that gendered people are produced and reproduced.

Such powers, constructions and controls of and on the body are thus both material and discursive.

Furthermore, within patriarchy and patriarchal relations the dominant, though not the only, powers, constructions and controls are those of men over women in heterosexuality. Simultaneously, such material and discursive processes *also* produce and reproduce 'women' and 'men' (Wittig, 1992; Butler, 1990; Hearn, 1994b). The operation of discourse is thus in this sense a part of the process of the maintenance, or subversion, of patriarchy, as, for example, in recent debates on re-eroticising the organisation and its critique (Brewis and Grey, 1994).

The framework we have developed has been to place sexuality, and particularly heterosexuality, in the context of patriarchy, and particularly public patriarchy. Accordingly, power, and specifically men's power, is understood as the root of the power of sexuality even though this process in turn constructs 'men'. Men's power in and through dominant forms of heterosexuality, that is hierarchic heterosexuality, is seen as one of the major bases of patriarchy and public patriarchy. The specific formation that we have labelled 'organisation sexuality' is a power-imbued and paradoxical effect of such public patriarchal relations. Again, it is important to emphasise both the persistence of patriarchies and patriarchal relations over time and space as well as the specification of different cultural forms.

FUTURE ISSUES

This section outlines some key issues that have become increasingly important in our recent works and thinking and which we consider are likely to have greater importance for both future practice and theory.

The deconstruction and transformation of sexuality, gender and organisations
a)   *From subtexts to multiple oppressions*
The idea of subtext is drawn from psychoanalytically-informed cultural studies (for example, Wood, 1987), in which the meaning of texts is understood more fully from their deep structure rather than their surface structure. For example, in

terms of sexuality, there has been extensive discussion of the ways in which men's overt heterosexuality may obscure a subtext of men's homosexuality/homosociality (for example, Irigaray, 1985; Hearn, 1992). In such analyses, women, heterosexually defined, may be understood as partly constructed as currency/signs between men.

Rather similarly, within organisational processes, some issues are organised in terms of overt politics, while others are organised outside of formal decision-making processes. The limitation of exploring only the conscious processes of organisations is recognised in many analyses of power. Issues organised outside of overt politics do not disappear but form part of organisational subtexts with the processes which locate them there being part of the often unrecognised, unacknowledged and unconscious processes. The subtext is also a powerful narrative and issues brought to organisational consciousness, whether for organisational members or organisational theorists, make clearer the components of these narratives. When gender was recognised as an issue, the subject of malestream theorising in the social sciences, and particularly organisational theory was demonstrated. Feminist theorising brought issues to consciousness, demonstrating the power of the male subtext to marginalise gender, and exclude and control women through the operation of public men, public patriarchies, public masculinities (Hearn, 1992).

Consciousness around gender demonstrated its obvious and powerful connection with sexuality, particularly with the increasing numbers of sexual harassment studies. The subtext exposed (sic) here was that of the male sexual narrative, further recognised as heterosexual, often mysogynist and homophobic. For example, of the powerful male subtext of deep mysogyny in the Church of England came to the fore when women were allowed to enter the priesthood.

Similarly, the emergence of policy and practice in the field of 'race relations' demonstrated a subtext of white racism. Attempts to recognise a subtext around age and ageism are increasing, for example, in redefinitions of what is meant by old age and retirement (Biggs, 1993; Bytheway, 1994).

The politics of disability highlight what is possibly and arguably the most powerful subtext of all. Increasing numbers of women and black people are in some organisations, so that those organisations have to respond to their issues, including challenges to dominant subtexts. Sexual harassment and other sexually abusive practices are being challenged. However, the relative absence of older people and disabled people means that their comparable issues are rarely raised. The subtext here is a powerful one and enmeshed with wider economic and political forms which demand that those in work increase output and productivity and performance through strategies of appraisal and performance related pay. This renders even more powerful a subtext which unconsciously defines organisational members in terms of physical and emotional strength. Sometimes it is brought to consciousness through organisational statements such as a bank to a job applicant who failed to progress beyond his second interview when declaring a depressive illness from which he was fully recovered. The bank said they did not employ anyone with anxiety, depression, nervous disorder or back trouble (Channel 4, *Pulse*, 17.2.94). One of the authors was in contact with a friend who had an amputation. This brought to consciousness much more awareness of the different paces of life. The speeding up of organisational life, through its demands to produce more, highlighted the growing gulf between the pace to which she was expected to perform and the pace dictated to the disabled person through the time and energy devoted to basic tasks of feeding, dressing and hygiene. Able-bodyism is an obvious part of *being in organisations* even when certain tasks are designated as for disabled people. Its very obviousness hides the powerful subtext and screening procedures which ensure that the organisation employs the able bodied and exclude those, through illness and early retirement, who cannot keep up the pace.

These subtexts can be viewed as separate strands added on to each other or intertwined with each other, but still separate. Another way is to recognise the subtexts as interconnected with the recognition of links between all of them, gender/sexuality, gender/sexuality/emotionality (Parkin, 1993; Hearn 1993), age/ class (Arber, 1989), disability (Oliver, 1990; Morris, 1991). Maybe these are not separate subtexts but rather the recognition of the multiplicity of oppressions in organisations would indicate the general subtext is that organisation = oppression. This analysis would move away from categorising and dividing oppressions in a way which would be competitive or 'adding on' and move towards the recognition of common themes and practices and interconnectedness.

Notions of hierarchies of oppression link with notions of categories of oppression which are compartmentalised as separate entities needing separate theorising. The subtext of organisation as oppression will always remain a massive unconscious process as the various oppressions around gender, sexualities, age, race, disability, appearance, emotionality are ranked and separated. The interconnectedness of these oppressions does not prevent the separate analysis of their ideologies and processes in organisations. Setting them up in competition diverts attention from the analysis of their interrelations, both within organisations and to organisations, as well as their relationship to the public/private divisions and differences. Stacey (1981) recognised the partial nature of sociological theory which was developed from the organisational world of labour relations, and took for granted the domestic sphere. This partial theory began to be redressed as feminist theory developed theorising around such issues as the private and personal, reproduction, family, and violence. The further development of theory around disabled, bereaved, ill, mentally ill, older and dependent people will demonstrate that this theorising is not just about 'private' life but about the powerful subtexts of oppressive and exclusionary organisational practices. Exclusion, categorisation and ranking are organisational processes which reduce resistance by reducing recognition of certain experiences. These processes operate both inside and outside organisations.

Organisational analyses around paradigms and metaphors have generally developed with little conscious recognition of subtexts. This links to Stacey's (1981) theory of the partiality of organisation theory being written exclusively around the public world. Similarly, we would argue that another partial theory is that which focuses on conscious processes and ignores the subtexts of organisational oppression. There is a need to recognise the tension between conscious and unconscious processes as between public and private definitions. These debates around the partiality of the malestream have been further complicated by the impact of postmodernism. Despite the disclaimer of being anti-grand theory, postmodernism has usually emerged both as such and genderless. In its focus on subjectivity, one might assume an accommodation to theorising around organisational oppression. Alternatively, the under-mining of materialist explanations of such oppressions could be argued as an even more powerful silencing, obscuring of power and thus a further subtext. The previous multiplicity of paradigms has thus, to some extent, been superseded by the multiplicity of oppressions. Meanwhile, those sets of multiplica-tions have been met by another set, namely those of postmodernism (Hearn and Parkin, 1993, 151). There is also the recognition that all oppressions contribute to the reproduc-tion and reinforcement of the others as well as being in contradiction with each other and in a contentious relationship to new theories. This is dealt with in an ambiguous way, to say the least, in most postmodern writing–often by reducing oppressions to differences (see Hearn and Parkin, 1993).

b)   *From sexuality to violence and the maintenance of subtexts and multiple oppressions*
The link between gender, sexuality and violence is most obvious with the recognition of sexual harassment, sexual violence and sexual abuse in organisations. Recent and current research on residential care institutions has demonstrated how a particular setting has highlighted sexual/physical violence towards vulner-able residents and the limitations of complaints procedures (Parkin and Green, 1994). While increasing numbers of sexual harassment studies demonstrate both the power of male heterosexuality and subtexts of men's violence in organisations, it is necessary and important not to ignore the harassment and violence that may be done by women and children in organisations.

The recognition of violence done by men within partriachy and capitalism clearly affects women and men quite differently. Not only do women suffer the violation of men's violence, but men experience each other's violence, whether through the military, in the upbringing as boys or on the streets. Violence may be done in the upbringing of boys as they are prepared for a male heterosexual able-bodied narrative through the control of certain emotions, violent sports, corporal punishment, rough play. Furthermore, violence in organisations, physical or otherwise, may, if conceived broadly, include the ridiculing of political correctness, the abusive use of language, and the various underminings of women through the creation of a backlash. On the other hand, such a perspective can mean that violence as violation blurs into power relations. These various violences can themselves be ways of maintaining both the subtexts already described, and indeed the complexity of multiple oppressions in both particular organisations and organisation more generally.

This raises the question of the usefulness of developing a violence perspective on organisations, in terms of making violence explicit, identifying different relations of different organisations to violence, the structure and process of violence in organisations, and the presence of violence in organisational work and cultures (Hearn, 1994a).

Particularities of sexuality, gender and organisation
a)   *Particular organisational settings*
A further set of complexities and contentions derive from the engagement with the particular, namely the specific form that processes of sexuality and gender take in particular organisations. For example, the publication of scandals in a variety of residential care settings moves us to consider further issues around sexuality, gender and violence in particular settings (Levy and Kahan, 1991).

The particular organisational setting of residential care offers a 'case study' approach, which exemplifies the connection of gender and sexuality, but draws us to consider the extremes of vulnerability of residents, increasingly very old, very dependent, very damaged, very disabled. The setting itself is complex and contradictory, located as it is between public and private. These are 'homes' where people live, but located in the public world of organisations. The units are self-contained and organisationally and ideologically isolated from public scrutiny and management scrutiny. Scandals have highlighted exploitation and abuse of vulnerable residents and also staff. The model of 'home' merges with a model of 'total institution', more to do with control than care, and gives rise to a potentially very exploitative situation where private rule and public rule merge (Parkin, 1989). The interconnection of gender and sexuality are apparent when male harassment of female staff to keep them quiet merges with male abuse of children which takes place in a particularly explotative setting. A recent study of issues of sexuality in residential care demonstrates levels of sexual abuse and homophobia (Parkin and Green, 1994). Detailed studies of the particular dynamic of sexuality and gender in particular organisations are urgently needed.

b) *Policies, practices and politics*
Many organisations adopt covering statements on equal opportunities, encompassing not only policies for gender and sexuality, but also statements about race, age, disability, for example. The effectiveness of such policies can only be judged through fundamental changes in organisational structures and reduction in sexual harassment. Cockburn's (1991) study of four organisations in respect of equal opportunities policies and practices identified the 'short agenda' of most organisations where a tokenistic and minimalistic approach was adopted to keep the organisation within the law. 'Long agenda' changes are more fundamental and involve a vision from below, with a restructuring of organisation from the basis of the most disadvantaged members.

In a recent study of residential care establishments (Parkin and Green, 1994) one of the issues identified was the presence or absence of complaints procedures for residents. This is not yet a restructuring from the basis of the most disadvantaged members of the organisation, but it is a recognition of the need for protection from abuse and exploitation. However, the study so far demonstrates the lack of effectiveness of such measures, especially when the route for the complaint is often through the internal hierarchy, which is imposing the exploitation in the first place. What is needed is a politics of equal opportunities which will be judged on its meaningfulness when the most vulnerable members of an organisation can change their situation through a fundamental change in power relations. Such organisational policies, practices and politics are indicative and constitutive of the politics of sexuality throughout society: the heterosexual domination of lesbian, gay and other sexualities (for example,

Burke, 1993; Hall, 1995). Sexuality, gender and organisation can be usefully studied through the analysis of practice and policy as part of the politics of organisation sexuality.

There are numerous legal and policy changes that have either occurred since the first edition or are in process of current debate. Relevant policy areas include: prisons, secure units for children, the armed forces; pornography; child care practices; adoption and fostering; abortion; sex education; housing and homelessness following sexual violence; age of consent; court practices, such as use of child witnesses and video evidence.

The history of sexuality, gender and organisations
a)   *History and historical location*
Such political changes are of course not just matters of the present and recent past, they are also matters of long-term historical concern and the very construction of history 'itself'. Indeed, the exclusion of organisations, gender and sexuality from many malestream accounts of history has to be contended with. Rewriting history includes writing in a history of organisations, gender and sexuality. For example, nineteenth century industrialisation can be reread as also a history of gender and sexuality in both public and private (Walby, 1986; Hearn, 1992). Late nineteenth century change includes a growing explicitness in concern not just about sexualisation of offices (Aron, 1987) but also the beginnings of women's/worker's/union resistance to sexual harassment by some women and men. A strike in Nelson, from December 1891 to March 1892, was at least in part a response to 'immoral language and conduct' by one of the overlookers (Fowler, 1985). In such ways changing over time are changing relationships between men and women, increasing the very categorisations of men, women, masculinity, femininity, gender, sexualities. Discourses around rationality, biology, medicine, psychiatry, morality and sexuality have emerged and offered different constructions and categorisations of these and other relevant concepts (Hearn, 1992). Historical transformations of gender relations, including representations of sexuality, masculinity and femininity, have entailed fundamental changes in public/private relations, with the growth of 'the public', especially in terms of public men, public masculinities and public patriarchies. However, further

examination of historical changes needs to go hand in hand with an enquiry as to how far there has been fundamental change in gendered power relations.

Contradictions lie in the new forms of patriarchies. The growth in size and complexity of the public domains produce new orders of men's power both individual and collective. Yet, within these are the seeds of post-public patriarchies bringing about their own possible de(con)struction. These conditions produce two major contradictions within which public men exist: 'First, there is the contradiction between *publicisation*– the dominance of the public–and the *fracturing of experience* in the public domains. Second, there is the contradiction between *the consolidation of men as a gender class* and the *fragmentation of men and masculinities* as the monolith of 'white heterosexual able-bodied men' is increasingly shown to be a myth' (Hearn, 1992, 228). There is a major need for research that addresses history and historical location, including questions of contradiction, in relation to change and continuity of sexuality, gender and organisation.

c) *Back to the problem of men*

A final issue that we wish to raise in this postscript is the way in which these concerns return us to the historical problem of men. This is not only in terms of men's violence, men's power, men as a gender class, but also slightly more subtly in the reformulation of new identities for men, such as the 'new(ish) man' (Mintel, 1994). Such reformulations may be further ways of obscuring relations of organisations, gender and sexuality. They are also another part of the history of sexuality, gender and organisations. As already noted, the sexual dynamics of men, and particularly relations between men, are especially complex in many organisations. While most organisations are dominated by heterosexuality and heterosexual men, this system usually operates through homosociable/homosocial/ homosexual relations between men, in which women may be reduced to commodities or signs between men. This theme fits with well established anthropological work (for example, Levi-Strauss, 1949; Rubin, 1975); it has also been taken up in poststructuralist feminism (for example, Irigaray, 1985; Game, 1989). And it is an emerging aspect of the recent analysis of men in organisations and management (for example, Hearn, 1992; Roper, 1996). These debates also highlight difficulties of the very terminology, 'homosociability', 'homosociality' and 'homosexual'. Whatever words are used, it is clear that in many organisations desire between men and men's preference for men is paramount. Research on the problem of men in these and other contexts is necessary.

CONCLUSION AND RESEARCH PRIORITIES

When we first wrote this book we were faced with the obvious and therefore paradoxical omission of sexuality in the study of organisations. In writing this postscript for the revised edition we have attempted to update the text and engage with subsequent debates and controversies in the field. This involves us in both clarifying our original ideas and broadening them to engage with wider issues. In the light of this, we conclude by summarising the following research priorities:

- The study of the relationship of sexuality and gender in organisations to other subtexts and thus multiple oppressions.
- The study of the interface between sexuality and violence in organisations.
- The study of the particular dynamics of particular organisations.
- The study of policies, practices and politics around sexuality, gender and organisations.
- The development of the historical sociology of sexuality, gender and organisations and the placing of contemporary studies in an historical perspective.
- The study of the problem of men in sexuality, gender and organisations.

All these research questions are issues for theoretical attention. Sexuality, gender and organisations are simultaneously material and discursive, hence the notion of discursive/material/ sexual practices.

Notes

FOREWORD

1. Marshall's (1984, 1) description of the backcloth to her research on women managers as 'fertile chaos' makes complete sense to us. We would also like to endorse her more gendered position on the humanisation of organisational analysis.
2. Much of this and the following paragraph are adapted from Hearn and Parkin (1984).
3. The seminar series has been organised under other titles since, including 'Women, Men and Organisations' and 'Gender, Power and Organisations'.

CHAPTER 1 SEXUALITY APPEARS

1. A British case is that of Cecil Parkinson, former chairman [sic] of the Conservative Party, who resigned from the Cabinet in October 1983 following his sexual relationship with his secretary, Sara Keays, and his fathering of her child (Keays, 1985). A contrasting American case is Mary Cunningham's (1984) exposure of sexual harassment in the Bendix boardroom.
2. The concept of patriarchy is open to many different interpretations and is the subject of intense debates. Some approaches emphasise the power of the father; others use the term to refer to male domination in a more general way; others, including some feminists, reject the concept as being unhelpful and ahistorically rigid. We find the term useful as one description of the power and domination of men, maleness, fatherhood and organisation, and their interrelationships.
3. This is part of the broad thesis within *The Archaeology of Knowledge* (Foucault, 1972). A recent discussion of the theme of discontinuity is in Poster (1984, 74–8).
4. Weber's theory of rationalisation applies not only and most obviously to economic life but also to more qualitative pursuits, such as culture

and aesthetics. Desexualisation could be a means of subordinating sexuality itself to the economic, or of rationalising the *form* of sexuality to produce more quantified variants. The growth of the pseudo-science of sexology would be relevant here.

5. Burrell (1984, 110−2) uses Goffman's (1968) analysis of total institutions to examine in a preliminary way 'resistance to organisational desexualisation'.

6. While there may be occasional exceptions to this statement (e.g. Steele, 1975), they still remain within the post-Human Relations framework (see chapter 2).

7. This parallels the use of the organisation as a defence by individuals and groups, particularly under stress as discussed by Menzies and Jacques (see chapter 2).

8. While particular sources and sites of power, for example, the wage relationship, may clearly have an impact on sexuality in organisations, it would be mistaken to reduce all sources of power to a single cause. Furthermore, simple notions of cause and effect do seem especially inappropriate in analysing sexuality. Beyond this there are important questions around the connection between what Cixous (1980) calls logocentrism and phallocentrism. Taking this seriously would seem to question all ideologies (Griffin, 1982).

CHAPTER 2   THE SEARCH FOR LITERATURE

1. This argument is elaborated by Child (1969) in terms of management thought serving both technical and legitimatory purposes.

2. For example, Larrain (1979, 46) suggests that: 'Ideology . . . appears as a sublimation in consciousness of the limitations of human practice which leads to the negation of social contradictions'.

3. Note, for example, Taylor's (1947, 46) statement that 'There is one illustration of the application of the principles of scientific management with which all of us are familiar, and with which most of us have been familiar since we were small boys . . . the management of a first-class American baseball team'.

4. Both managerial control and super ego, through excessive control, produce repression.

5. The relationship of organisational and especially managerial practice to Freudian and other psychoanalytic interpretations is a complex area, to which further attention is given below. At this stage we note that organisational and managerial authority in many ways parallels authority in the patriarchal family, against and in relation to which there are many resistances, internalisations and projections.

6. The disciplined control of the body in the factory and the office is comparable to the concerns of Foucault (1977) in his historical review of the custodial and institutional monitoring of the person qua body.

7. In Classical Theory and the associated managerial practice, the silence of asexuality creates the sexuality of persons just as the recognition of

persons simply as behaviours negates persons.

8. Mayo (1969, Chs 1 and 2) draws extensively on the work of the Industrial Fatigue Research Board of the British Medical Research Council, created in 1920.

9. This remains undefined by Mayo.

10. An unclear reference to the significance of the 'beneficial' effects of this information gathering by the nurse is noted by Mayo (1960, 70).

11. Contrast can be drawn with the research policy in the interviewing programme with the Western Electric Company where women were selected to interview women, and men to interview men (1960, 80).

12. These workers are repeatedly referred to by Mayo as 'girls' and 'girl workers', a practice that continues even in recent accounts (Pugh, Hickson and Hinings, 1983).

13. We are grateful to Peter Hitch for this concept.

14. Note, for example, Mayo's work on 'The Meaning of "Morale"' (1960, ch. 5), drawing extensively on the work of Janet and Freud. Indeed Mayo and Matthewson were from 1919 '. . . the first in Australia to use psychoanalysis as a therapeutic'. (Trahair, 1984, 105).

15. It must be stated very clearly that the identity of the woman, '. . . a highly trained and experienced Cambridge graduate, married, one child . . .' (sic) who undertook the 'greater part of the investigation' (p 6) is unrecorded. This omission by the male editor is glaring, especially as the '. . . book stands almost as originally drafted in report form. . .' (p 11). We are reminded of the use of women as informants and interviewers in the Hawthorne Experiments. The implicit sexism of the Mass Observation study has links with a more explicit racism in a vicious attack on the Austrian psychologist Marie Jahoda and her work on socio-psychological problems of factory life. She is criticised for her 'imperfect command of working language', and her generalised conclusions which happen to include the description of the management-worker relations as 'patriarchal'. These remarks on research methodology and sexism/racism should be seen in the context of men's uses of women within organisational sociology as peripheral researchers (Sheriff and Campbell, 1981).

16. A sociogroup refers to preferences arising from work in a group, such as task performance; a psychogroup arisen from personal preferences, such as external association.

17. The post-war period in Britain was one of major social and political change, in which not only was there a considerable growth in state welfare provision and the impact of welfare professions, but also a shift away from the war economy and the industrial work of women. A psychodynamic perspective on the deleterious effects of maternal deprivation amongst children in institutional care coincided conveniently with social and economic pressure on women to return to former domestic roles.

18. Very useful survey and discussion of different strands within feminism are to be found in Jaggar and Struhl (1978) and Elshtain (1981).

19. The critique of the hierarchical organisation and indeed preference for

the small group as the fundamental organising unit is a recurrent element in feminist theory and practice. In some versions of radical and anarchist feminism the very idea of organisation is held to be dominated by men, and so subject to critical theory and practice.

20. Co-writing as a woman and a man, this present study is informed by feminism but cannot be said to be feminist, as men cannot be feminists.

21. Leeds TUCRIC (1983) lists 73, mainly British, general publications and 11 British trade union publications. Alliance Against Sexual Coercion (1980) lists 171, mainly American, publications on sexual harassment to that date, including ten surveys. Other recent surveys include Morewitz (1981), Meyer et al. (1981), and Dziech and Weiner (1984) (Oxford University Students Union Women's Committee, 1984). Critical commentaries include Wilson (1983) and Krut and Otto (1984).

CHAPTER 3 THE PROCESS OF RESEARCH

1. Willis (1976, 136) discusses the way in which positivism's 'recognition of a *technical* inability to record all that is relevant—and its yielding of this zone to another technique ("qualitative" methodology)—. . . may actually preserve its deepest loyalty; the preservation of its object of enquiry truly as "object"'.

2. Sagarin (1978, 268 ff.) suggests four major problems in sex research: *ethical*, *ideological* (i.e. researchers' biases), *social* (the effects on behaviour and fulfilment), and *normative*. More entrenched problems arise from the established male domination of sexology and sex research, for example Ellis, Kinsey, Masters and Johnson (Jackson, 1984).

3. Clinical and sexological research has itself inherited a strangely quantitative tradition.

4. This list is adapted from Read (1982, 21). The inclusion or exclusion of non-contact harassment, such as pin-ups, is an important area of difference in surveys (Hearn, 1985a, 122−4).

5. For example, intentional harassment may not be noticed; unintentional harassment may be perceived as harassment.

6. This also applies to the narration of the research process.

7. Lehmann and Young (1974) suggest as possible techniques legal and adversarial involvement, ethnomethodology, community organising, accidents and scandals. Although these concentrate on technological scandal, e.g. pollution, the same can apply to sexual scandals.

8. This is comparable to the way so-called 'quality' papers report research findings on the question of sexuality (Rawnsley, 1985; Vines, 1985).

CHAPTER 4 SEXUALITY AND POWER

1. For a useful note on the debate between medical, physiological and the social, see Ryan (1985, 181−3) on the Donner−Money differences.

2. This false equation parallels Feldberg and Glenn's (1979) comments on

the use of gender models and job models for women and men. The problematic sexuality of men is explored in Metcalf and Humphries (1985).

3. The 'needs of capitalism' arguments can easily slip to a crude functionalism, justifying a lack of serious attention to the subject.

4. The sexology studies provide a mass of detailed information narrowly defining sexuality and the problems in a clinical and technical way.

5. A philosophical, especially analytical, approach to such questions is to be found in Soble (1980), and particularly the essay by Taylor (1967–8), which distinguishes 'being in love', 'sexual desire', 'sexual arousal', 'sexual excitement', and 'feeling sexy'.

6. Appealing though Foucault's (1981) and indeed Burrell's (1984) analyses of sexuality are, they contain an important flaw. This stems from their tendency to posit *overarching* structures of knowledge and control that *lie outside* sexuality and that accordingly produce or construct sexuality. Sexuality is relegated to the category of an object (or as if an object) to be moulded from outside itself, rather than seen as a series of relations. At times Foucault's work, despite his avowed critique of structuralism, approaches its own form of overdetermination, a kind of totalisation of non-totalisation(s). These analyses are also unsatisfactory in a second, and paradoxically almost opposite way. Foucault is profoundly ambiguous on the place of that which is *not determined*. For Foucault this is the possibility of transgression, across margins and silences: the power of the excluded, the deviant, not merely to act in a predefined role to strike back, but to act outside all of that. Sexuality has become a 'leftover' category, that which is left over when other 'more rational' analysis has been exhausted. Taken together, however, these critiques do point to the complex interrelation of power and sexuality.

7. Despite his interest in sexuality, Foucault (1981) says very little of sexual relations as they could be described or experienced, of even *women* and *men*, of gender relations. Despite his own critique of experts, intellectuals and ideologues, he himself produces another bland, male gloss on history. He tells us little of the lives of others, including women. In *The History of Sexuality Volume 1*, you would hardly know women existed or that sex was something usually involving more than one person. He writes of 'sexuality' hardly mentioning sex. He indexes 'women' on four pages out of 159. There is no 'reference' to 'men'. Men, male, masculinity have been taken for granted; the whole is abstract, neutered and implicitly patriarchal. His categories are sex- and gender-blind.

8. See, for example, Vance (1984), Dickson (1985) for explicit attempts to focus on women's sexuality.

9. This is particularly important within object relations psychology, and related feminist developments by, amongst others, Eichenbaum and Orbach (1982).

10. In the light of Foucault's work, increasing 'explicitness' may also be treated with some doubt. The creation of sexual discourses may be a means, however indirect, of power, of certain people claiming the power to speak over sexuality, and even desexualising it.

11. These definitions are developed from Hearn and Parkin (1984; 1985). "'Desire'", MacKinnon (1982, 2) comments, is a 'a term parallel to "value" in marxist theory to refer to that substance felt to be primordial or aboriginal but posited by the theory as social and contingent'.

12. Rubin (1984, 282) argues that a 'sex hierarchy' of sexual preferences based on the power of moral and similar judgements has more in common with ideologies of racism than true ethics. Connell (1983, 41–2) argues against 'a graduated scale of sex-power, as seems to be implied in some sociological discussions of "sexual stratification" (bearded Marlboro advertising executives with 100, pregnant teenage lesbians with 0) . . . gender categories, in social interaction as well as ideology, are composite, constructed'.

13. There are of course further differences between these various parties, interests, even sub-classes (Hearn, 1983, ch. 4).

14. This concept is developed further in Hearn (1987) in relation to the power of men.

CHAPTER 5 THE ORGANISATIONAL CONSTRUCTION OF SEXUALITY

1. The thesis that large organisations are producers of greater collective and class consciousness is a central part of the Marxian tradition. Large organisations may in the broad historical perspective produce comparable effects upon consciousness and alliances around sexuality.

2. Vaught and Smith (1980) refer to the presence of 'encapsulated enclaves' with strong mechanical solidarity within United States coal mines.

3. The question of sexuality, and particularly homosexuality and the use of prostitutes, as 'security risks', looms large in popular portrayals of the security services, for example in Britain, the Profumo case; the Burgess–Philby–Maclean case; the cases of Sir Geoffrey Harrison, (British Ambassador to Moscow 1965–8), Edward Scott (senior diplomat in Prague 1956), Rhona Ritchie (senior diplomat in Tel-Aviv in 1981), all of whom became involved in sexual entanglements; and the Sir Anthony Blunt case (Parry, 1985). A relevant popular account of the activities of 'sex spies' is provided by Boar and Blundell (1984, 121–46).

4. A vivid account of the sexual ambiguities of such work is given in Beattie (1985); a more academic analysis is provided by Rasmussen and Kuhn (1976).

5. Tomkinson (1982) discusses the close interrelation of sexploitation agencies, police corruption and protection rackets in London.

6. The hazards of making a 'soft porn' calendar for Unipart were shown in the independent television film *The Making of a Model* (1985) with women models having to position their bodies for the camera of Patrick Litchfield to avoid the display of tropical insect bites. One model halfway through a camera sequence was heartily sick before continuing her work.

7. The undervaluation of most of these types of people also contributes

to the undervaluation of their sexuality.

8. Graphic descriptions of this problem are found in Boyle (1977).

9. The understanding of the effects of severity of initiation (e.g. Aronson and Mills, 1959), is clearly relevant to the effects of sexual initiation on subsequent sexual life in organisations.

10. A woman fire officer was found to have had to endure at least two forms of initiation with the London Fire Service, including being strapped to a fire ladder and having urine poured over her and suffered indecent exposure from one of the male fire officers (Ballantyne, 1985).

11. Limitations on prison visiting may clearly contribute to marital breakdown and divorce (Rosie, 1983).

12. Okely (1978a; 1978b) writes of the 'processes of body containment' that comprise part of the 'curriculum of the unconscious' in girls' boarding schools. Arnold and Laskey's (1985) history of life in an Irish orphanage notes the girls' entire ignorance of sex, their subsequent vulnerability to commands and the merest affection, frequently resulting in 'illegitimate' births.

13. An example of such allegations was as part of controversies surrounding the Johnson-Mathey banking collapse in 1985 in Britain.

14. This raises particular difficulties when spouses separate, for example, the wives of male clergy who are either divorced or widowed or do not share their partner's beliefs (cf. note 11).

15. An interesting comparison is that of 'less masculine' male nurses as subordinates to 'less feminine' female senior nurses (Gray, 1985).

16. Up to about ten years ago, at least one social work qualifying course used 'appearance' as one evaluative criterion for admission. It remains an issue in the selection of teachers and in the practice of social work in court and other formal settings.

17. The Policy Study Institute's confidential report to the Metropolitan Police was revealed in the press on 29 October 1983 and refers to the 'cult of masculinity' within that force.

18. Waldron *et al.*'s (1984) study of the occurrence of scrotal cancer in the West Midlands, during the period 1936–76, found three-fifths of cases had been employed in jobs entailing some exposure to oil, such as tool setters and tool fitters.

19. The heading is taken from the newspapers at the time (Berlinguer, 1985, 5).

20. Close working involvements can of course arise for many other reasons, such as participative structures and management styles.

21. Such personal 'exposure' both of direct and indirect feelings and stresses, has sexual connotations. Counter-transference of a sexual nature can become a 'double-bind' both encouraged and condemned as 'over-exposure'.

22. The sexual mythology surrounding powerful people such as royalty, pop and film stars and business magnates is well documented, for example, Summers (1985) study of Marilyn Monroe. For a general popular account see Nicholas (1985). Such powerful people may become involved, socially and sexually, with others of power, such as diplomats and

politicians, leading to security risk and scandals (see note 3 and p. 70).

23. Zita (1982, 162) and MacKinnon (1982, 16) both discuss the relationship of hierarchy and heterosexuality; Reynaud (1981) relates hierarchy and men's fear of homosexuality; Hearn (1987) locates 'hierarchic heterosexuality' as a major institution of patriarchy.

24. A closed space of special interest is that of 'car space' and journeys within cars which are usually less closely monitored (Hearn, 1982b).

CHAPTER 6   THE SEXUAL CONSTRUCTION OF ORGANISATIONS

1. The term 'fronts' has diverse possible interpretations. The ambiguity of displaying and obscuring may apply to both individuals and collectivities. We find the term useful because, apart from its literal meanings, it suggests by analogy, and even as allegory, some of the complexities of the impact of sexuality.

2. Although this chapter is dominantly concerned with the qualitative it is impossible to escape the interplay of quantitative and qualitative within that. There are further dialectical relationships between the visible and secret; the visible and unseen; secret and unseen; and all these and the elusive.

3. This may have been due to a combination of sexism and anti-royalist republicanism amongst the men.

4. Such uses of speech are often seen by the participants as either non-sexual or only implicitly sexual, and are therefore included in this section. However, these behaviours are being increasingly recognised as sexual harassment.

5. Loring and Wells (1972, 119) discuss the development of joint hiring policies for executive couples.

6. Airedale and Craven Marriage Guidance Council initiated a service to companies by which personnel managers may refer employees showing signs of marital or other personal problems, to the detriment of organisational performance.

7. The power of records is likely to remain even with the movement to 'open files' in social work and elsewhere, and new controls under the Data Protection Act, 1984; obvious 'professional' strategies include the use of 'unofficial' files, and the preference for paper over computerised recording.

8. An interesting contrast is to be made here with Ferris' (1977, 23–5) discussion of the citing of 'professional neutrality' as a euphemism for concealing any sign of not conforming to dominant heterosexual norms of behaviour in social work.

9. Although both officers were demoted, the main media attention was focused upon W.P.C. Wendy de Launay, the woman officer in the case, rather than on her male colleague, P.C. Trevor Attfield. A tribunal found that W.P.C. Wendy de Launay had suffered sexual discrimination (Moncur, 1983).

10. An industrial tribunal found that the woman booking clerk had been unlawfully discriminated against and she was awarded damages (Singer, 1981). A similar finding was made by an industrial tribunal in 1979 in favour of a sales manager demoted to salesperson after an affair with another member of staff (Askill, 1979).
11. The industrial tribunal in this case dismissed the nurse's application on the grounds of bringing the nursing service into disrepute ('Topless nurse . . .', 1984).
12. Loring and Wells (1972, 150−2) critically discuss Berman's dismissal of women's potential for executive posts on the grounds of their 'raging hormones'.
13. A speculative point is that there is a broad parallel between fantasy and reality on the one hand, and sexuality and organisations on the other. This may be in a number of ways: firstly the assumption that there is a clear separation between each with mutual exclusion of the other; secondly the assumption that both fantasy and sexuality can possibly be excluded as relatively inferior to reality and organisations respectively; thirdly, the practical experience that both fantasy and sexuality are intimately present in the public world of reality and organisation; and fourthly, that the individual mind, and its fantasies in their social milieu can be seen as a microcosm of sexuality in relation to organisational life.

CHAPTER 7 ORGANISATION SEXUALITY: A PARADOX

1. This phrase is used by Petchesky (1979) in discussing the interrelationship of marxism and feminism.
2. Precedents for this kind of usage include *Organization Woman* (Stott, 1978) and *The Organization Man* (Whyte, 1956), which also often happens to refer to the intimate relationship of organisations and the person.
3. Organisation sexuality and street sexuality are clearly not discrete and separate entities. Actions and behaviours in the one are likely to have effects on and similarities to those in the other. Furthermore, particular locations may stand ambiguously across the organisation−street 'divide', such as cinemas, libraries, mass spectator sports, discos, buses and trains, where in different ways the 'street' may be temporarily brought within an organisation.
4. Within organisations, toilets are ambiguous in relation to sexuality. Although many would see toilets in organisations and 'rules' surrounding them as merely functional, they have many connections with sexuality and its control. These range from their association with hidden sexual states to their use as refuges for emotionality, intimacy and sexual acts, and to their ambiguity as meeting places, which could be interpreted as either secret organisational conversations or implicitly homosexual. In such subtleties organisational toilets differ from 'public toilets', and both can be distinguished from toilets in ambiguous organisation/street

locations (see note 3 above).

5. Henley (1977, 163—6) discusses the variety of connections between gaze and superordination/subordination distinguishing between gaze that is dominant staring and that which is subordinate attentiveness.

6. Earlier discussions of total institutions are clearly relevant (see pp. 72—9). In addition to the obvious ways in which such institutions construct sexuality, totality is usually a statement on sexuality. This is most obvious in the possibility of voyeurism from within or of those visiting and temporarily observing. Foucault's discussion of Bentham's Panopticon (Foucault, 1977) is an extreme case. This raises the further complication of the link between punishment by others or self and sexuality as in sado-masochism.

7. Indeed Seidenberg (1970, 13—4, cited in Loring and Wells, 1972, 101) suggests:

> that our society is overwhelmingly dominated by male 'homosexuality' in religion, politics, higher education, law, big business, the armed forces, and practically all other important [sic] institutions . . . the reality that men in general prefer to spend most of their time in each others' company. . . . Very little time is spent with women. . . . They are sexual partners but this only takes a few minutes a week, just enough time to establish that the male is a heterosexual, which he obviously is not, based on his apparent preferences as found in time-spent studies. . . . For most men, women are good to sleep with—not to stay awake with.

8. We are grateful to John Barker for drawing our attention to this point.

9. Moye (1985, 55) notes that:

> There are certain conventions that pornography requires its women models to adapt in their poses and gestures, the most significant of these being the gaze directed to return the reader's gaze. This gaze emphasises the woman's presence in a manner which is personalised and colludes with the reader's interest. It establishes the ground upon which the male reader can enact his sexual desire in fantasy, by positing him as sexually desirable. With relief the reader can mingle his fantasies of desire with the images of the woman offering herself to him.

10. The term 'whitepower' has clear racist/fascist overtones with the implication that terms such as 'manpower' etc. are examples of 'gender fascism'.

11. The public presentation of the Playboy organisation is further complicated by its own repeated claims that the company is like a family (Amis, 1985).

CHAPTER 8 NARRATIVE: HISTORY, EXPERIENCE AND CHANGE

1. This theme is explored at length in *The Gender of Oppression* (Hearn, 1987).

2. The reason for elaborate, ceremonial dressing by men, such as priests and other patriarchal 'authorities' (Daly, 1978, 112) may appear 'mere tradition'. Alternatively, it may represent the symbolic paraphernalia of men's domination of the ceremonies and rituals of the public domain,

against and obscuring women's power and creativity in childbirth and elsewhere. (cf. O'Brien, 1981).

3. This remark was made by a tank commander interviewed on the BBC1 television programme on 'Tanks' in 'Soldiers', introduced by Frederick Forsyth, 30 October 1985.

4. This remark was part of the Keynote address at the Men's Gathering, 'In Celebration of the New Emerging Male—Looking at Men's Roles and Men's Lives', held at the College of Marin, California, 15 September 1984 (Bliss, 1985).

5. A more accurate description of sexual harassment and other forms of sexual oppression is sexualism, based as it is around sexuality, rather than sexism.

6. Genderism, being oppression and discrimination on the basis of gender, is a more accurate term than sexism for describing generic power relations.

POSTSCRIPT TO THE REVISED EDITION: UPDATING THEORY AND PRACTICE

1. This section draws on Burrell and Hearn (1989).
2. This and the following section draws on Hearn and Parkin (1994).

Bibliography

Acker, J. and Van Houten, D.R., 'Differential recruitment and control: the sex structuring of organizations', *Administrative Science Quarterly*, 19, (1974).

Adams, C., and Laurikietis, R., *The Gender Trap. 1: Education and Work* (Virago, London, 1980; 1st pub. 1976).

Adkins, L., 'Hors d'oeuvres', *Trouble and Strife*, 24 (1992a).

Adkins, L., 'Sexual work and the employment of women in the service industries' in *Gender and Bureaucracy*, ed. M. Savage and A. Witz (Basil Blackwell, Oxford, 1992b).

Adkins, L., *Gendered Work. Sexuality, Family and the Labour Market* (Open University Press, Buckingham and Philadelphia, Pa, 1995).

Adler, P.A., 'The irony of secrecy in the drug world'. *Urban Life*, 8 (1980).

Alfred Marks Bureau, *Sex in the Office: An Investigation of the Incidence of Sexual Harassment* (Alfred Marks Bureau, London, 1982).

Alliance Against Sexual Coercion, *Sexual Harassment: An Annotated Bibliography* (Alliance Against Sexual Coercion, Cambridge, Mass., 1980).

Amis, M., 'Mr. Hefner and the desperate pursuit of happiness', *The Observer* (22 September 1985).

Arber, S., 'Class and the elderly', *Social Studies Review* 4 (3) (1989).

Ardener, S., 'Nudity, vulgarity and protest', *New Society*, 27 (1974).

Ardill, S., and O'Sullivan, S., 'Upsetting an applecart: difference, desire and lesbian sadomasochism', *Feminist Review*, 23 (1986).

'Armagh picket', *Class Struggle*, 9 (1985).

Arnold, M., and Laskey, H., *The Children of the Poor Homes, The Story of an Irish Orphanage* (Apple Tree, Belfast, 1985).

Aron, C. S., *Ladies and Gentlemen of the Civil Service. Middle Class Workers in Victorian America* (Oxford University Press, New York, 1987).

Aronson, E., and Mills, J., 'Effect of severity of initiation on liking for a group', *The Journal of Abnormal and Social Psychology*, 59 (1959).

Askill, J., 'Licence to love', *The Sun* (8 September 1979).

Aubrey, C., *Who's Watching You?* (Penguin, Harmondsworth, 1981).

Ballantyne, A., 'Council clash on baptism of fire woman', *The Guardian* (1 February 1985).

Barker, J., and Downing, H., 'Word processing and the transformation of the patriarchal relations of control', *Capital and Class*, 10 (1980).

Barrett, M., *Women's Oppression Today* (Verso, London, 1980).

Barry, K., *Female Sexual Slavery* (New York University, New York, 1984).

Beattie, G., 'The masseuse's tale', *The Guardian* (27 April 1985).

Beechey, V., 'Women and production: a critical analysis of some sociological theories of women's work' in *Feminism and Materialism: Women and Modes of Production*, ed. A. Kuhn and A.-M. Wolpe (Routledge and Kegan Paul, London, 1978).

Beechey, V., 'Some notes on female wage labour in capitalist production' in *The Woman Question: Readings on the Subordination of Women*, ed. M. Evans (Oxford University Press, Oxford, 1982).

Beer, C., Jeffery, R., and Munyard, T., *Gay Workers: Trade Unions and the Law* (NCCL, London, 2nd Edn, 1983).

Bell, A.P., and Weinberg, M.S., *Homosexualities: A Study of Diversity among Men and Women* (Simon and Schuster, New York, 1978).

Berlinguer, G., 'The effects of working conditions on sexuality', *Planned Parenthood in Europe*, 14 (1985).

Betzold, M., 'How pornography shackles men and oppresses women' in *A Book of Readings for Men Against Sexism*, ed. J. Snodgrass (Times Change, Albion, Ca., 1977).

Beynon, H., and Blackburn, R.M., *Perceptions of Work, Perceptions within a Factory* (Cambridge University, Cambridge, 1972).

Biggs, S., *Understanding Ageing* (Open University Press, Buckingham and Philadelphia, Pa., 1993).

Bion, W., 'Experiences in groups'. *Human Relations*, 1, 2, 3 (1948, 1949, 1950).

Blanchard, K., and Johnson, S., *The One Minute Manager* (Willow, London/Toronto, 1983).

Bland, L., Brunsdon, C., Hobson, D., and Winship, J., 'Women "inside and outside" the relations of production' in *Women Take Issue*, Women's Studies Group, Centre for Contemporary Cultural Studies, University of Birmingham (Hutchinson, London, 1978).

Blau, P., and Scott, W.R., *Formal Organisations* (Routledge & Kegan Paul, London/Boston, 1963).

Bliss, S., 'Fathers and sons', *The Men's Journal* (Spring 1985).

Blundy, D., 'Lovely Rita's acts of congress give Washington the shudders', *The Sunday Times* (March 1981).

Boar, R., and Blundell, N., *The World's Greatest Spies and Spymasters* (Octopus, London, 1984).

Bologh, R.W., 'Max Weber on erotic love: a feminist inquiry' in *Max Weber, Rationality and Modernity*, ed. S. Lash and S. Whimster (Allen & Unwin, London, 1987).

Bologh, R.W., *Love or Greatness? Max Weber and Masculine Thinking—A Feminist Inquiry* (Unwin Hyman, Winchester, Mass., 1990).

Boseley, S., 'Disabled sit in over hostel sacking', *The Guardian* (29 October 1983).

Bowlby, J., *Child Care and the Growth of Love* (Penguin, Harmondsworth, 1953).

Boyle, J., *A Sense of Freedom* (Pan, London, 1977).

Bradford, D.L., Sargent, A.G., and Sprague, M.S., 'Executive man and woman: the issue of sexuality' in *Bringing Women into Management*, ed. F.E. Gordon and M.H. Strober (McGraw-Hill, New York, 1975).

Brake, M., 'Sexuality as praxis—the consideration of the contribution of sexual theory to the process of sexual being' in *Human Sexual Relations*, ed. M. Brake (Penguin, Harmondsworth, 1982).

Brampton, S., 'City slickers', *The Observer* (9 December 1984).

Brant, C., and Too, Y. L. (ed.), *Rethinking Sexual Harassment* (Pluto, London, 1994).

Braverman, H., *Labor and Monopoly Capital* (Monthly Review, New York, 1974).

Brenton, M., *The American Male* (Fawcett, Greenwich, Conn., 1966).

Brewis, J., and Grey, C., 'Re-eroticizing the organization: an exegesis and critique' *Gender, Work and Organization* 1 (2) (1994).

Brooks, V., *Minority Stress and Lesbian Women* (Lexington Press, Lexington, Mass., 1981).

Bruegel, I., 'Women as a reserve army of labour: a note on the recent British experience' in *The Changing Experience of Women*. ed. E. Whitelegg (Martin Robertson, Oxford, 1982).

Buffum, I.C., *Homosexuality in Prisons* (US Department of Justice, Law Enforcement Assistance Administration, National Institute of Law Enforcement and Criminal Justice, Washington DC, 1982).

Burke, M.E., *Coming Out of the Blue. British Police Officers talk about their lives in 'The Job' as lesbians, gays and bisexuals* (Cassell, London and New York, 1993).

Burrell, G., 'Sex and organisational analysis', *Organization Studies*, 5 (1984).

Burrell, G. and Hearn, J., 'The sexuality of organization' in *The Sexuality of Organization*, ed. J. Hearn, D.L. Sheppard, P. Tancred-Sheriff and G. Burrell (Sage, London, 1989).

Burrell G., and Morgan, G., *Sociological Paradigms and Organisational Analysis* (Heinemann, London, 1979).

Burstyn, V., 'Masculine dominance and the state' in *The Socialist Register 1983*, ed. R. Miliband and J. Saville (Merlin, London, 1983).

Burton, A., *A Programmed Guide to Office Warfare* (Panther, London, 1971).

Butler, J., *Gender Trouble. Feminism and the Subversion of Identity* (Routledge, New York and London, 1990).

Byrne, D., Allgeier, A., Winslow, L., and Buckman, L., 'The situational facilitation of interpersonal attraction: a three factor hypothesis', *Journal of Applied Social Psychology*, 5 (1975).

Bytheway, B., *Ageism* (Open University Press, Buckingham and Philadelphia, Pa., 1994).

Callan, H., 'The premiss of dedication: notes towards an ethnography of diplomats' wives' in *Perceiving Women*, ed. S. Ardener (J.M. Dent, London, 1977).

Campaign for Homosexual Equality, *What About the Gay Workers?* (CHE, London, 1981).

Cardwell, L., 'Managing women–a man's view', *Management Education and Development*, 16 (1985).

Cavendish, R., *Women on the Line* (Routledge & Kegan Paul, London/Boston, 1982).

Chafetz, J., Sampson, P., Beck, P., and West, J., 'A study of homosexual women', *Social Work*, 19 (6) (1974).

Child, J., *British Management Thought* (Allen & Unwin, London, 1969).

Cixous, H., 'Sorties' in *New French Feminisms*, ed. E. Marks and I. de Courtivron (Harvester, Brighton, 1981; University of Massachusetts, Amherst, 1980; 1st pub. 1975).

Cleugh, J., *Love Locked Out* (Hamlyn, London, 1963).

Cleverley, G., *Managers and Magic* (Penguin, Harmondsworth, 1973).

Cockburn, C., *Brothers. Male Dominance and Technological Change* (Pluto, London, 1983).

Cockburn, C., 'Masculinity, the Left and Feminism' in *Male Order: Unwrapping Masculinity*, ed. R. Chapman and J. Rutherford (Lawrence and Wishart, London, 1988).

Cockburn, C., 'Equal opportunities: the short and the long agendas', *Industrial Relations Journal*, 20 (1989).

Cockburn, C., 'Men's power in organisations: "equal opportunities" intervenes' in *Men, Masculinity and Social Theory*, ed. J. Hearn and D. Morgan (Unwin Hyman, London and Winchester, Mass., 1990).

Cockburn, C., *In the Way of Women: Men's Resistance to Sex Equality in Organisations* (Macmillan, London, 1991).

Cohen, S., Green, S., Merryfinch, L., Jones, G., Slade, J., Walker, M., *The Law and Sexuality. How to Cope with the Law if You're not 100% Conventionally Heterosexual* (Grassroots, Manchester, 1978).

Coles, A., 'Interviews. Sex: an optional extra?', *Honey* (July 1978).

Collins, E.G.C., 'Managers and lovers', *Harvard Business Review*, 61 (1983).

Collinson, D., 'Managing the Shopfloor', unpub. M.Sc. thesis, University of Manchester I.S.T., Manchester (1981).

Collinson, D.L., *Managing the Shopfloor: Subjectivity, Masculinity and Workplace Culture* (de Gruyter, Berlin and New York, 1992).

Collinson, D.L., and Collinson, M., 'Sexuality in the workplace: the domination of men's sexuality' in *The Sexuality of Organization*, ed. J. Hearn, D. Sheppard, P. Tancred-Sheriff and G. Burrell (Sage, London, 1989).

Collinson, D.L., Knights, D., and Collinson, M., *Managing to Discriminate* (Routledge, London and New York, 1990).

Connell, R.W., *Which Way Is Up?* (Allen & Unwin, London/Boston, 1983).

Cooper, C.L., and Cooper, R.D., 'Stress and breast cancer: is there a link', *Leadership and Organization Development Journal*, 5 (1984).

Cooper, C.L., and Davidson, M., *High Pressure: Working Lives of Women Managers* (Fontana, Glasgow, 1982).

Corless, F., 'The 100 sexy secrets of a secretary's diary', *Daily Mirror* (5 October 1983).

Corzine, J., and Kirby, R., 'Cruising the truckers. Sexual encounters in a highway rest area', *Urban Life*, 6 (1977).

Costello, J., *Love Sex and War. Changing Values 1939–45* (Collins, London, 1985).

Courtney, A.E., and Whipple, T.W., *Sex Stereotyping in Advertising* (D.C. Heath, Lexington, Mass., 1983).

Coveney, L., Jackson, M., Jeffreys, S., Kaye, L., and Mahoney, P., *The Sexuality Papers: Male Sexuality and the Social Control of Women* (Hutchinson, London, 1984).

Coward, R., *Patriarchal Precedents. Sexuality and Social Relations* (Routledge & Kegan Paul, London/Boston, 1983).

Coward, R., Lipshitz, S., and Cowie, E., 'Psychoanalysis and patriarchal structures' in *Papers on Patriarchy*, Conference Papers (London, 1978).

Cunningham, M., with Schumer, F., *Powerplay–What Really Happened at Bendix* (Ballantine, New York, 1984).

Cunnison, S., *Wages and Work Allocation* (Tavistock, London, 1966).

Curb, R., and Manahan, N. ed., *Breaking Silence: Lesbian Nuns on Convent Sexuality* (Columbia, London; Naiad, New York, 1985).

Daly, M., *Gyn/ecology: The Metaethics of Radical Feminism* (The Women's Press, London, 1978).

Davies, B., 'The problem of desire', *Social Problems*, 37 (1990).

Davies, N., 'Kangaroo courts abuse young girls in prison', *The Observer* (10 February 1985).

Davies, N., and Foster, J., 'Police use "snoops" to compile personal files', *The Observer* (8 December 1985).

Davies, R., *Women and Work* (Arrow, London, 1975).

Dean, M., 'Decency allows gaol jobs bias', *The Guardian* (29 December 1983).

de Board, R., *The Psychoanalysis of Organizations* (Tavistock, London, 1978).

Delacoste, F., and Alexander, P. ed., *Sex Work, Writings by Women in the Sex Industry* (Virago, London, 1988).

Diamond, I., and Quinby, L., 'American Feminism in the age of the body', *Signs*, 10 (1984).

Diamond, I., and Quinby, L., *Feminism and Foucault: Reflection or Resistance* (Northeastern University Press, Boston, Mass., 1988).

Dicks, H.V., *50 Years of the Tavistock Clinic* (Routledge & Kegan Paul, London, 1970).

Dickson, A., *Mirror Within: New Look at Sexuality* (Quartet, London, 1985).

Dienhart, L., and Pinsel, M., 'Sex and the power lunch. Touching moments at table', *Weekend* (25–31 July 1984).

Dimock, H., *Rediscovering the Adolescent* (Association, New York, 1941).

DiTomaso, N., 'Sexuality in the workplace: discrimination and harassment' in *The Sexuality of Organization*, ed. J. Hearn, D. Sheppard, P. Tancred-Sheriff and G. Burrell (Sage, London, 1989).

Dixon, N., *On The Psychology of Military Incompetence* (Jonathan Cape, London, 1976).

Dorn, N., and South, N., *Of Males and Markets: A Critical Review of 'Youth Culture' Theory* (Centre for Occupational and Community Research, Middlesex Polytechnic, Middlesex, n.d.).

Due Billing, Y., 'Gender and bureaucracies: a critique of Ferguson's "The Feminist Case Against Bureaucracy"', *Gender, Work and Organization*, 1 (1994).

Due Billing, Y., and Alvesson, M., *Gender, Managers and Organization* (de Gruyter, Berlin and New York, 1994).

Dutton, D., and Aron, A., 'Some evidence of hightened sexual attraction under conditions of high anxiety', *Journal of Personality and Social Psychology*, 30 (1974).

Dyer, G., *Advertising as Communication* (Methuen, London and New York, 1982).

Dyer, R., 'Male sexuality in the media' in *The Sexuality of Men*, ed. A. Metcalf and M. Humphries (Pluto, London, 1985).

Dziech, B. W., and Weiner, L., *The Lecherous Professor. Sexual Harassment on Campus* (Beacon, Boston, 1984).

Edwards, A.R., 'The prison', in *Processing People*, ed. J.B. MacKinlay (Holt, Rinehart & Winston, New York and London, 1975).

Edwards, T., *Erotics and Politics: Gay Male Sexuality, Masculinity and Feminism* (Routledge, London and New York, 1994).

Eichenbaum, L., and Orbach, S., *Outside In. Inside Out* (Penguin, Harmondsworth, 1982).

Elias, N., *The Civilising Process* (Basil Blackwell, Oxford, 1978).

Elshtain, J.B., *Public Man, Private Woman* (Martin Robertson, Oxford, 1981).

Emerson, J., 'Behavior in private places: sustaining definitions of reality in gynecological examinations' in *Recent Sociology No. 2, Patterns of Communicative Behavior*, ed. H.P. Dreitzel (Macmillan, New York, 1970).

Eribon, D., *Michel Foucault* (Faber, London, 1992).

Farley, L., *Sexual Shakedown* (Melbourne House, London; McGraw-Hill, New York, 1978).

Feigelman, W., 'Peeping: the pattern of boyeurism among construction workers', *Urban Life*, 3 (1974).

Feldberg, R.L., and Glenn, E.N., 'Male and female: job versus gender models in the sociology of work', *Social Problems*, 26 (1979).

Feminism & Psychology, Special Issue on Heterosexuality, 2 (3) (1992).

Ferguson, K.E., *The Feminist Case Against Bureaucracy* (Temple University Press, Philadelphia, Pa., 1984).

Fernbach, D., *The Spiral Path: A Gay Contribution to Human Survival* (Gay Men's Press, London, 1982).

Ferris, D., *Homosexuality and the Social Services* (NCCL, London, 1977).

Finch, J., *Married to the Job: Wives' Incorporation in Men's Work* (Allen & Unwin, London, 1983).

Finkelstein, C.A., 'Women managers: career patterns and changes in the United States' in *Access to Power: Cross-National Studies of Women and Elites*, ed. C.F. Epstein and R.L. Coser (Allen & Unwin, London/Boston, 1981).

Fitzgerald, M., and Sim, J., *British Prisons* (Basil Blackwell, Oxford, 1979).

Fletcher, A.C., *Reproductive Hazards of Work* (Equal Opportunities Commission and ASTMS, Manchester, 1985).

Foucault, M., *The Archaeology of Knowledge* (Tavistock, London, 1972; 1st pub. 1969).

Foucault, M., *The Birth of the Clinic* (Tavistock, London, 1973; 1st pub. 1963).

Foucault, M., *Discipline and Punish. The Birth of the Prison* (Allen Lane, Harmondsworth, 1977; 1st pub. 1975).

Foucault, M., *The History of Sexuality Volume 1* (Penguin, Harmondsworth/New York, 1981; 1st pub. 1976).

Fowler, L., 'Women and Work–sexual harassment, patriarchy and the labour process'. Unpub. ms. MSc Industrial Sociology, University of Bradford (1985).

Freud, S., *Civilization and its Discontents* (Norton, New York, 1962).

Game, A., 'Research and writing: "secretaries and bosses"', *Journal of Pragmatics*, 13 (1989).

Game, A., and Pringle, R., *Gender at Work* (Allen & Unwin, London, 1983).

Georgiou, P., 'The goal paradigm and notes towards a counter paradigm', *Administrative Science Quarterly*, 18 (1973).

Giallombardo, R., *Society of Women: A Study of a Woman's Prison* (Wiley, New York, 1966).

Giddens, A., *Central Problems in Social Theory* (Macmillan, London/New York, 1979).

Goffman, E., *Asylums* (Penguin, Harmondsworth, 1968; Doubleday, New York, 1961).

Goffman, E., *Gender Advertisements* (Macmillan, London, 1979; Society for the Anthropology of Visual Communication, Washington, 1976).

Goodison, L., 'Really being in love means wanting to live in a different world' in *Sex & Love. New Thoughts on Old Contradictions*, ed. S. Cartledge and J. Ryan (The Women's Press, London, 1983).

Gould, R.E., 'Measuring masculinity by the size of a paycheck' in *Men and Masculinity*, ed. J.H. Pleck and J. Sawyer (Prentice-Hall, New York, 1974).

Gray, H.L., 'Men with women bosses: some gender issues', *Management Education and Development*, 16 (1985).

Gray, S., 'Romance in the workplace: corporate rules for the game of love', *Business Week* (18 June 1984).

Greater London Council, *Danger! . . . Heterosexism at Work* (GLC, London, 1985).

Griffin, S., 'The way of all idealogy' in *Feminist Theory*, ed. N.O. Keohane, M.Z. Rosaldo and B.C. Gelpi (Harvester, Brighton; University of Chicago, Chicago, 1982).

Gutek, B.A., *Sex and the Workplace. The Impact of Sexual Behavior and Harassment on Women, Men and Organizations* (Jossey-Bass, San Francisco, 1985).

Gutek, B.A., and Dunwoody, V., 'Understanding sex in the workplace' in *Women and Work: An Annual Review*, vol 2, ed. A. Stromberg, L. Larwood and B.A. Gutek (Sage, Newbury Park, Ca., 1987).

Gutek, B.A., and Morasch, B., 'Sex-ratios, sex-role spillover, and sexual harassment of women at work', *Journal of Social Issues*, 38 (1982).

Gutek, B.A., and Nakamura, C.V., 'Gender roles and sexuality in the world of work' in *Changing Boundaries. Gender Roles and Sexual Behavior*, ed. E.R. Allgeier and N.B. McCormick (Mayfield, San Francisco, 1982).

Haavio-Mannila, E., 'Erotic relations at work' in *The Transformation of Europe*, ed. M. Alestalo, E. Allardt, A. Rychard, and W. Wesolowski (IFIS Publisher, Warsaw, 1994).

Haavio-Mannila, E., 'Attraction and love at work' forthcoming in *Nordic Feminist Thought* ed. D. van der Fehr, A. Jónasdóttir and B. Rosenbeck, Mimeo, University of Helsinki (1995).

Hales, M., *Living Thinkwork. Where do labour processes come from?* (CSE, London, 1980).

Hall, E., *We Can't Even March Straight* (Vintage, London, 1995).

Hall, M., 'Private experiences in the public domain: lesbians in organisations' in *The Sexuality of Organization*, ed. J. Hearn, D.L. Sheppard, P. Tancred-Sheriff and G. Burrell (Sage, London, 1989).

Hare, A.P., *Handbook of Small Group Research* (Free Press, Glencoe, Ill., 1962).

Harrison, R., and Lee, R., 'Love at work', *Personnel Management* (January 1986).

Harrison, T. ed. (Mass Observation) *War Factory: A Report* (Victor Gollancz, London, 1943).

Hasenfeld, Y., 'People processing organizations', *American Sociological Review*, 37 (1972).

Health Education Council, *Stay Fit in the Office* (HEC, London, n.d.).

Hearn, J., 'The professions and the semi-professions: the control of emotions and the construction of masculinity', paper at British Sociological Association, Manchester University, Mimeo, University of Bradford (April 1982a).

Hearn, J., 'Womb with a view'. *Social Work Today*, 13 (1982b).

Hearn, J., *Birth and Afterbirth: A Materialist Account* (Achilles Heel, London, 1983).

Hearn, J., 'Men's sexuality at work' in *The Sexuality of Men*, ed. A. Metcalf and M. Humphries (Pluto, London, 1985a).

Hearn, J., 'Sexism, men's sexuality and management: the seen but unnoticed case of men's sexuality', paper in symposium 'Sexuality, Power and Organization Theory', Academy of Management, San Diego, Ca. (August 1985b).

Hearn, J., *The Gender of Oppression. Men, Masculinity and the Critique of Marxism* (Wheatsheaf, Brighton, 1987).

Hearn, J., *Men in the Public Eye: The Construction and Deconstruction of Public Men and Public Patriarchies* (Routledge, London and New York, 1992).

Hearn, J., 'Emotive subjects: organizational men, organizational masculinities and the (de)construction of emotions' in *Emotion in Organizations*, ed. S. Fineman (Sage, London, 1993).

Hearn, J., 'The organisation(s) of violence: men, gender relations, organisations and violences', *Human Relations*, 47 (1994a).

Hearn, J., 'Research in men and masculinities: some sociological issues and possibilities', *Australian and New Zealand Journal of Sociology*, 30 (1994b).

Hearn, J., and Parkin, P.W., 'Gender and organizations: a review and a critique of a neglected area'. *Organization Studies* 4 (1983). Reprinted in *Gendering Organizational Analysis*, ed. A.J. Mills and P. Tancred (Sage, Newbury Park, Ca., 1992).

Hearn, J., and Parkin, P.W., '"Sex" at "Work": methodological and other difficulties in the study of sexuality in work organizations', paper at British Sociological Association Conference, University of Bradford (April 1984), mimeo, University of Bradford.

Hearn, J., and Parkin, P.W., 'Sex at work', *Planned Parenthood in Europe*, 14 (1985).

Hearn, J., and Parkin, P.W., 'Women, men and leadership: a critical review of assumptions, practices and changes in the industrialized nations', *International Studies of Management and Organization*, 16 (1986–7).

Hearn, J., and Parkin, P.W., 'Women, men and leadership: a critical review of assumptions, practices and change in the industrialized nations' in *Women in Management Worldwide*, ed. N.J. Adler and D. Izraeli (M.E. Sharpe, New York, 1988).

Hearn, J., and Parkin, W., 'Organizations, multiple oppressions and postmodernism' in *Postmodernism and Organizations*, ed. J. Hassard and M. Parker (Sage, London, 1993).

Hearn, J., and Parkin, W., 'Sexuality, gender and organisations: acknowledging complexities', British Sociological Association

Annual Conference, University of Central Lancashire, mimeo, University of Bradford (1994).

Hearn, J., Sheppard, D., Tancred-Sheriff, P., and Burrell, G. (ed.), *The Sexuality of Organization* (Sage, London, 1989).

Henley, N.M., *Body Politics. Power, Sex and Nonverbal Communication* (Prentice-Hall, Englewood Cliffs, NJ, 1977).

Henslin, J.M., and Biggs, M.A., 'Dramaturgical descualization: the sociology of the vaginal examination' in *The Sociology of Sex*, ed. J.M. Henslin and E. Sagarin (Schocken, New York, 1978).

Hey, V., *Patriarchy and Pub Culture* (Tavistock, London and New York, 1986).

Hogbacka, R., Kandolin, I., Haavio-Mannila, E., and Kauppinen-Toropainen, K., *Sexual Harassment*, Equality Publications, Series E, Abstracts 2/1987, Helsinki (Ministry of Social Affairs, Finland, 1987).

Hollibaugh, A., and Moraga, C., 'What we're rollin around in bed with: sexual silences in feminism' in *Desire. The Politics of Sexuality*, ed. A. Snitow, C. Stansell and S. Thompson (Virago, London, 1984; Monthly Review, New York, 1983).

Hollway, W., 'Heterosexual sex: power and desire for the Other' in *Sex & Love. New Thoughts on Old Contradictions*, ed. S. Cartledge and J. Ryan (The Women's Press, London, 1983).

Hollway, W., and Mukurasi, L., 'Women managers in the Tanzanian Civil Service' in *Competitive Frontiers: Women Managers in a Global Economy*, ed. N.J. Adler and D.N. Izraeli (Blackwell, Cambridge, Mass., 1994).

Horn, P.D., and Horn, J.C., *Sex in the Office. Power and Passion in the Workplace* (addison-Wesley, Reading, Mass., 1982).

'How long could you spend with this girl?', *Sunday* (19 December 1982).

Huston, T.L., and Cate, R.M., 'Social exchange in intimate relationships' in *Love and Attraction*, ed. M. Cook and G. Wilson (Pergamon, Oxford, 1979).

Irigaray, L., 'That sex which is not one', trans. R. Albury and P. Foss from *Ce sexe qui n'en est pas un* (Les Editions de Minuit, Paris, 1977, pp. 23–32) in *Language, Sexuality and Subversion*, ed. P. Foss and M. Morris (Feral, Darlington, Australia, 1978).

Irigaray, L., *This sex which is not one* (Cornell University Press, New York, 1985) in print in French 1977.

Itzin, C. (ed.), *Pornography: Women, Violence and Civil Liberties* (Oxford University Press, Oxford, 1992).

'J', *How to become The Sensuous Woman* (Granada, St Albans, 1978; 1st pub. 1969).

Jacklin, C.N., and Maccoby, E.E., 'Sex differences and their implications for management' in *Bringing Women into Management*, ed. E. Gordon and M.H. Strober (McGraw-Hill, New York, 1975).

Jackson, M., 'Sex research and the construction of sexuality: a tool of male supremacy?', *Women's Studies International Forum*, 7 (1984).

Jaggar, A., and Struhl, P., *Feminist Frameworks* (McGraw-Hill, New York, 1978).

Jaques, E., 'Social systems as a defence against persecutory and depressive anxiety' in *New Directions in Psychoanalysis*, ed. M. Klein, P. Heimann and R. Money-Kyrle (Tavistock, London, 1955).

Jenkins, D., *Job Power: Blue and White Collar Democracy* (Heinemann, London, 1974).

Kane, P., 'Notes on the pink economy', *The Bi-Monthly*, 1 (1984).

Kanter, R.M., 'Women in organizations: sex roles, group dynamics, and change strategies' in *Beyond Sex Roles*, ed. A. Sargent (West, St Paul, Minn., 1975).

Kanter, R.M., *Men and Women of the Corporation* (Basic, New York, 1977).

Keat, R., and Urry, J., *Social Theory as Science* (Routledge & Kegan Paul, London/Boston, 2nd edn, 1982).

Keays, S., *A Question of Judgement* (Quintessential, London, 1985).

Keller, E.F., 'The gender/science system: or is sex to gender as nature is to science?', *Hypatria*, 2 (1987).

Kelly, L., *Surviving Sexual Violence* (Polity, Cambridge, 1988).

Kendrick, D.T., Cialdini, R.B., and Linder, D.E., 'Heterosexual attraction and attributional processes in fear-producing situations' in *Love and Attraction*, ed. M. Cook and G. Wilson (Pergamon, Oxford, 1979).

Klein, J., *The Study of Groups* (Routledge & Kegan Paul, London, 1956).

Kohn, M., 'Bureaucratic man: a portrait and an interpretation', *American Sociological Review*, 36 (1971).

Konecki, K., 'Dependency and worker flirting' in *Organisational Symbolism*, ed. B.A. Turner (de Gruyter, Berlin and New York, 1990).

Korda, M., *Male Chauvinism! How It Works* (Random House, New York, 1972).

Korda, M., *Power!* (Coronet, London, 1976).

Kosok, M., 'The phenomenology of fucking', *Telos*, 8 (1971).

Kristeva, J., *Desire in Language* (Blackwell, Oxford, 1980).

Krut, R., and Otto, E., 'Danger! Male bonding at work', *Trouble and Strife*, 4, (1984).

Labour Research Department, *Out at Work: Lesbian and Gay Workers' Rights* (LRD, London, 1992).

Lakoff, R., *Language and Woman's Place* (Harper & Row, New York, 1975).

Laming, S., 'Sex in the suburbs', *News of the World* (22 December 1985).

Larrain, J., *The Concept of Ideology* (Hutchinson, London, 1979).

Laws, S., 'Male power and menstrual etiquette' in *The Sexual Politics of Reproduction*, ed. H. Homans (Gower, Aldershot/Brookfield, Vt, 1985).

Leapman, M., *The Last Days of the Beeb* (Allen & Unwin, London, 1986).

Leavitt, H., 'Some effects of certain communication patterns on group performance', *Journal of Abnormal and Social Psychology*, 46 (1951).

Leclerc, A., 'Woman's word' in *New French Feminisms*, ed. E. Marks and I. de Courtivron (Harvester, Brighton, 1981; University of Massachusetts, Amherst, 1980; 1st pub. 1974).

Leeds TUCRIC, *Sexual Harassment of Women at Work* (Leeds TUCRIC, Leeds, 1983).

Lehmann, T., and Young, T.R., 'From conflict theory to conflict methodology: an emerging paradigm for sociology', *Sociological Inquiry*, 44 (1974).

Levi-Strauss, C., *The Elementary Structure of Kinship* (Beacon, Boston, Mass., 1949).

Levine, M.P., 'Employment discrimination against gay men', *International Review of Modern Sociology*, 9 (1979).

Levine, M.P., and Leonard, R., 'Discrimination against lesbians in the workforce', *Signs*, 9 (1984).

Levy, A., and Kahan, B., *The Pindown Experience and the Protection of Children—The Report of the Staffordshire Child Care Inquiry 1990* (Staffordshire County Council, Stafford (1991).

Lewenhak, S., *Women and Work* (Fontana, Glasgow, 1980).

Lipman-Blumen, J., 'Towards a homosocial theory of sex roles: an explanation of the sex segregation of social institutions' in *Women and the Workplace*, ed. A. Blaxall and B. Reagan (University of Chicago, Chicago, 1976).

Lippert, J., 'Sexuality and consumption' in *A Book of Readings for Men Against Sexism*, ed. J. Snodgrass (Times Change, Albion, Ca., 1977).

'Lords approve marriages in prison', *The Guardian* (29 January 1983).

Loring, R., and Wells, T., *Breakthrough: Women into Management* (Van Nostrand-Reinhold, New York, 1972).

Lukes, S., *Power: A Radical View* (Macmillan, London, 1974).

Lundman, R.J., and McFarlane, P.T., 'Conflict methodology: an inquiry and preliminary assessment', *The Sociological Quarterly*, 17 (1976).

Lupton, T., *On the Shop floor* (Pergamon, Oxford, 1963).

MacEwen Scott, A. (ed.), *Gender Segregation and Social Change. Men and Women in Changing Labour Markets* (Oxford University Press, Oxford, 1994).

Macey, D., *The Lives of Michel Foucault* (Hutchinson, London, 1993).

McIntosh, J., 'Sexual harassment: you tell us it's *not* a joke', *Cosmopolitan* (October 1982).

Mackie, L., and Pattullo, T., *Women at Work* (Tavistock, London, 1977).

MacKinnon, C.A., *The Sexual Harassment of Working Women* (Yale University, New Haven, 1979).

MacKinnon, C.A., 'Feminism, Marxism, method and the State: an agenda for theory' in *Feminist Theory*, ed. N.O. Keohane, M.Z. Rosaldo and B.C. Gelpi (Harvester, Brighton; University of Chicago, Chicago, 1982).

McNally, F., *Women for Hire* (Macmillan, London, 1979).

McNay, L., *Foucault and Feminism* (Polity, Cambridge, 1992).

Mahony, P., *Schools for the Boys? Co-education reassessed* (Hutchinson, London, 1985).

Manning, P.K., 'Metaphors of the field: variations of organizational discourse' in *Qualitative Methodology*, ed. J. Van Maanen (Sage Publications, Beverly Hills, 1983).

Marcuse, C., *Eros and Civilization* (Vintage, New York, 1955).

Marshall, J., *Women Managers. Travellers in a Male World* (John Wiley, Chichester/New York, 1984).

Marx, K., 'Economic and philosophical manuscripts' in *Early Writings* (Penguin, Harmondsworth, 1975).

Mayes, S.S., 'Women in positions of authority', *Signs*, 4 (1979).

Mayo, E., *The Human Problems of an Industrial Civilization* (Viking, New York, 1960; 1st pub. 1933).

Mayo, E., *The Social Problems of an Industrial Civilization* (Routledge & Kegan Paul, London, 1962; 1st pub. 1949).

Menzies, I.E.P., 'A case-study in the functioning of social systems as a defence against anxiety: a report on a study of the nursing service in a general hospital', *Human Relations*, 13 (1960).

Metcalf, A., and Humphries, M. ed., *The Sexuality of Men* (Pluto, London, 1985).

Meyer, M.C., Oestriech, J., Collins, F.J., and Berchtold, I., *Sexual Harassment* (Petrocelli, New York, 1981).

Mieli, M., *Homosexuality and Liberation. Elements of a Gap Critique* (Gay Men's Press, London, 1980; 1st pub. 1977).

Miles, J., 'Punk policeman', *Daily Telegraph* (23 July 1985).
Miles, R., *Danger! Men at Work* (Macdonald, London, 1983).
Miles, R., 'Sex on the job', *Cosmopolitan* (July 1985).
Miller, J., *The Passion of Michel Foucault* (HarperCollins, London, 1993).
Mills, A.J., 'Gender, sexuality and organisation theory' in *The Sexuality of Organization*, ed. J. Hearn, D. Sheppard, P. Tancred-Sheriff and G. Burrell (Sage, London, 1989).
Mills, A.J., and Tancred, P. (ed.), *Gendering Organisational Analysis* (Sage, Newbury Park, Ca., London, New Delhi, 1992).
Mills, A.J., and Simmons, T., *Reading Organization Theory: A Critical Approach* (Garamond, Toronto, 1995).
Mintel, *Men 2000* (Mintel, London, 1994).
Moncur, A., 'Policewoman wins sex discrimination', *The Guardian* (22 December 1983).
Morewitz, S.J., 'The sexual harassment of working women', paper to Annual Meeting of the American Sociological Association, Toronto, Canada (1981).
Morgan, D., 'Men, masculinity and the process of sociological enquiry', in *Doing Feminist Research*, ed. H. Roberts (Routledge & Kegan Paul, London/Boston, 1981).
Morris, J., *Pride Against Prejudice. Transforming Attitudes to Disability* (Women's Press, London, 1991).
Morris, W.N., Worchel, S., Bois, J.L., Pearson, J.A., Rountree, C.A., Samaha, G.M., Wachtler, J., and Wright, S.L., 'Collective coping with stress: group reactions to fear, anxiety and ambiguity', *Journal of Personality and Social Psychology*, 33 (1976).
Moye, A., 'Pornography' in *The Sexuality of Men*, ed. A. Metcalf and M. Humphries (Pluto, London, 1985).
Mumford, E., and Banks, O., *The Computer and the Clerk* (Routledge & Kegan Paul, London, 1967).
NALGO, Liverpool, Equal Opportunities Working Party, *Report on Sexual Harassment* (NALGO, Liverpool, 1982).
'Navy scuttles Gilly, the ship's sexy pin-up', *News of the World* (19 December 1982).
Nelson, R., *Success Without Tears* (Star, London, 1980).
Neugarten, D.A., and Shafritz, J.M. (ed.), *Sexuality in Organizations: Romantic and Coercive Behavior at Work* (Moore, Oak Park, Ill., 1980).
Neville, K., 'Classes of '85', *The Observer* (20 June 1985).
Nicholas, M., *The World's Greatest Lovers* (Octopus, London, 1985).
Oakley, A., *The Sociology of Housework* (Martin Robertson, London, 1974).

O'Brien, M., *The Politics of Reproduction* (Routledge & Kegan Paul, London/Boston, 1981).

Okely, J., 'Girls and their bodies: or how to make one sex invisible', *New Society*, 46 (1978a).

Okely, J., 'Privileged, schooled and finished: boarding education for girls' in *Defining Females. The Nature of Women in Society*, ed. S. Ardener (Croom Helm, London, 1978b).

Oliver, M., *The Politics of Disability* (Macmillan, London, 1990).

Oxford University Students Union Women's Committee, '*The Ones Who Just Patronise seem Genial by Comparison. . . .' An Enquiry into Sexual Harassment of Women in Oxford University* (Oxford University Students Union, Oxford, 1984).

Parker, T., *Soldier, Soldier* (Heinemann, London, 1985).

Parkin, P.W., and Hearn, J., 'Frauen, Männen und Führung' in *Handwörterbuch der Führung*, ed. A. Kieser, G. Reber and R. Wunderer (C.E. Poeschel, Stuttgart, 1987, 2nd ed. 1995).

Parkin, W., 'Private experiences in the public domain: sexuality in residential care organizations' in *The Sexuality of Organization.* ed. J. Hearn, D.L. Sheppard, P. Tancred-Sheriff and G. Burrell (Sage, London, 1989).

Parkin, W., 'The public and the private: gender, sexuality and emotion' in *Emotion in Organizations*, ed. S. Fineman (Sage, London, 1993).

Parkin, W., and Green, L., 'Sexuality and residential care', British Sociological Association Annual Conference, University of Central Lancashire, Mimeo, University of Huddersfield (1994).

Parry, G., 'Equal rights on the wedding night', *The Guardian* (26 July 1983).

Parry, G., '"Spy" cases that reveal lapses at GCHQ', *The Guardian* (20 Ocrober 1985).

Parsons, T., and Bales, R.F. ed., *Family, Socialization and Interaction Process* (Free Press, New York, 1955; Routledge & Kegan Paul, London, 1956).

Parsons, T., Bales, R.F., and Shils, E.A., *Working Papers in the Theory of Action* (Free Press, New York, 1951; Collier-Macmillan, London, 1953).

Pascall, J., 'Sex appeal matters again', *Company* (April 1984).

Petchesky, R., 'Dissolving the hyphen: a report on Marxist feminist groups 1-5', *Capitalist Patriarchy and the Case for Socialist Feminism*, ed. Z. Eisenstein (Monthly Review, New York, 1979).

Pollert, A., *Girls, Wives, Factory Lives* (Macmillan, London, 1981).

Poster, M., *Foucault, Marxism and History* (Polity, Cambridge; Blackwell, New York, 1984).

Pringle, R., *Secretaries' Talk* (Verso, London, 1989a).

Pringle, R., 'Bureaucracy, rationality and sexuality: the case of secretaries' in *The Sexuality of Organization*, ed. J. Hearn, D.L. Sheppard, P. Tancred-Sheriff and G. Burrell (Sage, London, 1989b).

Pringle, R., 'Male secretaries' in *Doing "Women's Work. Men in Nontraditional Occupations*, ed. C.L. Williams (Sage, Newbury Park, Ca., 1993).

Pugh, D.S., Hickson, D., and Hinings, C., *Writers on Organisations* (Penguin, Harmondsworth, 3rd ed, 1983).

Quinn, R.E., 'Coping with Cupid: the formation, impact and management of romantic relationships in organizations', *Administrative Science Quarterly*, 22 (1977).

Ramazanoglu, C. (ed.), *Up Against Foucault: Explorations of Some Tensions between Foucault and Feminism* (Routledge, London, 1994).

Rasmussen, P.K., and Kuhn, L.L., 'The new masseuse. Play for pay', *Urban Life*, 5 (1976).

Rawnsley, A., 'Affairs that put industry off its stroke', *The Guardian* (30 December 1985).

Read, S., *Sexual Harassment at Work* (Hamlyn, Feltham, 1982).

Red Collective, *The Politics of Sexuality in Capitalism* (Red Collective, London, 1978).

Reich, W., *The Function of the Orgasm* (Noonday, New York, 1942).

Reid, C., 'Upstaged by my being King Lear', *The Sunday Times* (15 March 1981).

Reskin, B., and Padavic, I., *Women and Men at Work* (Pine Forge Press, Thousand Oaks, London, New Delhi, 1994).

Reynaud, E., *Holy Virility. The Social Construction of Masculinity* (Pluto, London, 1981).

Rich, A., 'Compulsory heterosexuality and lesbian existence', *Signs*, 5 (1980).

Rohlen, T.P., *For Harmony and Strength. Japanese White-Collar Organisation in Anthropological Perspective* (University of California, Berkeley, 1974).

Roman, K., and Maas, J., *How to Advertise* (Kogan Page, London, 1979; St Martin's, New York, 1976).

Roper, M., '"Seduction and succession": male bonding in business' in *The Men of Management*, ed. D.L. Collinson and J. Hearn (Sage, London, 1996).

Rose, G.L., and Andiappon, P., 'Sex effects on managerial hiring decisions', *Academy of Management Journal*, 21 (1978).

Rosie, G., 'Wife seeks jail sex', *The Sunday Times* (27 February 1983).

Roy, D.F., 'Banana time: job satisfaction and informal interaction', *Human Organization*, 18 (1960).

Rubenstein, D., 'Love and work', *Sociological Review*, 26 (1978).

Rubin, G., 'The traffic in women: notes on the political economy of sex' in *Towards an Anthropology of Women*, ed. R. Reiter (Monthly Review Press, New York, 1975).

Rubin, G., 'Thinking sex: notes for a radical theory of the politics of sexuality' in *Pleasure and Danger: Exploring Female Sexuality*, ed. C.S. Vance (Routledge & Kegan Paul, London/Boston, 1984).

Ryan, T., 'Roots of masculinity', in *The Sexuality of Men*, ed. A. Metcalf and M. Humphries (Pluto, London, 1985).

Sagarin, E., 'Sex research and sociology: retrospective and prospective' in *The Sociology of Sex*, ed. J.M. Henslin and E. Sagarin (Schocken, New York, 1978).

Saghir, M.T., and Robins, E., *Male and Female: A Comprehensive Investigation* (Williams and Wilkins, Baltimore, Md., 1973).

Salvage, J., *The Politics of Nursing* (Heinemann, London, 1985).

Savage, M. and Witz, A. (ed.), *Gender and Bureaucracy* (Blackwell/The Sociological Review, Oxford, 1992).

Sawicki, J., *Disciplining Foucault: Feminism, Power and the Body* (Routledge, London and New York, 1991).

Scacco, A.M. Jr., *Rape in Prison* (Charles C. Thomas, Springfield, Ill., 1975).

Schneider, B.A., 'The office affair: myth and reality for heterosexual and lesbian women', *Sociological Perspectives*, 27 (1984).

Schneider, B.E., 'Coming out at work: detriments and consequences of lesbians' openness at their workplaces'. Paper presented at Annual Meeting for the Society for the Study of Social Problems, Toronto (1981).

Schuler, H., and Berger, W., 'The impact of physical attractiveness on an employment decision' in *Love and Attraction*, ed. M. Cook and G. Wilson (Pergamon, Oxford, 1979).

Scobie, W., '$18m bid for a brothel', *The Observer* (15 September 1985).

'Secretary kept diary of "sex harassment"', *The Guardian* (5 October 1983).

Seddon, V., 'Keeping women in their place', *Marxism Today*, 27 (1983).

Seidenberg, R., *Marriage in Life and Literature* (Philosophical Library, New York, 1970).

Sharron, H., 'Getting personal', *Social Work Today*, 15 (1983).

Sheppard, D.L., 'Organisation, power and sexuality: the image and self-image of women managers' in *The Sexuality of Organization*, ed. J. Hearn, D.L. Sheppard, P. Tancred-Sheriff and G. Burrell (Sage, London, 1989).

Sheriff, P., and Campbell, L.J., 'La place des femmes: un dossier sur la sociologie des organisations', *Sociologie et Sociétés*, 13 (1981).

Shibutani, T., *Improvised News* (Bobbs-Merrill, Indianapolis, 1966).

Shop Stewards T&GWU 9/12 Branch, *Stress at Work. Final Report* (T&GWU, Leeds, March 1981).

Silverman, D., *Qualitative Methodology and Sociology. Describing the Social World* (Gower, Aldershot/Brookfield, Vermont, 1985).

Simpson, R.L., and Simpson, I.H., 'Women and bureaucracy in the semi-professions' in *The Semi-Professions and their Organization* ed. A. Etzioni (Free Press, New York, 1969).

Singer, A., '£100 for sacking with sex bias', *The Guardian* (25 July 1981).

Sjoberg, G., and Miller, P.J., 'Social research and bureaucracy: limitations and opportunities', *Social Problems*, 21 (1973).

Soble, A. ed. *The Philosophy of Sex: Contemporary Readings* (Rowman & Littlefield, Totowa, NJ, 1980).

Sofer, C., *Organizations in Theory and Practice* (Heinemann, London, 1972).

Solomons, H.H., and Cramer, A., 'When the differences don't make a difference', *Management Education and Development*, 16 (1985).

Spender, D., *Man Made Language* (Routledge & Kegan Paul, London/Boston, 1980).

Stacey, M., 'The division of labour or overcoming the two Adams', in *Practice and Progress. British Sociology 1950–1980*, ed. P. Abrams, R. Deem, J. Finch and P. Rock (Allen & Unwin, London, 1981).

Stacey, M., and Price, M., *Women, Power and Politics* (Tavistock, London, 1981).

Stanley, L., 'Whales and minnows: some sexual theorists and followers and how they contribute to making feminism invisible', *Women's Studies International Forum*, 7 (1984).

Stanley, L., and Wise, S., 'Feminist research, feminist consciousness, and experiences of sexism', *Women's Studies International Quarterly*, 2 (1979).

Stanley, L., and Wise, S., *Breaking Out: Feminist Consciousness and Feminist Research* (Routledge & Kegan Paul, London/Boston, 1983).

Steele, F., *The Open Organization* (Addison-Wesley, Reading, Mass., 1975).

Stone, L., *The Family, Sex and Marriage in England 1500–1800* (Weidenfeld & Nicolson, London, 1977).

Stott, M., *Organization Woman* (Heinemann, London, 1978).

Streich, C., 'A groom with a view', *The Guardian* (11 April 1985).

Strodtbeck, F.L., and Mann, R.D., 'Sex role differentiation in jury deliverations', *Sociometry*, 19 (1956).

Summers, A., *Goddess: The Secret Lives of Marilyn Monroe* (Gollancz. London, 1985).

Systems and Procedures Association, *A Guide of Office Clerical Time Standards: A Compilation of Standard Data used by Large American Companies* (SPA, Detroit, 1960).

Tancred-Sheriff, P., 'Gender, sexuality and the labour process' in *The Sexuality of Organization*, ed. J. Hearn, D.L. Sheppard, P. Tancred-Sheriff and G. Burrell (Sage, London, 1989).

Tatchell, P., *Democratic Defense. A Non-Nuclear Alternative* (GMP, London, 1985).

Taylor, F., 'Taylor's testimony to the Special House Committee, 1912' in *Scientific Management* (Harper, New York, 1947).

Taylor, N. ed., *All in a Day's Work. A Report on Anti-lesbian Discrimination in Employment and Unemployment in London* (Lesbian Employment Rights, London, 1986).

Taylor, R., 'Sexual experiences' in *The Philosophy of Sex: Contemporary Readings*, ed. A. Soble (Royman & Littlefield, Totowa, NJ, 1980).

Thomas, A., and Kitzinger, C., 'It's just something that happens: the invisibility of sexual harassment in the workplace', *Gender, Work and Organization,* 1 [3] (1994).

Tittle, C.R., 'Inmate organization: sex differentiation and the influence of criminal subcultures', *American Sociological Review*, 34 (1969).

Tomkinson, M., *The Pornbrokers. The Rise of the Soho Sex Barons* (Virgin, London, 1982).

'Topless nurse loses her fight', *Daily Mirror* (13 June 1984).

Trahair, R.S.C., *The Humanist Temper. The Life and Work of Elton Mayo* (Transaction, New Brunswick/London, 1984).

Tysoe, M., 'The sexual harassers', *New Society*, 62 (1982).

Underwood, L., 'Executive marriages: the hidden stress', *Chief Executive* (March 1982).

Urban Life, Special Issue on Secrecy, Informational Control and Uncertainty, 8 (1980).

Vance, C.S. ed., *Pleasure and Danger: Exploring Female Sexuality* (Routledge & Kegan Paul, London/Boston, 1984).

Vaught, C., and Smith, D.L., 'Incorporation and mechanical solidarity in an underground coal mine', *Sociology of Work and Occupations*, 7 (1980).

Veitch, A., 'Sex row health booklet rescued', *The Guardian* (18 February 1983).

Vines, S., 'Office romantics–who fall down on the job', *The Observer* (29 December 1985).

Walby, S., *Patriarchy at Work: Patriarchal and Capitalist Relations in Employment* (Polity, Cambridge, 1986).

Walby, S., *Theorizing Patriarchy* (Basil Blackwell, Oxford and Cambridge, Mass., 1990).

Waldron, H.A., Waterhouse, J.A.H., and Tesseme, N., 'Scrotal cancer in the West Midlands 1936–76', *British Journal of Industrial Medicine*, 41 (1984).

Ward, D.A., and Kassebaum, G.G., *Women's Prison: Sex and Social Structure* (Aldine, Chicago, 1965).

Watts, J., '. . . if you've got to cry then cry in the loo', *The Observer* (29 October 1978).

Webb, S., 'Gender and authority in the workplace', paper at British Sociological Association Conference, Manchester University (April 1982), mimeo, Manchester University.

Weeks, J., *Coming Out: Homosexual Politics in Britain from the Nineteenth Century to the Present* (Quartet, London, 1977; New York, 1978).

Weiss, C., and Friar, D.J., *Terror in the Prisons: Homosexual Rape and Why Society Condones It* (Bobbs-Merrill, Indianapolis, 1974).

Weston, K.M., and Rofel, L.B., 'Sexuality, class and conflict in a lesbian workplace' in *The Lesbian Issue. Essays for Signs Chicago*, ed. E.B. Freedman, B. Gelpi, S.L. Johnson and K.M. Weston (Chicago University Press, Chicago, Ill., 1985).

Whyte, W.H., *The Organization Man* (Simon and Schuster, New York, 1956).

Wilkinson, S. and Kitzinger, C. (ed.), *Heterosexuality. A Feminism & Psychology Reader* (Sage, London, 1993).

Williamson, J., *Decoding Advertisements: Ideology and Meaning in Advertising* (Marion Boyars, London, 1978).

Willis, P.E., 'The man in the iron cage: notes on method', *Working Papers on Cultural Studies*, 9 (1976).

Willis, P.E., 'Shop-floor culture, masculinity and the wage form' in *Working Class Culture. Studies in History and Theory*, ed. J. Clarke, C. Critcher and R. Johnson (Hutchinson, London, 1977).

Wilson, E., *What Is To Be Done About Violence Against Women?* (Penguin, Harmondsworth, 1983).

Wilson, F.M., *Organizational Behaviour and Gender* (McGraw-Hill, London and New York, 1995).

Wilson, G., and Nias, P., *Love's Mysteries* (Open Books, London, 1976).

Wittig, M., *The Straight Mind and Other Essays* (Harvester Wheatsheaf, Hemel Hempstead, 1992).

Witz, A., *Professions and Patriarchy* (Routledge, London and New York, 1992).

Witz, A., and Savage, M., 'The gender of organisation' in *Gender and Bureaucracy*, ed. M. Savage and A. Witz (Blackwell, Oxford, 1992).

Wolff, J., 'Women in organizations' in *Critical Issues in Organizations*, ed S. Clegg and D. Dunkerley (Routledge & Kegan Paul, London, 1977).

'Women sailors quit U.S. Navy in sex row', *Daily Telegraph* (3 September 1982).

Wood, J., 'Raging Bull: the homosexual subtext in film' in *Beyond Patriarchy: Essays by Men on Power, Pleasure and Change*, ed. M. Kaufman (Oxford University Press, Toronto, 1987).

Wooden, W.S., and Parker, J., *Men Behind Bars: Sexual Exploitation in Prison* (Plenum, New York, 1982).

Wyatt, S., and Fraser, J.A., *The Effects of Monotony in Work* (Industrial Health Research Board, London, 1929).

Zaretsky, E., *Capitalism, The Family and Personal Life* (Pluto, London, 1976).

Zetterberg, H., 'The secret ranking', *Journal of Marriage and the Family*, 28 (1966).

Zita, J.N., 'Historical amnesia and the lesbian continuum' in *Feminist Theory*, ed. N.O. Keohane, M.Z. Rosaldo and B.C. Gelpi (Harvester, Brighton; University of Chicago, Chicago, 1982).

Author Index

Subject Index

Advertisement, 39, 108, 122, 142–3, 163
Advertising, 15, 60, 68, 71, 95, 102, 140–3, 148
Affairs, 14, 38, 72, 114–17, 124, 201n
Age, 172, 176, 178, 184–6, 188–90
Air cabin staff/air hostesses, 82, 143
Airlines, 142–3
Alienation, 12–13, 71, 84–6, 106, 147–8, 152–3
Allusion *see* Innuendo
Ambiguity, 44, 80, 89, 97, 105–6, 123–7, 148–9, 159, 200–1n
Anti-Organisation theory *see* Organisation theory
'Apartment, The', 149
Appearance, 3ff, 25–8, 58, 82, 107–8, 113–4, 140, 142–3, 176, 180, 186, 199n
Armagh Jail, 73
Army *see* Military
Asexuality, 3–4, 93, 103, 148, 152, 156, 159, 202–3n
Ashton, Joe, 117
Attractiveness, 26–7, 37, 93, 113–14, 133, 142, 147

Auschwitz-Birkenau, 73
Authority, 5, 18–19, 27–9, 36–7, 60, 79, 97, 101–3, 105–7, 109, 120, 123–4, 126, 160, 194n, 202n; Division of, 64–5, 81, 90–5, 171; Divisions of sexuality, 90–5

Barker, John, 140, 202n
Barmaids/barworkers, 144
Bendix Corporation, 193n
Beneficiaries *see* Prime beneficiaries
Bentham, Jeremy, 202n
Biology, 5–6, 23, 53–6, 196n 140, 202n
Birth defects, 87
Bisexuality, 58, 60, 62, 138, 140, 202n
Black, Christopher, 73
Blunt, Anthony, 198n
Body, 9, 20–1, 24, 43, 57–8, 61, 64, 69–70, 72–81, 102, 118–19, 121, 127, 132, 134–5, 141–2, 150, 152, 156, 171, 175–6, 182, 194n, 198–9n; politics 57–9, 61, 72–3, 199n; rhythms, 88–9
Bolton school, 133
Boss *see* Manager